Extending Microsoft Dynamics AX 2012 Cookbook

A practical guide to extending and maximizing the potential of Dynamics AX using common Microsoft technologies

Murray Fife

[PACKT] enterprise ⧉
PUBLISHING
professional expertise distilled

BIRMINGHAM - MUMBAI

Extending Microsoft Dynamics AX 2012 Cookbook

First published: August 2013

Production Reference: 1190813

Published by Packt Publishing Ltd.
Livery Place
35 Livery Street
Birmingham B3 2PB, UK.

ISBN 978-1-78216-833-1

www.packtpub.com

Cover Image by Sandeep Vaity (sandeep.vaity@yahoo.com)

Credits

Author
Murray Fife

Reviewers
Angela Buchanan
Kamalakannan Elangovan
Chris Merchant
Muhammad Amir Nazim

Acquisition Editor
Joanne Fitzpatrick

Lead Technical Editor
Antony Lowe

Technical Editors
Larissa Pinto
Amit Ramadas

Project Coordinator
Kranti Berde

Proofreader
Julie Jackson

Indexers
Monica Ajmera Mehta
Rekha Nair

Production Coordinator
Shantanu Zagade

Cover Work
Shantanu Zagade

About the Author

Murray Fife is a Microsoft Dynamics AX MVP, a presenter, and an author with over 18 years of experience in the software industry.

Like most people he has paid his dues as a developer, as an implementation consultant, and a trainer. He has a hard-to-find blend of technical and interpersonal skills and spends his days working with companies solving their problems with the Microsoft suite of products, specializing in Dynamics AX solutions.

No ideas are ever created in a vacuum, and there were a lot of people that helped and inspired a lot of what is in this book. Some of the people that I need to thank in particular are Jack Payne, for letting me experiment with coding examples over the many years that we worked together; Larry Farley, for introducing me to Dynamics AX and giving me a whole new world of tools to tinker with; Ryan Kaul, for helping me with my first line of X++ code; Chris Hoer, for showing me all of the ins and outs of Dynamics AX, and for answering all of my many questions; and Andy Vabulas, for supporting me throughout the book.

About the Reviewers

Angela Buchanan is a Software Developer and Technical Consultant for Dynamics AX. She is currently working as a freelance consultant in the United Kingdom.

Angela began working with AX in 2001, while completing her Computer Science degree at The University of Waikato in New Zealand. After a successful implementation of version 2.5, and later upgrade to 3, the husband and bags were packed up and moved over to England to seek out bigger project challenges, and for a taste of world travel.

Since this move, Angela has worked on many AX implementations, specializing in business solutions design, X++ programming, reporting, and business intelligence. She is a Microsoft Certified Professional for AX: Development, Installation, and Configuration, as well as key modules: Finance, Projects, Production, Trade, and Logistics; and is also a Microsoft Certified Trainer for AX.

A big thanks to the author for all his efforts in writing this book and for inviting me to be one of the reviewers. I've learned lots of useful tricks through the process.

Kamalakannan Elangovan started his career in 2005 as a Technical Consultant in ERP for Sonata, where he played a key role in the development of Business Integration solutions for Microsoft. He later moved on to head the Business Integration Development Team. He spearheaded the development of a commodity trading vertical for a U.K.-based ISV. It is through his experience that Kamal picked up his passion for product development, and this passion has driven his career since then.

In 2008 Kamal joined InnoVites and led their product development team, creating one of the first verticals, such as cable and wires, for Dynamics AX on multidimension industry. Currently, he works with CuroGens, Inc. as a Development Manager overseeing the product development efforts. As a Microsoft Dynamics AX enthusiast and architect, he shares his insights by contributing to the Microsoft Dynamics community through his blog http://kamalblogs.wordpress.com.

I would like to thank Packt Publishing and the author for offering me the chance to review and read this wonderful book. It has been a great learning experience.

www.PacktPub.com

Support files, eBooks, discount offers and more

You might want to visit www.PacktPub.com for support files and downloads related to your book.

Did you know that Packt offers eBook versions of every book published, with PDF and ePub files available? You can upgrade to the eBook version at www.PacktPub.com and as a print book customer, you are entitled to a discount on the eBook copy. Get in touch with us at service@packtpub.com for more details.

At www.PacktPub.com, you can also read a collection of free technical articles, sign up for a range of free newsletters and receive exclusive discounts and offers on Packt books and eBooks.

http://PacktLib.PacktPub.com

Do you need instant solutions to your IT questions? PacktLib is Packt's online digital book library. Here, you can access, read and search across Packt's entire library of books.

Why Subscribe?

- Fully searchable across every book published by Packt
- Copy and paste, print and bookmark content
- On demand and accessible via web browser

Free Access for Packt account holders

If you have an account with Packt at www.PacktPub.com, you can use this to access PacktLib today and view nine entirely free books. Simply use your login credentials for immediate access.

Instant Updates on New Packt Books

Get notified! Find out when new books are published by following @PacktEnterprise on Twitter, or the *Packt Enterprise* Facebook page.

Table of Contents

Preface

Dynamics AX is a great application for businesses, but if you are just using it to track customers, sales, vendors, purchase orders, and inventory, you are not getting the most out of the system. There is a lot of free functionality that is built into Dynamics AX, and because it is also built and integrated with all of the other Microsoft tools such as Microsoft SQL Server, Microsoft SharePoint, and the Microsoft Office Suite, there is so much more that you can use to help you make Dynamics AX even more productive.

This book will take you through a number of recipes that will help you extend and personalize your Dynamics AX installation with very little to no coding using Microsoft technologies that should already be available and configured as part of your default installation. As a result, it will just cost you a little elbow grease and a little investment in time.

Each recipe will guide you through all the configurations that you need to make to your Dynamics AX system, and also give you examples of how you can use them in the real world. Although you may not need the particular examples that we show in this book, it should be easy to find situations that you will be able to apply techniques and tools that we will show in this book that will make your life just a little easier.

What the book covers

Chapter 1, Extending Out with SharePoint, will show you how to take advantage of some of the features within SharePoint to help you augment data within Dynamics AX through My Sites and Document Repositories.

Chapter 2, Reports and Dashboards, shows you how to create your own ad hoc reports and dashboards by using tools that you are already using such as Excel, or by using PowerPivot and Power View to create interactive dashboards and reporting galleries.

Chapter 3, Dashboards, Charts, and Scorecards, will focus on how you can extend out Role Centers by using PerformancePoint charts and reports, and also how you can add external data such as RSS feeds and internal blog posts to Role Centers to get real-time information.

Chapter 4, Communication and Collaboration, will show how to link and use the productivity and collaboration tools such as Outlook and Lync to keep an up-to-date track on all your tasks and appointments, and also to contact others inside and outside your organization.

Chapter 5, Using Cases to Manage Incidents and Requests, will give examples of how you can use the new cases capabilities within Dynamics AX 2012 to manage and streamline your business processes.

Chapter 6, Organizing Your Workflows, shows how to take advantage of the in-built workflow capabilities in Dynamics AX 2012 to manage common business processes, and also how to develop your own workflows to manage the not so common processes.

Chapter 7, Reporting in Office, focuses on how you can use the Microsoft Dynamics AX Office Add-Ins to create report and form templates in Word and Excel that are then accessed through Dynamics AX, and also how you can use Visio to create unstructured dashboards.

Chapter 8, Talking to the Outside World, will show how you can use the Customer and Vendor portals that are delivered with Dynamics AX to share information with people outside the organization.

Chapter 9, Creating Help, will introduce the help authoring system that is built into the Dynamics AX framework, and show you how you can take advantage of it to build your own integrated help system and knowledge base.

Chapter 10, Web Services and Forms, will show you how you can use Microsoft InfoPath to create custom forms that are linked to Microsoft Dynamics AX, and also how you can use these forms to capture information for your business.

Chapter 11, Role Center Personalization and Customization, will review all of the user personalization that is available within Dynamics AX such as filtering, cues, showing, hiding and adding fields to screens, and also the creation of custom user menus.

What you need for this book

All the examples shown in this book were done with the Microsoft Dynamics AX 2012 virtual machine image that was downloaded from the Microsoft CustomerSource or PartnerSource site. If you don't have your own installation of Microsoft Dynamics AX 2012, you can also use the images found on the Microsoft Learning Download Center. The following list of software from the virtual image was leveraged within this book:

- Microsoft Dynamics AX 2012 (both R1 and R2)
- Microsoft Windows Server 2008 R2 Enterprise
- Microsoft SQL Server 2008 R2 (both Standard and Enterprise)
- Microsoft SharePoint 2010 (both Foundation and Enterprise)
- Microsoft Office Excel 2010

- ▶ Microsoft Office Word 2010
- ▶ Microsoft Office Outlook 2010
- ▶ Microsoft Office InfoPath 2010
- ▶ Microsoft Office Visio 2010
- ▶ Microsoft Lync 2010
- ▶ Microsoft Visual Studio 2010 Developer Edition
- ▶ Microsoft Internet Explorer 8
- ▶ Notepad

Even though all the preceding software was used during the development and testing of the recipes in this book, they may also work on earlier versions of the software with minor tweaks and adjustments, and should also work on later versions without any changes. You can download this software from the links mentioned in the following table:

Sr No.	Software name	URL
1	Microsoft Dynamics AX 2012 (both R1 and R2)	http://www.microsoft.com/
2	Microsoft Windows Server 2008 R2 Enterprise	http://www.microsoft.com/
3	Microsoft SQL Server 2008 R2 (both Standard and Enterprise)	http://www.microsoft.com/
4	Microsoft SharePoint 2010 (both Foundation and Enterprise)	http://www.microsoft.com/
5	Microsoft Office Excel 2010	http://www.microsoft.com/
6	Microsoft Office Word 2010	http://www.microsoft.com/
7	Microsoft Office Outlook 2010	http://www.microsoft.com/
8	Microsoft Office InfoPath 2010	http://www.microsoft.com/
9	Microsoft Office Visio 2010	http://www.microsoft.com/
10	Microsoft Lync 2010	http://www.microsoft.com/
11	Microsoft Visual Studio 2010 Developer Edition	http://www.microsoft.com/
12	Microsoft Internet Explorer 8	http://www.microsoft.com/
13	Notepad	

Who this book is for

Although in some of the recipes that we will show there may be some coding required, the code itself is very simple; so you don't have to have to be a developer, just be willing to get under the Dynamics AX hood for a short time.

And, although we will be using SharePoint and Microsoft SQL Server to configure some of the examples, you don't have to be a SharePoint guru or a DBA in order to make the changes; you just need to be willing to roll your sleeves up and make a few simple tweaks here and there.

Whether you are a power user looking to fill a need, a systems administrator looking for a inexpensive solution to a solve a business problem, or a developer wanting to try out other technologies rather than spend hours coding, this is the book for you.

Conventions

In this book, you will find a number of styles of text that distinguish between different kinds of information. Here are some examples of these styles, and an explanation of their meaning.

Code words in text are shown as follows: "From the **Organization administration** area page, click on the **Case workflow** menu item in the Cases folder of the **Setup** group to view all the workflows associated with cases."

A block of code is set as follows:

```
<entry>
  <text>Walkthroughs</text>
  <Microsoft.Help.F1></Microsoft.Help.F1>
  <children>
    <entry>
      <text>Released Product Inventory Lookup</text>
      <Microsoft.Help.F1>108B0027-6EF1-4F3F-80A4-5A5A416FDC2C</
Microsoft.Help.F1>
    </entry>
  </children>
</entry>
```

New terms and **important words** are shown in bold. Words that you see on the screen, in menus or dialog boxes for example, appear in the text like this: "Then, click on the **Save as HTML** button within the **Save** group of the **Microsoft Dynamics Help** tab to publish the HTML files."

[![note icon] Warnings or important notes appear in a box like this.]

[![tip icon] Tips and tricks appear like this.]

Reader Feedback

Feedback from our readers is always welcome. Let us know what you think about this book—what you liked or may have disliked. Reader feedback is important for us to develop titles that you really get the most out of.

To send us general feedback, simply send an e-mail to feedback@packtpub.com, and mention the book title via the subject of your message.

If there is a topic that you have expertise in and you are interested in either writing or contributing to a book, see our author guide on www.packtpub.com/authors.

Customer Support

Now that you are the proud owner of a Packt book, we have a number of things to help you to get the most from your purchase.

Errata

Although we have taken every care to ensure the accuracy of our content, mistakes do happen. If you find a mistake in one of our books—maybe a mistake in the text or the code—we would be grateful if you would report this to us. By doing so, you can save other readers from frustration and help us improve subsequent versions of this book. If you find any errata, please report them by visiting http://www.packtpub.com/support, selecting your book, clicking on the **errata submission form** link, and entering the details of your errata. Once your errata are verified, your submission will be accepted and the errata will be uploaded on our website, or added to any list of existing errata, under the Errata section of that title. Any existing errata can be viewed by selecting your title from http://www.packtpub.com/support.

Piracy

Piracy of copyright material on the Internet is an ongoing problem across all media. At Packt, we take the protection of our copyright and licenses very seriously. If you come across any illegal copies of our works, in any form, on the Internet, please provide us with the location address or website name immediately so that we can pursue a remedy.

Please contact us at copyright@packtpub.com with a link to the suspected pirated material.

We appreciate your help in protecting our authors, and our ability to bring you valuable content.

Questions

You can contact us at questions@packtpub.com if you are having a problem with any aspect of the book, and we will do our best to address it.

1

Extending Out with SharePoint

In this chapter, we will show you how to take advantage of some of the features within SharePoint, to help you add value to Dynamics AX through My Sites and Document Repositories. This chapter will cover:

- ▶ Configuring a My Site host site
- ▶ Using note boards to microblog from the Role Centers
- ▶ Adding My Site profile links to the Role Centers
- ▶ Creating shared document libraries
- ▶ Linking document libraries to Dynamics AX records

Introduction

SharePoint is one of the core Microsoft technology platforms which allows you to organize your files with shared document libraries, collaborate with others through shared task lists and calendars, communicate with others with blogs, and much more, all through a web portal. Something that makes SharePoint even more useful is that you don't have to be a developer to configure these features.

If you have Dynamics AX up and running, then chances are you should already have SharePoint installed and configured, since it is also the foundation for all of the Role Centers and enterprise portals that are delivered with Dynamics AX. Although the Role Centers and portals are preconfigured and use a lot of the features of SharePoint, there are still more features that you can take advantage of in conjunction with Dynamics AX that will make your system even better.

First we will show how to configure the My Sites feature so that the users are able to microblog and maintain their personal information within SharePoint. Once you have this configured, then you are able to add content from your personal My Site, or links to other My Sites into the Role Centers in Dynamics AX. This provides a better collaboration system for the business, and also adds a social element to the application.

We will also show how you can create your own document libraries within SharePoint to allow users to store documents, such as scanned invoices, and then index and link them back to Dynamics AX. This is an alternative to the standard document attachments feature within Dynamics AX. SharePoint document libraries allow multiple records to be linked to the same document list, and also give you document management features, such as file check-in and out to control who updates the documents.

None of these examples are hard to set up or configure, but since they require you to add to your existing SharePoint sites, you will need to have administrator rights to SharePoint. Also, for the last two examples, there is some X++ coding required. Each has only about 10 lines of simple code, so even novices should be able to work through the examples.

Configuring a My Site host site

SharePoint My Sites give your users the chance to have their very own part of SharePoint that they can use to store documents, to update their own personal profile and description, to make notes and blog entries and also to connect with other people within the organization. In a socially connected workplace, My Sites are great tools to allow the users to post and capture knowledge.

If you do not have My Sites configured, then the first step is to create a My Sites site within SharePoint and link it to your Role Centers so that the users will then be able to access their personal profile and content.

Getting ready

Before you start on this example, you will need to make sure that you have access to the SharePoint Central Administration console. To check this:

1. Access your server that has SharePoint installed on it.

2. From the program menu, you should be able to find the **SharePoint Central Administration Console** in the **Microsoft SharePoint Products** group.

3. When you open the application, you should see a screen similar to this:

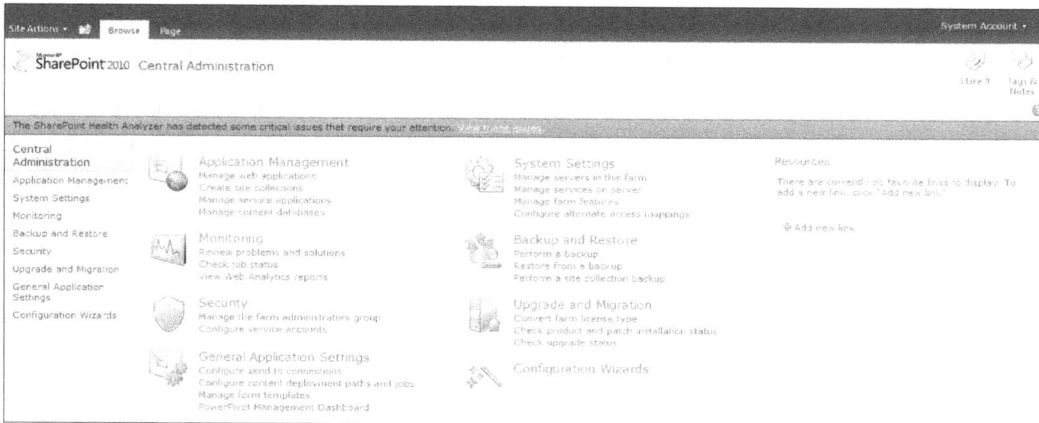

How to do it...

To create and link your own My Sites site, follow these steps:

1. From your SharePoint Central Administration console, navigate to the **Application Management** group.

2. Select the **Create Site Collection** from the **Site Collections** group.

3. Name your application `My Sites`.

4. Set the website address to be in the `my/personal` folder, and name the subfolder `My Sites`.

5. From the **Enterprise** tab on the **Template** selection choose **My Site Host**.

6. Don't forget to assign the **Primary** and **Secondary** administrators to the site that you are creating:

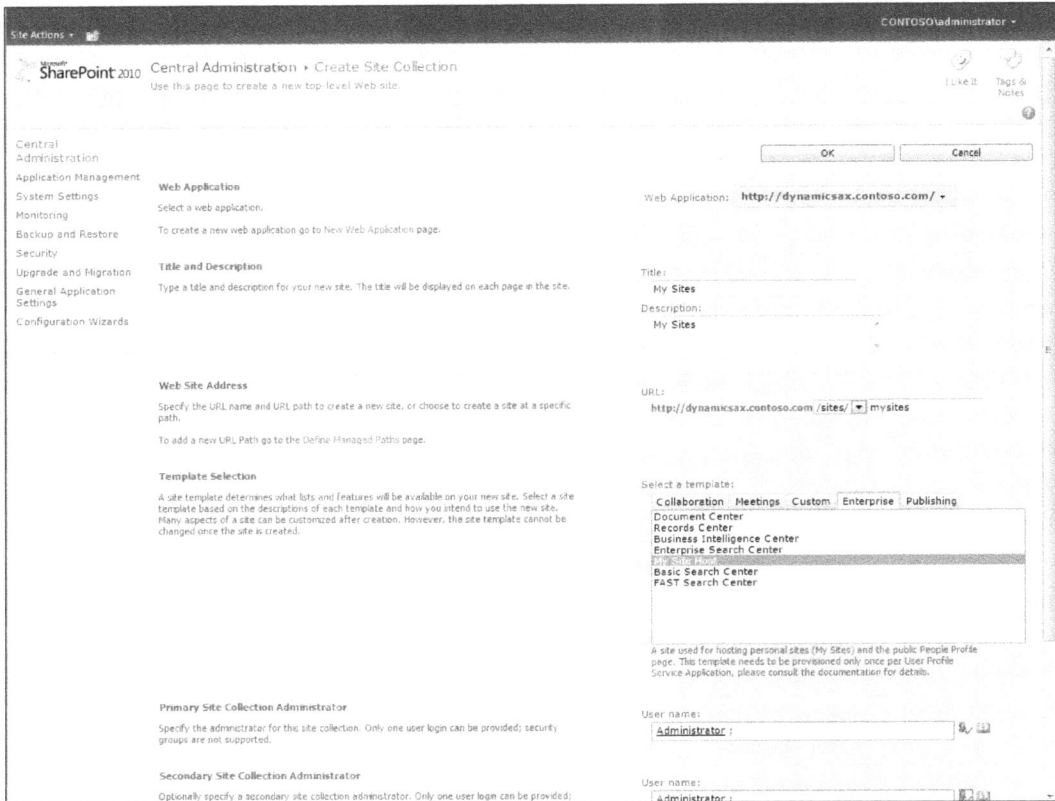

7. Click on **OK** to create your site.

8. From the **Application Management** option in **Central Administration**, select the site that we added the My Sites host site to.

9. Click on the **Define** button in the ribbon bar, and then select the **Managed Paths** option:

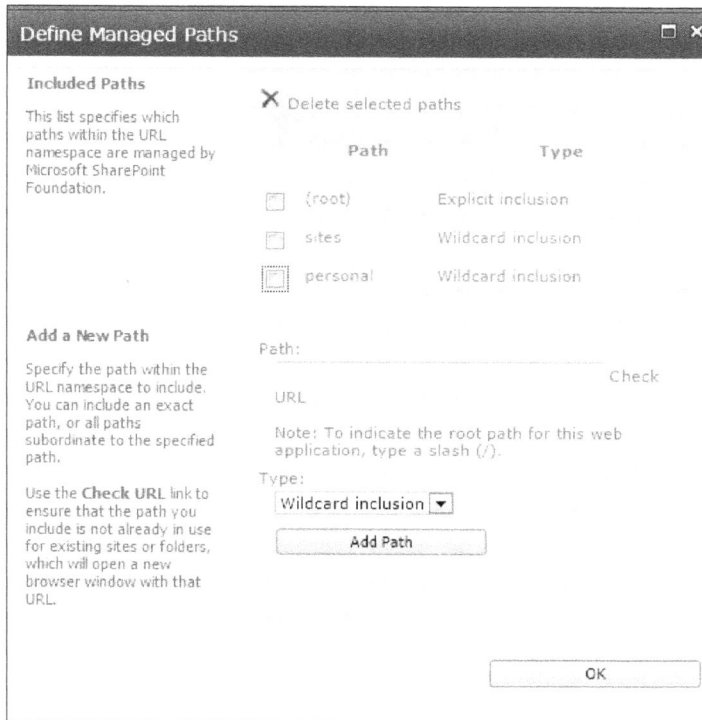

10. Here we will add our new My Site link. You don't need to type in the full URL, so you can skip the host prefix.

11. Also, you may just want to check the **Self-Service Site Creation** option, to make sure that the feature is turned **On**:

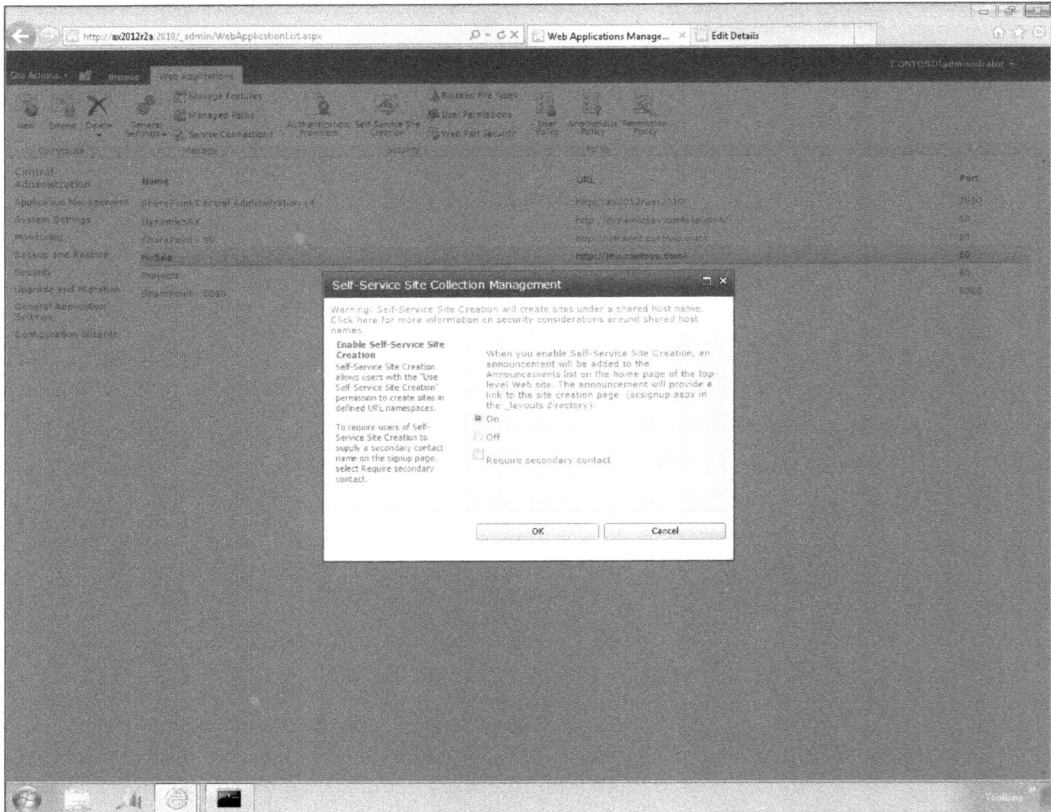

12. Finally, we need to configure the **User Profile Service** application.

13. When you select the application, you will be able to see all of the My Site and user profile configuration options. From here you need to choose the **Setup My Site** menu option.

> Remember this link because you may need to come back here later to configure profiles, and so on.

14. We just need to configure the site parameters, the administrator users, and so on.

> Make sure that the host URL matches, that is, SharePoint.

How it works...

Once you have My Sites configured, you will see a **My Site** option when you select the drop-down menu under the user name within SharePoint, as follows:

Opening up your My Site will take you to your personal site within SharePoint. Initially it will be a little dull, but since you will be the administrator of this little slice of SharePoint, you can add information and pictures to your profile, create your own blogs, and browse through the organization to see other's My Sites to see what they are up to. You also have your own personal documents area that you are able to save files to, that you can then share with other users in the organization.

Using note boards to microblog from the Role Centers

A part of your My Site is a personal note board. If you don't want to create a full-fledged blog, then you can use this to take quick notes for yourself or others within the organization, such as reminders that you will be on vacation, alerts about upcoming events, and much more that you can publish to the entire organization.

In this recipe, we will show you how to make this even more useful by adding the note board directly into the Dynamics AX Role Center. This will allow your users to view your posts quickly and get back to work, without having to open another window.

How to do it...

To add a note board panel to the Role Center, follow these steps:

1. From within the Role Center, click on the **Personalize this page** link in the top-right hand corner to enter into the edit mode.
2. Click on the **Add a Web Part** link where you would like to add the note board.
3. This will open up the web part explorer. From the categories, select the **Social Collaboration** group and this will filter the available web parts to the My Site controls.
4. Select the **Note Board** control and click on the **Add** button:

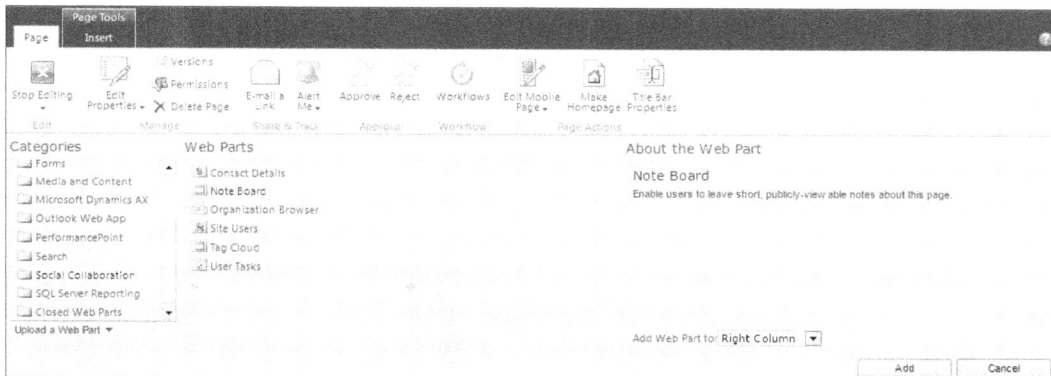

5. Now click on the **Stop Editing** button to return to the view mode for the Role Center.

How it works...

Since the Note Board is a direct link to the user's personal My Site Notes, they are able to post directly from Dynamics AX without opening up another browser window:

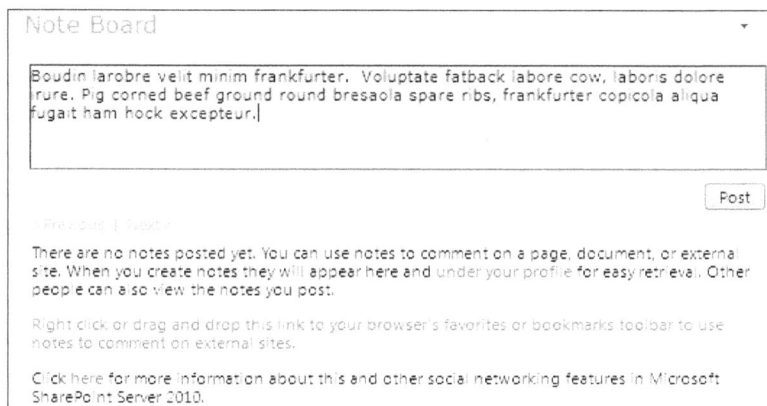

The notes that are posted on the Note Board on the Role Center will show up on the **Tags** and **Notes** panel within the user's My Site page. Additionally, if the user makes notes from their My Site, then these will show up on the wall of the Role Center.

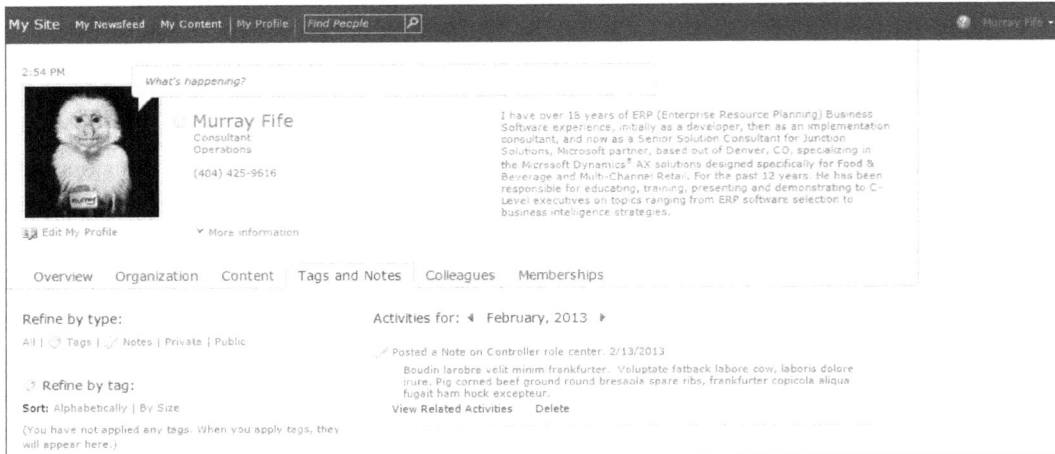

Adding My Site profile links to the Role Centers

Another feature of My Sites is the ability for users to personalize their own profile with descriptions, contact details, profile pictures, and also personal notes and interests. Users configure and update their profiles, and then these can be used as a company directory, and an easy way to get to know the people you work with.

In this recipe, we will show how you can add your profile link to the Dynamics AX Role Center to give you quick access to your own My Site, and also how to add people that you frequently contact on your Role Center for quick access. Getting ready

Before you start on this example, you will need to make sure that you have configured your own personal profile within your My Site. To do this carry out the following steps:

1. Access your My Site by selecting the **My Site** option on the drop-down menu under your name in SharePoint.

2. Once you are in your My Site, click on the **My Profile** link in the top-left hand corner to access your profile page.

3. Click on the **Edit My Profile** link under your profile picture.

   This will open up the Profile Maintenance page allowing you to add descriptions, avatars, and any other information that you may want to include on your profile:

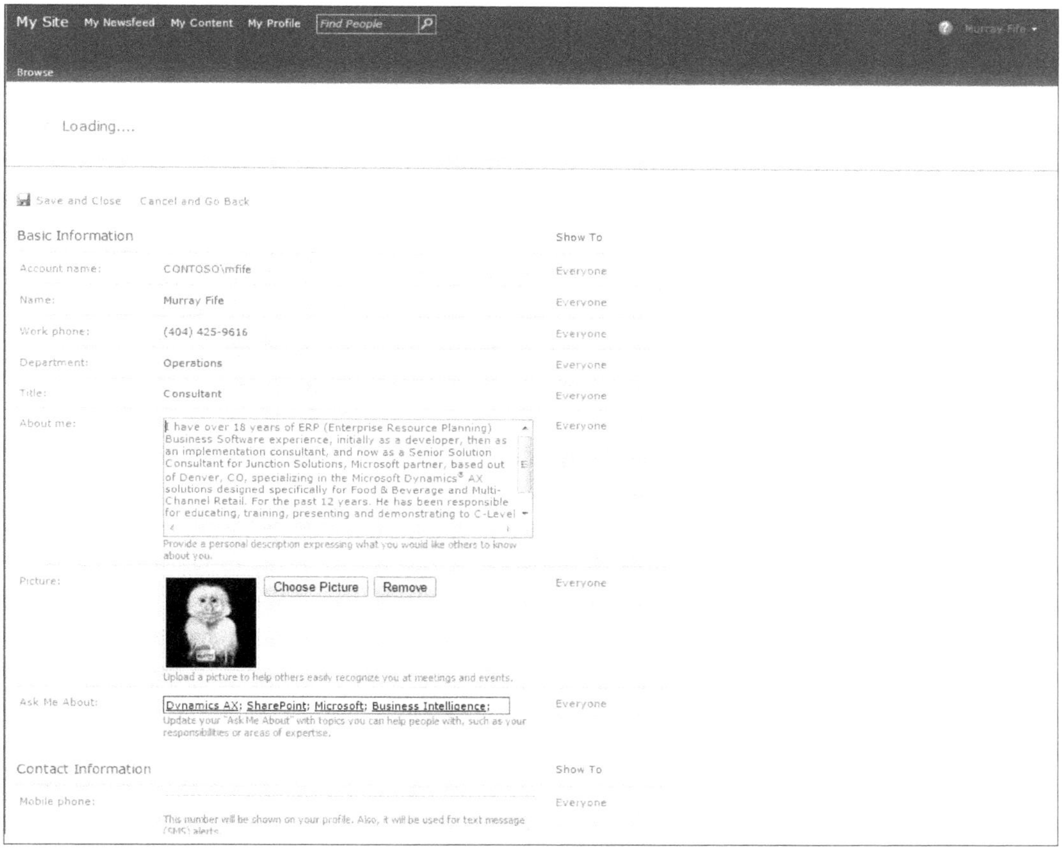

How to do it...

To add a **Contact Details** panel to the Role Center, follow these steps:

1. From within the Role Center, click on the **Personalize this page** link in the top-right hand corner to enter into the edit mode.

2. Click on the **Add a Web Part** link where you would like to add your contact information.

3. This will open up the web part explorer. From the categories, select the **Social Collaboration** group and this will filter the available web parts to the My Site controls.

4. Navigate to the **Contact Details** control, and then click on the **Add** button:

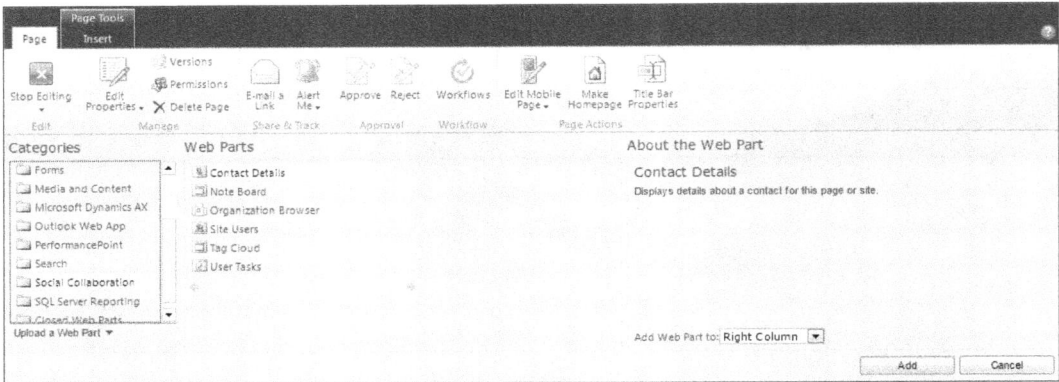

5. This will add the **Contact Details** web part to the Role Center, but you need to configure it with a contact. To do that, navigate to **Click here** to add or modify a contact link.

6. This will open up the **Web Part properties** panel, and you will be able to select a contact from the address book:

7. Click on the **Stop Editing** button and you are done.

How it works...

Once you have defined a contact for Contact Details, then the information from the My Site of that person will be displayed on the Role Center:

If you click on the name of the person, then that will take you directly to their personal site:

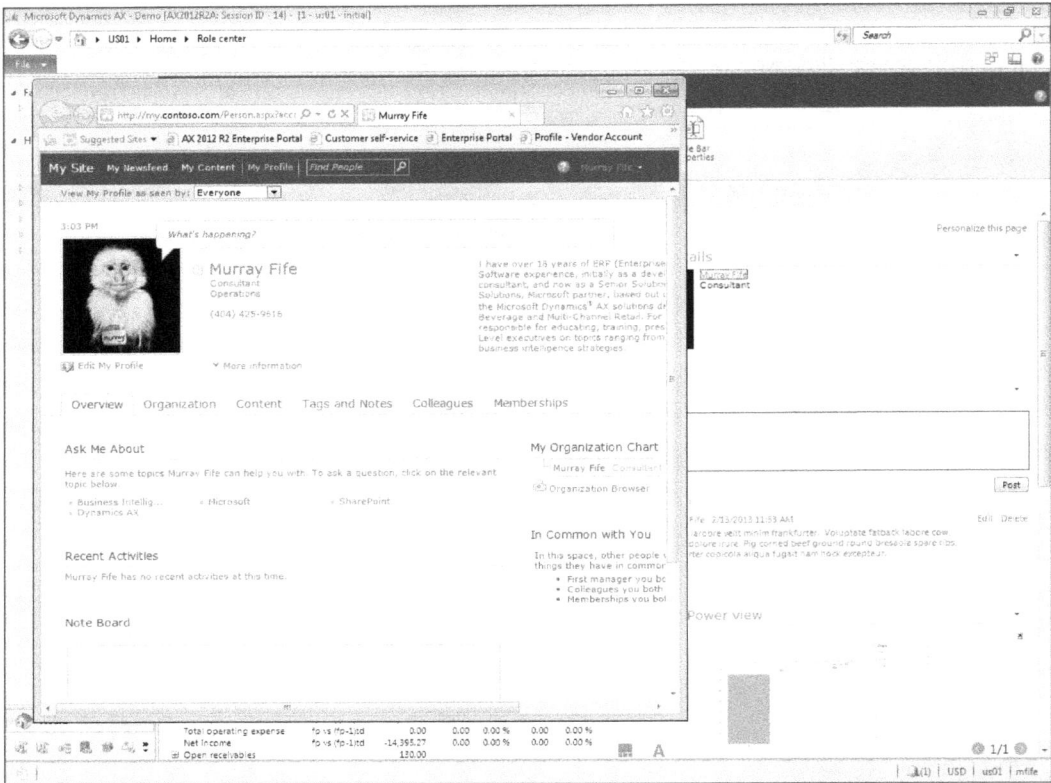

Creating shared document libraries

One of the strengths of SharePoint is that it is a great document management system. Although you can attach documents to records directly within Dynamics AX, you may want to use SharePoint as a store, so that people without access to Dynamics AX can still have access to the documents. SharePoint also allows you to index documents a number of different ways, allowing them to link to more than one record within Dynamics AX.

For this recipe, we will show how you can create an Accounts Payable document library to store all of your vendor invoices and scanned documents.

Before we show you how to access these documents from within Dynamics AX, you need to create a library to store the documents.

Getting ready

Before you start on this example, you will need to make sure that you have administrator privileges on your document management site. To check this carry out the following step:

1. Access the site, and open up the **Site Actions** menu. You need to make sure that you have the ability to create a **New Document Library**:

How to do it...

To create a new document library for your Accounts Payable scans and images, follow these steps:

1. From your SharePoint site that you want to store your documents in, access the **Site Actions** menu, and then select the **New Document Library** menu item:

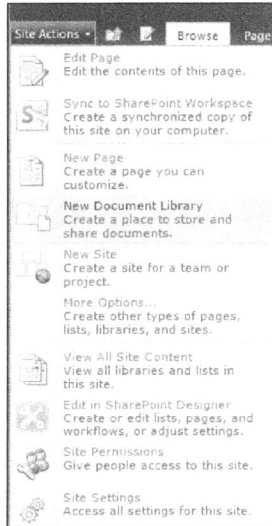

2. This will open up the Document Library creation form. Give the library a name for the area of the business that will be using the documents, and then click on the **Create** button:

3. Now you should have a generic document library. We want to be able to index and search through our documents though. So we will add a few index fields to the document library. To do this, click on the **Create Column** button in the **Library/ Manage Views** section of the ribbon bar:

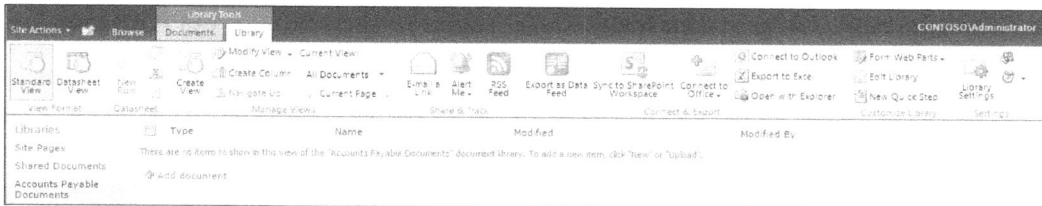

4. This will open up the **Create Column** dialog box, and we will create a column for **Vendor Account Number**:

5. After doing that, create non-required columns for Invoice Number (AccountNum), Document Amount (Amount), Document Date (Date), Purchase Order Number (PurchaseOrder), and Company ID (Company).

6. From the **Library/Manage Views** tab on the ribbon bar, you may also want to rearrange and hide the columns to make the library tidier.

How it works...

From the document library, we can now upload our scanned documents and images to SharePoint through the **Upload Documents** button.

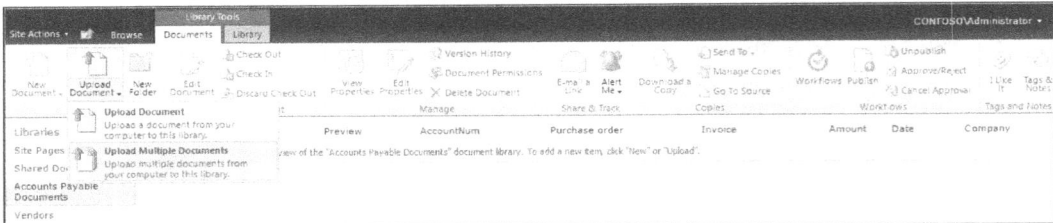

Once you have your documents uploaded, you can the open up the **Properties** panel for the document through the drop-down box beside the document name.

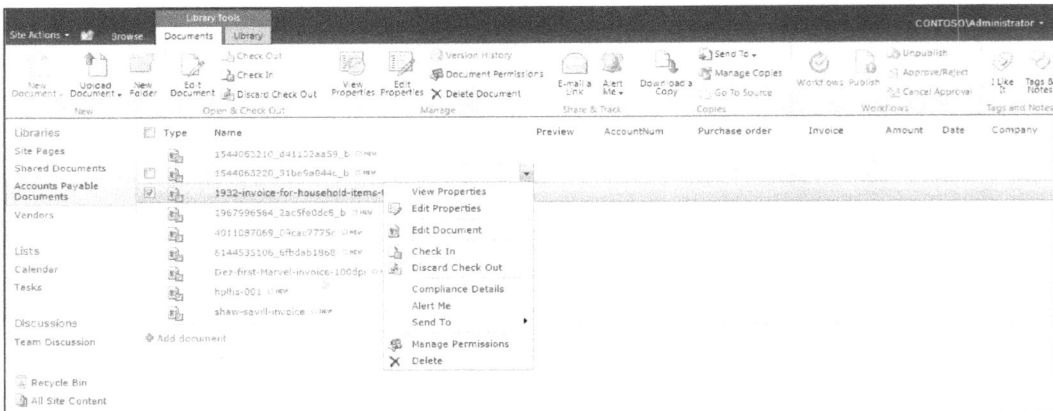

The column properties allow you to add additional index information to documents, so that later on we are able to search and find documents that relate to specific data in the database.

As we index these documents we are able to see the indexed column values in the main view of the document library.

Additionally, if you have a number of documents in your library, you can use the filter button to just find the documents that you are looking for.

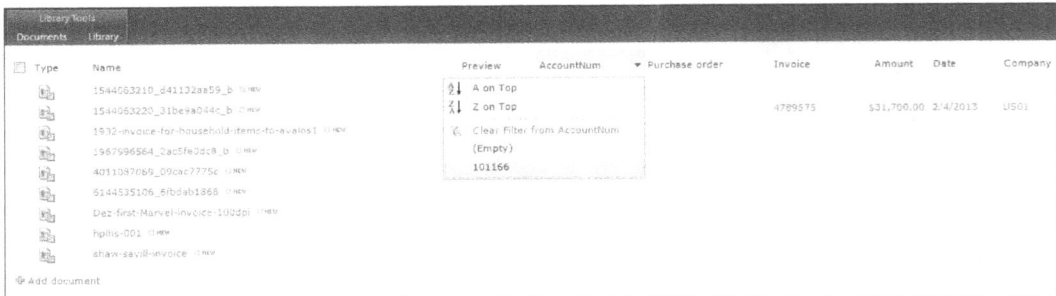

Linking document libraries to Dynamics AX records

Now that you have a document library configured, you can make it accessible directly from the Dynamics AX forms, and have it automatically filtered so that you just see the documents that are associated to the information that you are looking for.

In this recipe, we will show how you can link the document library that we just created to the Vendor form, and do just that.

Getting ready

This example requires that you access the development environment and make changes to forms. Before you start on this example, make sure that you have developer rights on your installation of Dynamics AX. To check this carry out the following steps:

1. Open up the form that you are going to modify.

2. Right-click on the form and navigate to the **Personalize** option.

3. Click on the **Information** tab and you should be able to see the system form name:

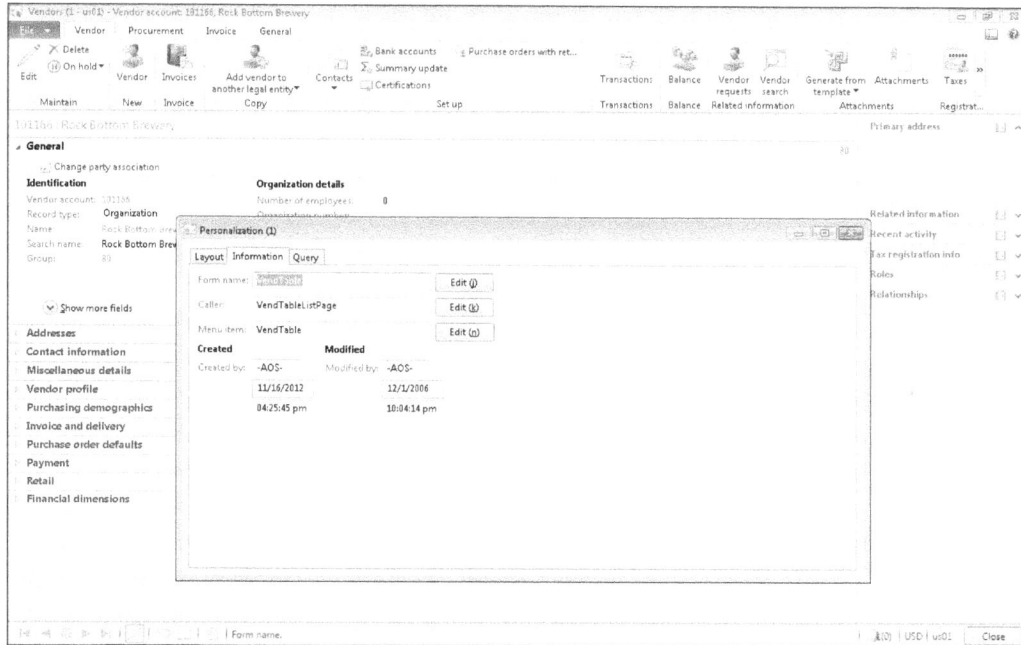

4. Click on the **Edit** button to the right of the form name and you should be taken into the AOT development environment.

How to do it...

To add a link to a SharePoint document library within a form, follow these steps:

1. Create a new development project in AOT, **AccountsPayableSharePointDocs**. Add the **VendorTable** form to the project:

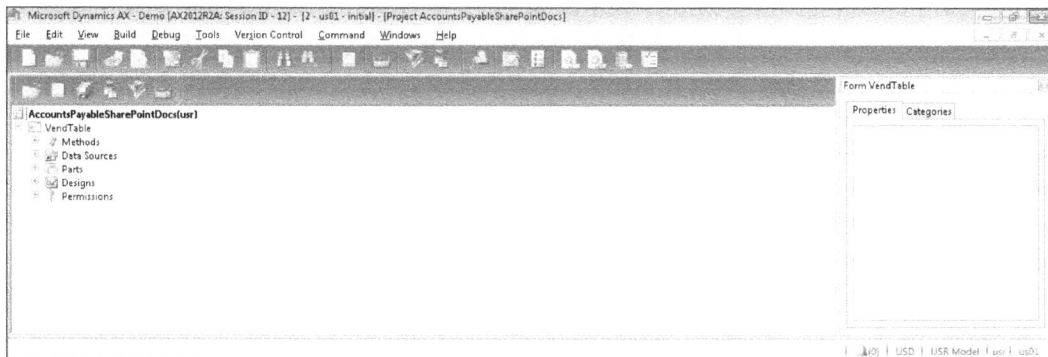

2. We are going to add a new tab group to the **VendorTable** form to show the documents that relate to the Vendor record. To do that expand the **Designs** group and find the **Design form** definition. Expand **MainTab** and **TabPageDetails**, and then right-click on the **Tabs** group, navigate to **New Control**, and then **TabPage**:

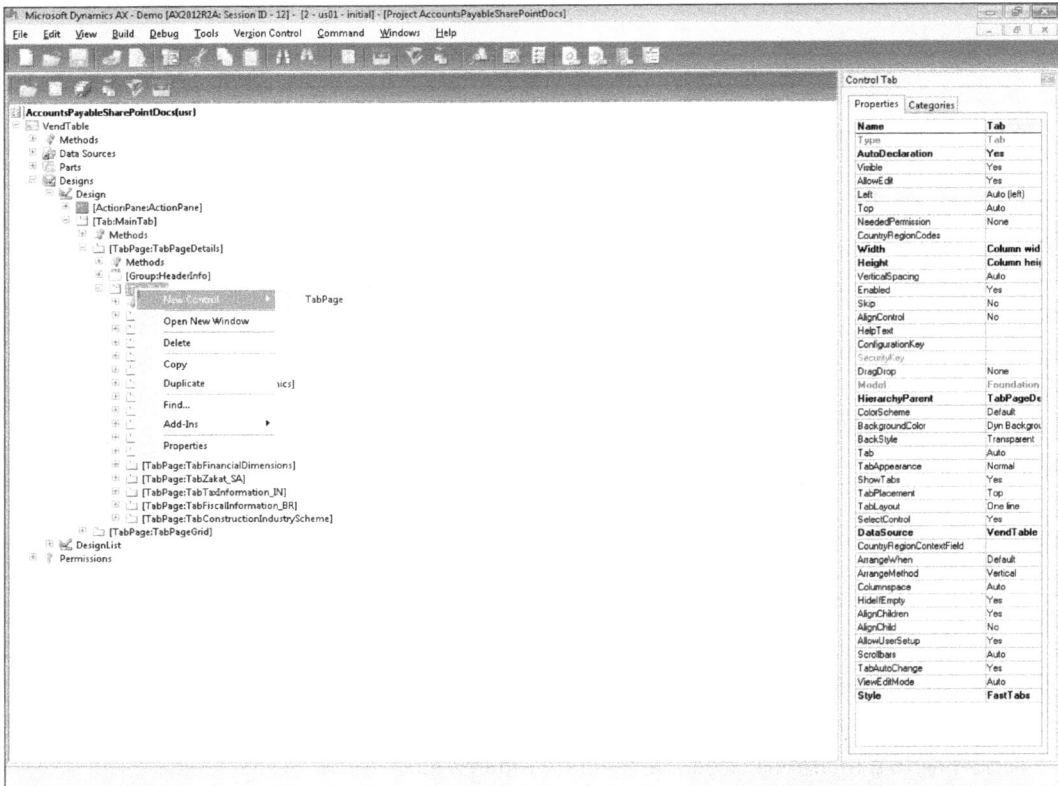

3. Rename **TabPage** to **AccountsPayableDocuments** and also add a caption for **TabPage** in the properties box of **Vendor Documents**.

4. We need to add a browser to the form so that we can display the SharePoint documents window. To do this, right-click on the new tab that we created, navigate to the **New Control** menu, and then select the **ActiveX** control.

5. When the ActiveX control browser shows up, navigate to the **Microsoft Web Browser** control, and add it to the tab.

6. In the properties panel for the **Web Browser** control, set the **Name** property to Documents, set the **Width** property to Column width, and the **Height** property to Column height, so that the control will fill the space that is available in the tab control:

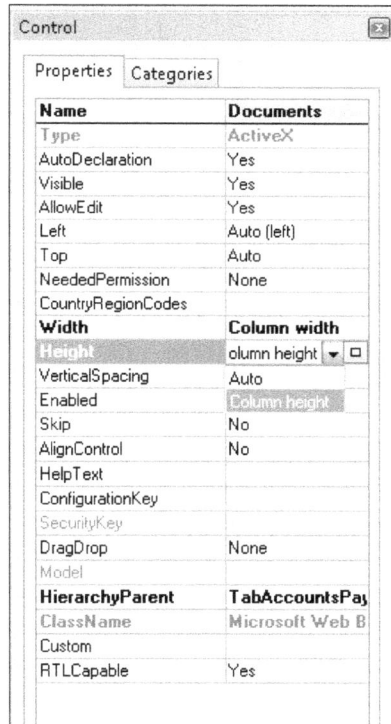

Control	
Properties	Categories

Name	Documents
Type	ActiveX
AutoDeclaration	Yes
Visible	Yes
AllowEdit	Yes
Left	Auto (left)
Top	Auto
NeededPermission	None
CountryRegionCodes	
Width	**Column width**
Height	olumn height
VerticalSpacing	Auto
Enabled	Column height
Skip	No
AlignControl	No
HelpText	
ConfigurationKey	
SecurityKey	
DragDrop	None
Model	
HierarchyParent	**TabAccountsPa**
ClassName	Microsoft Web B
Custom	
RTLCapable	Yes

7. Now that we have a control to show the SharePoint site with the documents, we just need to initialize it when entering the vendor form. To do this, right-click on the **Methods** group in the **VendTable** form, select the **Override method** menu, and then **activate**:

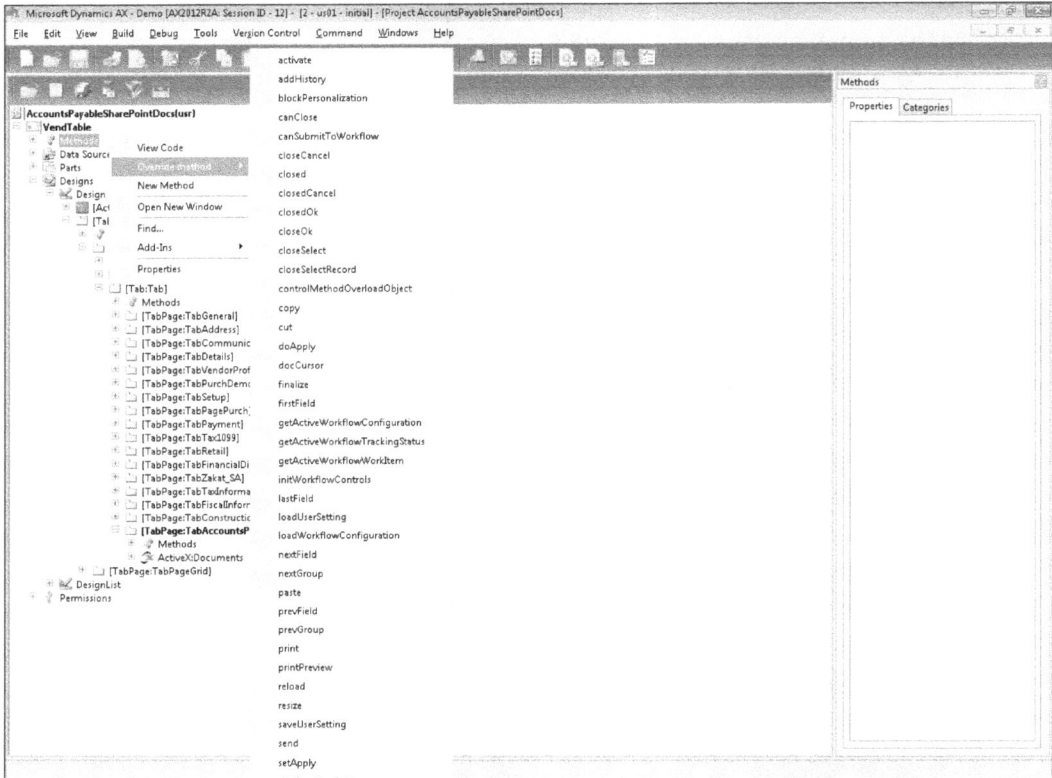

8. This will open up the code editor for the activate method. We will change this by creating a URL string that references the Accounts Payable document library in SharePoint, and then navigate the browser control to the URL, as follows:

```
public void activate(boolean _active)
{
    String255 url = "http://intranet.contoso.com/
      Accounts%20Payable%20Documents/Forms/
        AllItems.aspx?IsDlg=1";

    url = url + "&FilterField1=AccountNum&
      FilterValue1=" + VendTable.AccountNum;
    url = url + "&FilterField2=Company&
```

```
        FilterValue2=" + VendTable.dataAreaId;
    Documents.Navigate(url);

    super(_active);
}
```

Code Snippet 1: VendTable Form activate method

9. Two items to note, we added the `IsDlg=1` qualifier to the URL which removes all of the navigation and gutter options on the page, and also the Filter qualifiers will automatically add a filter on the `AccountNum` field, and the Company indexes.

10. Now we can save the project, and we are finished.

How it works...

When we open up the **Vendor Detail** form, we will see a new tab at the bottom of the page that will list the documents that are indexed with **Vendor Account Number**:

At any time, the users are able to open up the documents, and view the scanned images.

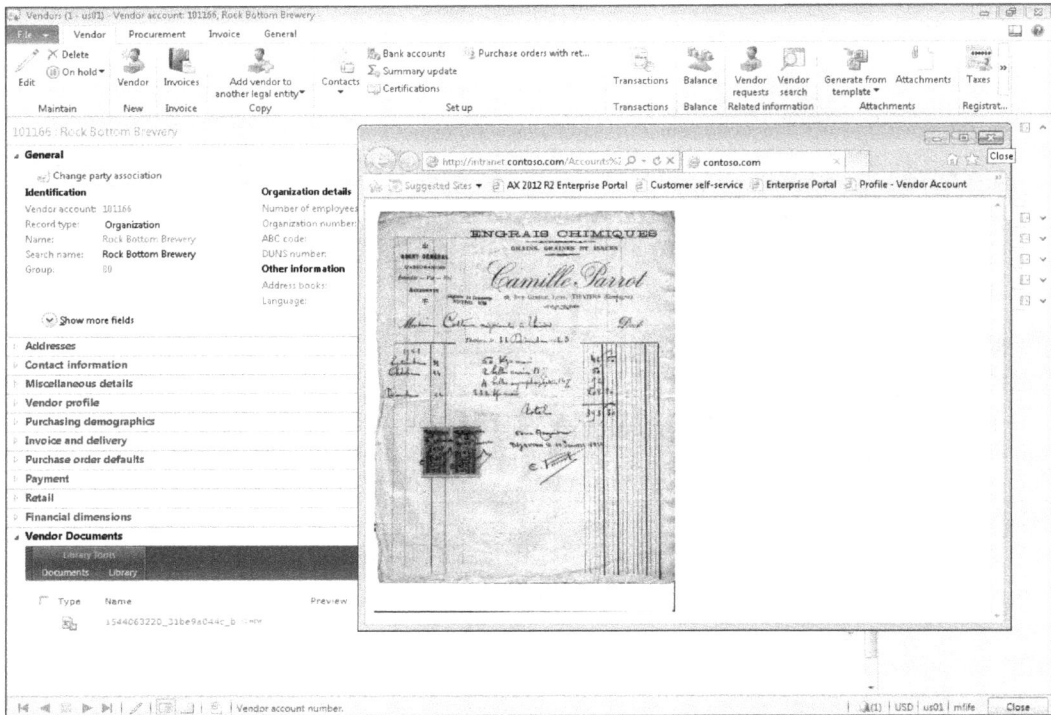

Summary

SharePoint is a great tool for sharing and collaborating, and is even more useful because you don't need to be a developer in order to set it up. In this chapter we looked at just a couple of the features that you can use with Dynamics AX, but there are a lot more that you can take advantage of.

Some other ways that you can use SharePoint include:

▶ Creating knowledge bases with Wiki's, allowing the users to collaboratively update information related to products, customers, vendors, or other records in the system

▶ Enabling blogging within SharePoint so that users can share business insights with everyone else in the organization

▶ Adding document workflows to manage the approval of documents such as Invoices

Since you probably have SharePoint up and running, then it would be a shame not to take advantage of it.

2
Reports and Dashboards

In this chapter, we will show you how to create your own ad-hoc reports and dashboards by using tools that you are already using such as Excel, or by using PowerPivot and Power View to create interactive dashboards and reporting galleries. This chapter will cover:

- ▶ Creating a Power View report from Dynamics AX
- ▶ Creating a Power View report from Power View cubes
- ▶ Saving Power View dashboards and reports
- ▶ Adding a Power View report to a Role Center
- ▶ Exporting a Power View report to PowerPoint
- ▶ Creating a PowerPivot gallery in SharePoint
- ▶ Creating a PowerPivot data source for Power View
- ▶ Creating a Power View report via the PowerPivot gallery
- ▶ Linking Power View reports to Dynamics AX forms

Introduction

Power View is a new reporting tool that was introduced by Microsoft with the release of Microsoft SQL Server 2012. Unlike many of the other reporting tools that are available, this one is designed so that users can create their own dashboards and reports without needing a lot of help, making everyone just a little more productive. Gone are the days where you have to export data from Dynamics AX to Excel, and then create a one-off dashboard when you want to analyze some data. Now you can create a dashboard in Power View, save it, and return to it any time you like.

With the R2 release of Microsoft Dynamics AX 2012, Power View was also embedded directly into the forms allowing users to create dashboards and reports on the fly without even knowing that they are using Power View.

In this chapter we will show how you can use Power View with the Dynamics AX 2012 R2 to create reports, how the users are able to save the reports for others to use, and also how you can export the reports to PowerPoint to create interactive presentations that include the Power View dashboards.

Later on we will also show how you can use PowerPivot for Excel and PowerPivot galleries in SharePoint to create data sources for Power View dashboards and reports, and then even embed links within the Dynamics AX forms for the users to quickly access them regardless of the version of Dynamics AX that you are running.

The later examples in this chapter may require configuration to your SharePoint sites in order to create the PowerPivot gallery, requiring administrator access, and the last example does have a little bit of X++ coding, but apart from that, these examples shouldn't require much technical expertise to set up and configure.

Creating a Power View report from Dynamics AX

The Dynamics AX 2012 R2 release has links to Power View embedded directly into the application, allowing the users to create their own reports and dashboards with just a click of a button.

In this quick recipe, we will show how you can quickly create a report directly from the Dynamics AX application.

Getting ready

In order to work through this example, you need to be running Microsoft Dynamics AX 2012 R2, or later.

How to do it...

To create a simple ad-hoc report from Dynamics AX, follow these steps:

1. Open up the **Customers** list from within **Accounts Receivable**.

2. In the far right corner of the ribbon bar, in the **Customer** tab there is an **Analyze data** button. Click on this button to open up Power View:

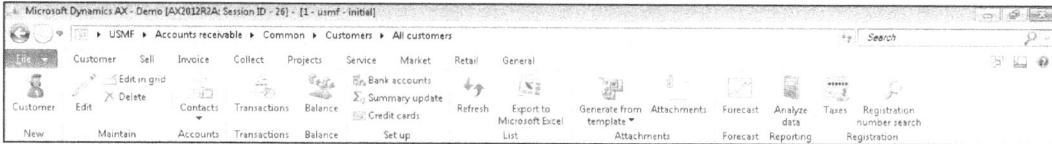

3. When the Power View window opens up, find the **Accounts receivable open transactions measure** from the field list on the right and select the checkbox to add it to the report canvas:

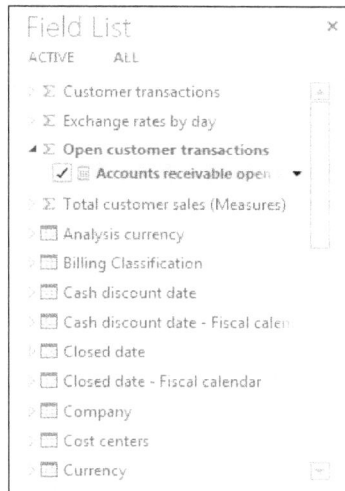

4. Find the **Month** dimension that is in the **Transaction Date** group in the field list and add it to the report.

5. Change the report design to be a column chart by clicking on the **Column** chart type in the **Visualizations** group on the **Design** tab of the ribbon bar:

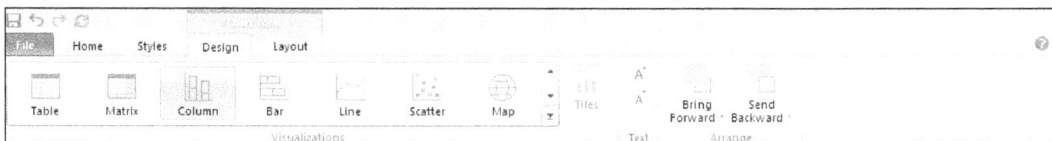

6. To show some segregation of the data, you can find the **Customer group name** field that will be in the **Customer** field group, and drag it into the legend properties box:

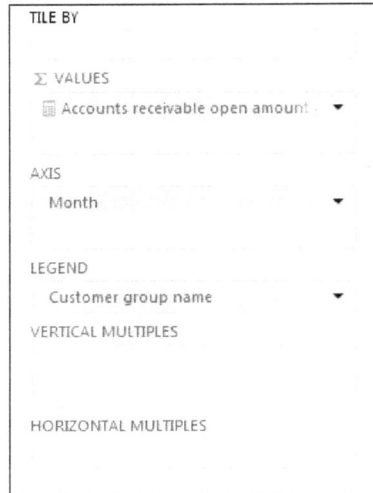

```
TILE BY

Σ VALUES
    Accounts receivable open amount     ▼


AXIS
    Month                               ▼


LEGEND
    Customer group name                 ▼
VERTICAL MULTIPLES



HORIZONTAL MULTIPLES
```

7. To finish off the dashboard, we can update the title so that it shows something a little more descriptive.

How it works...

Once we have generated our Power View report on the fly, we are able to click on any of the groupings or data within the report and the dashboard will filter out the data for us, or show related information in the chart:

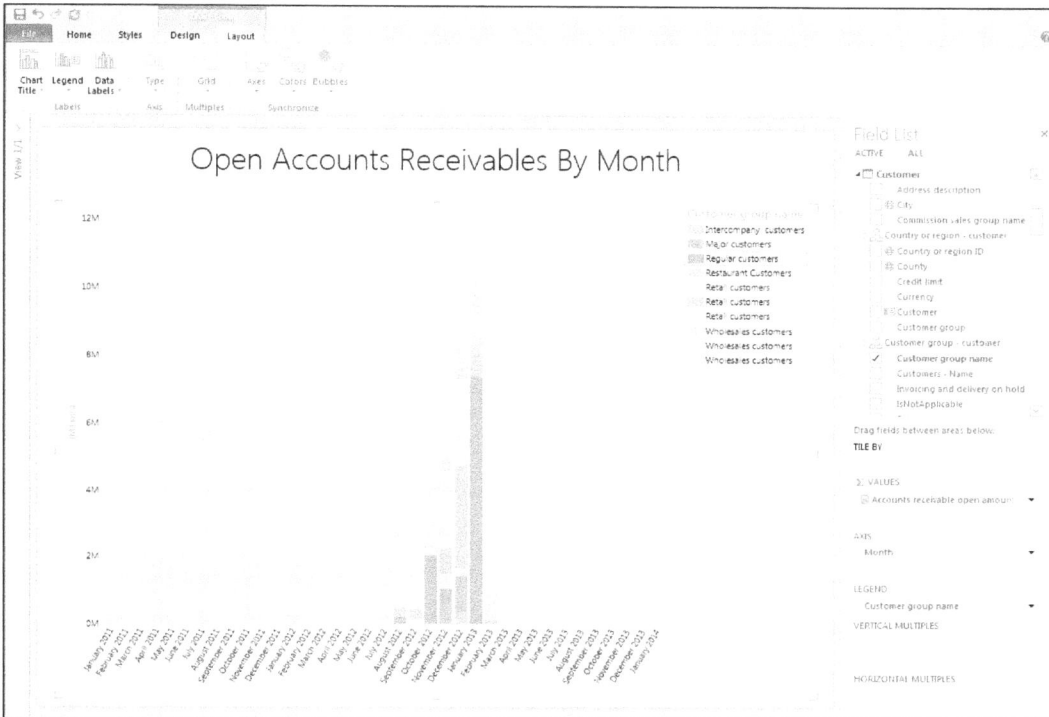

Open Accounts Receivables By Month

Creating a Power View report from Power View cubes

With the Dynamics AX 2012 R2 release, there are additional reporting cubes hidden within SharePoint that are not currently linked to the main forms. If you find them, then you are able to create Power View dashboards and reports.

In this example we will show how you can use the **Sales cube** to build a more elaborate Power View dashboard.

Getting ready

Before you start this recipe, you need to find where the Power View dashboards are stored. You may need to have administrator access to SharePoint for this step. To find the Power View Reports library follow these steps:

1. Open up any Dynamics AX Role Center, and from the **Site Actions** drop-down menu in the top left corner, select the **View All Site Content** menu option:

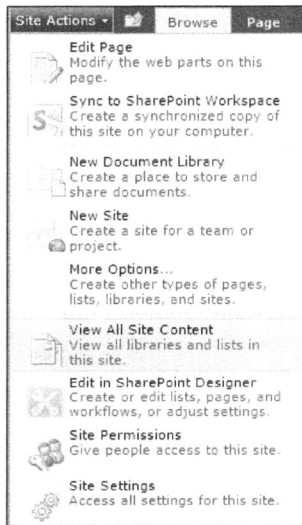

2. This will open up the Site Content browser. Here you should be able to see a **Power View Reports** document library and drill down into the contents to see all of the reports that have been saved, and also all of the available cubes:

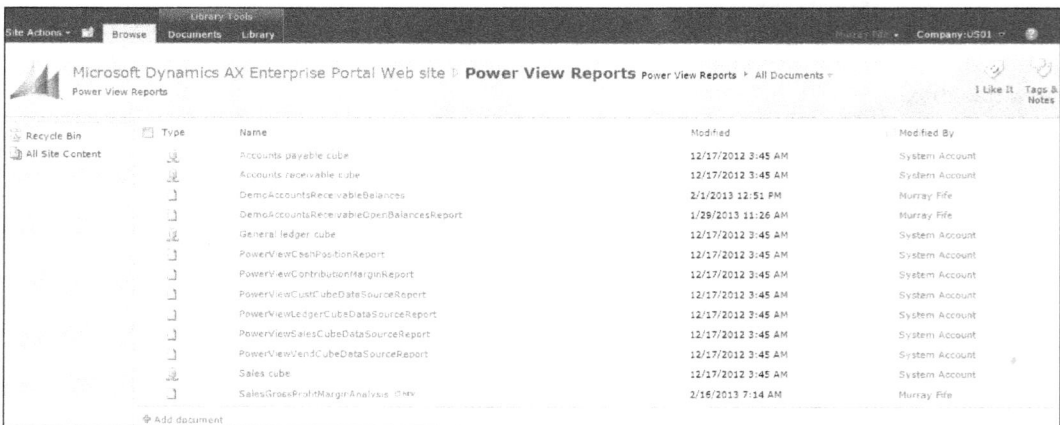

How to do it...

To create a dashboard directly from a Power View cube, follow these steps:

1. Open the drop-down menu for the cube that you want to report off and select the **Create Power View Report** option. In this case we are choosing the Sales cube which hasn't been linked to the Dynamics AX client yet:

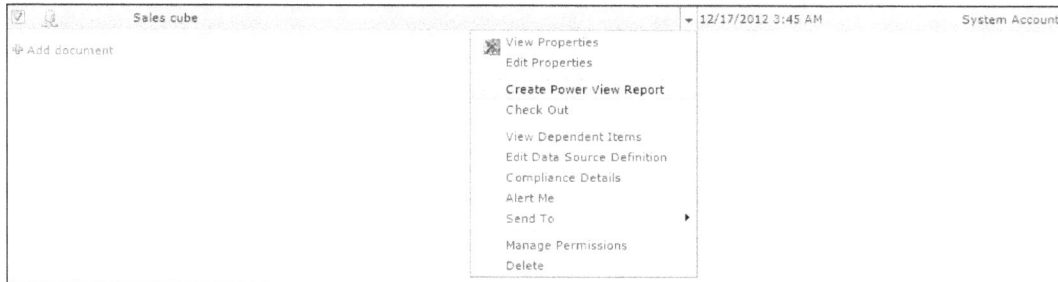

2. This will open up a blank Power View canvas. We will start off the by adding a title to the dashboard:

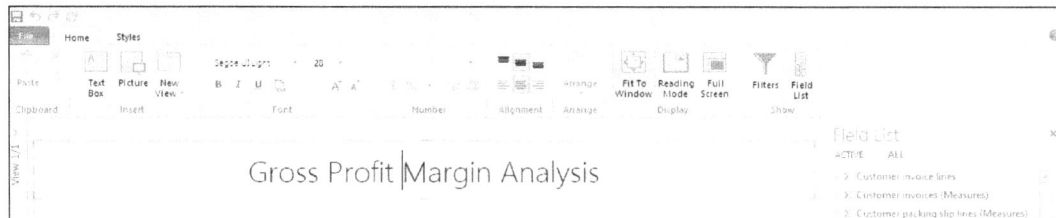

3. Create a new dashboard panel by checking the **Gross profit margin** measure from the **Measures** field group, and also the **Month** dimension from the **Transaction date** field group:

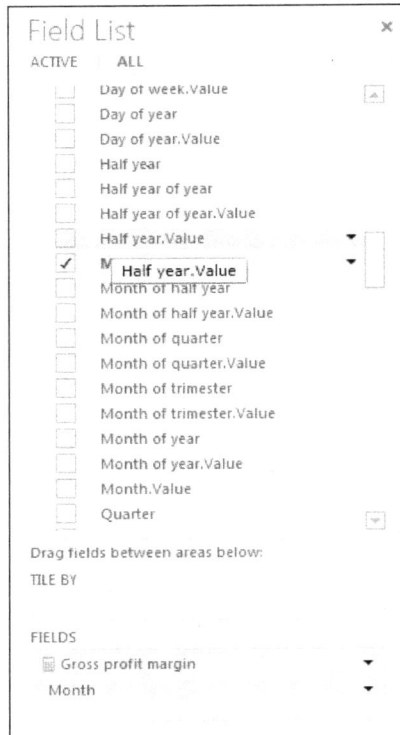

4. From the **Design** tab on the ribbon bar, select the **Column** chart type from the **Visualizations** group to convert the report to a column chart:

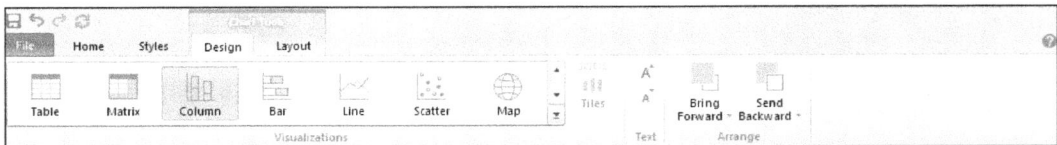

5. Drag the **Item group name** measure from the **Released products** field group into the **Legend** box on the right of the dashboard designer:

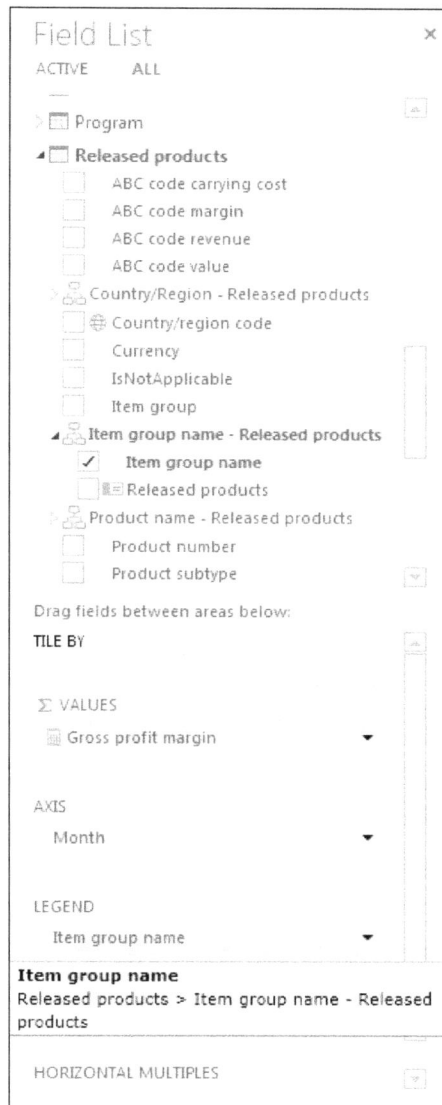

6. Add another panel to the report by clicking on the blank canvas. Select the **Month** and **Item group name** dimensions and the **Gross profit margin** percent measure. Then change the visualization type to be **Bar**.

7. For the third dashboard, create a new **Column** chart using the **Month** and **Item group name** dimensions, the **Invoice amount** measure.

8. For the final chart, create a **Column** chart with the **Item group name** as the only dimension, and add the **Commission line amount**, **Cost of goods sold**, and **Sales tax measures**:

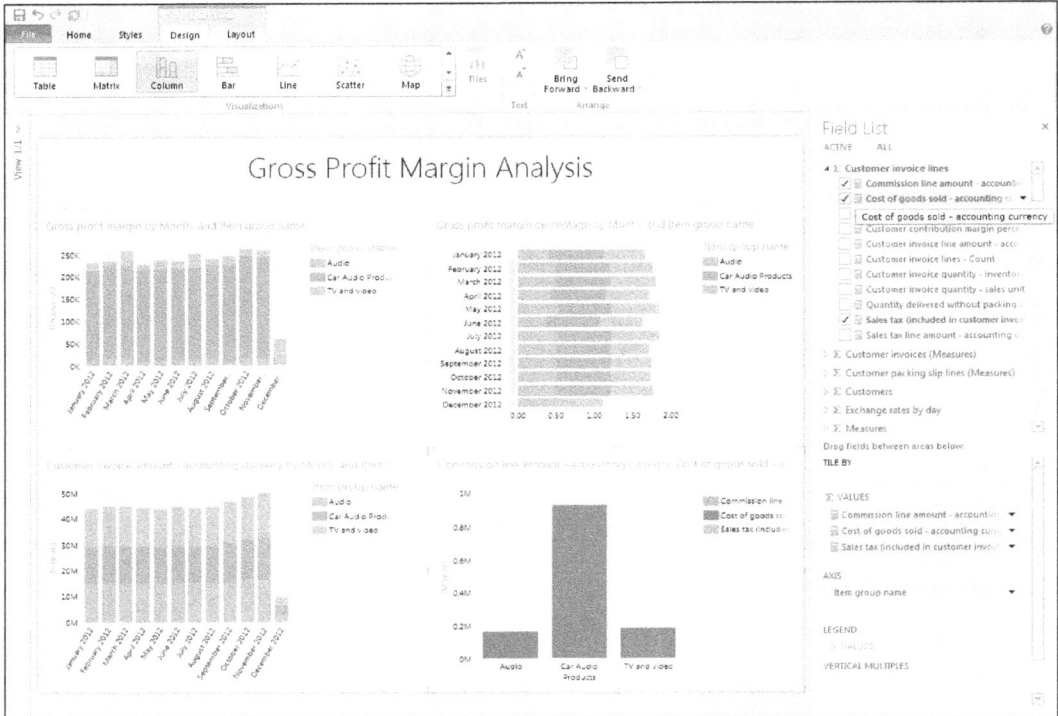

How it works...

Now you should have a multipanel dashboard. Clicking on any of the elements will filter out the view to show you the related data in the other views:

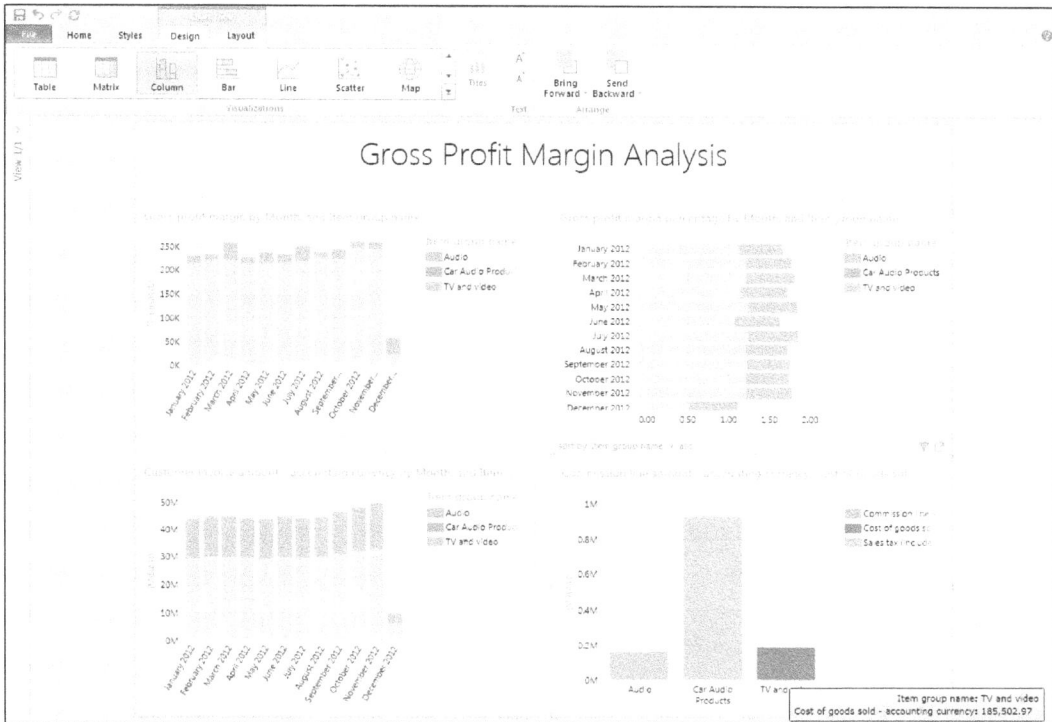

Gross Profit Margin Analysis

Saving Power View dashboards and reports

Although creating a Power View dashboard is a simple task, you probably don't want to recreate the same report over and over again, and others may be interested in using your dashboard as well.

In this quick recipe, we will show how you can save your dashboards back to the `Power View Reports` folder in Dynamics AX so that you and others are able to access the data at any time.

How to do it...

If you have a Power View report that you would like to use again, you can save it by following these steps:

1. From the **File** menu on the Power View report designer, just select the **Save As** option:

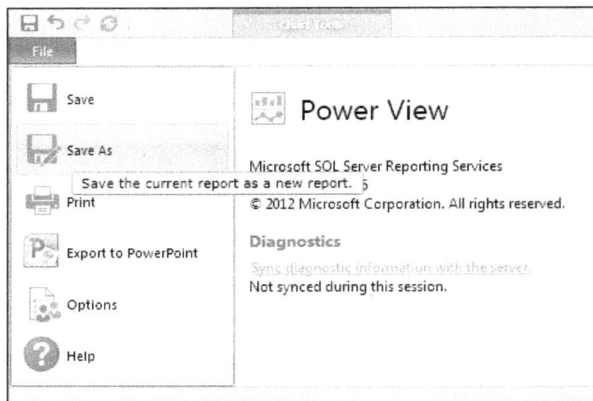

2. Then give your report a name and save it:

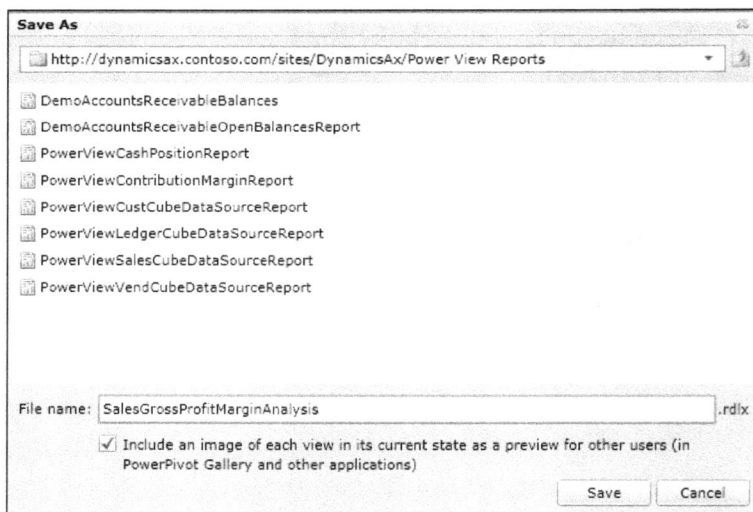

How it works...

Once your dashboard is saved, you can access it from the `Power View Reports` folder within your Role Center content:

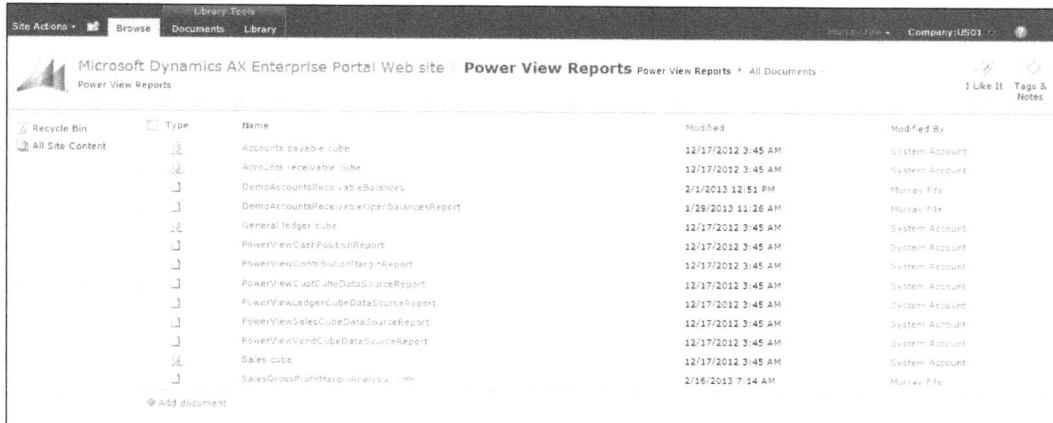

Adding a Power View report to a Role Center

With Microsoft Dynamics AX 2012 R2, a new Web Part was added that allows you to easily embed your Power View dashboards into the Role Centers. Any report or dashboard that you create may be added this way, and users are able to view and filter the information directly within the Role Center, or pop the dashboard out of the Role Center and edit the report on the fly.

This recipe will show you how to customize your Role Center and add a Power View report or dashboard.

How to do it...

To add a Power View dashboard to a Role Center, follow these steps:

1. Click on the **Personalize this page** link in the top-right of your Role Center within Dynamics AX.

2. Click on the **Add a Web Part** link on the panel that you would like to add the Power View dashboard to.

3. This should open up the Web Part browser. Find the **Microsoft Dynamics AX** category group and you should see an **SQL Server Power view** web part:

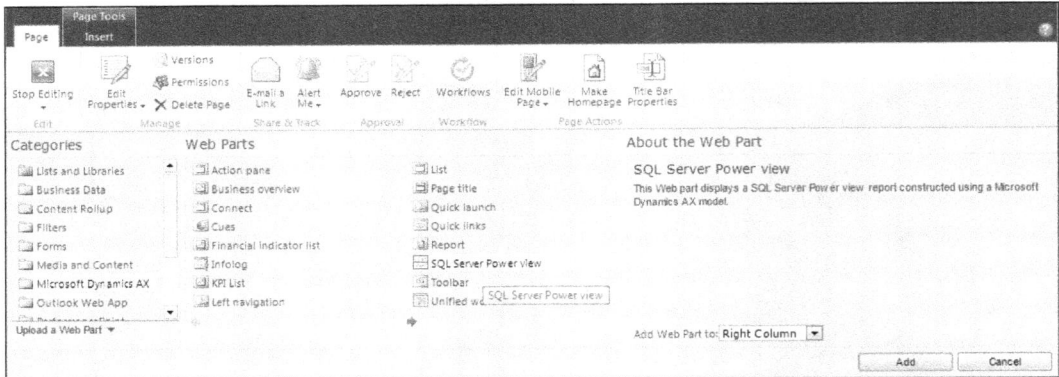

4. Select the **SQL Server Power view** web part and then click on the **Add** button.

5. Now that you have the web part on your Role Center, configure it by choosing **Edit My Web Part** option from the context menu of the web part.

6. In the properties box for the SQL Power View web part, click on the list browser icon to the right of the **Select a report** field to open up the report browser:

7. This will take you to the **Power View Reports** document library on SharePoint and you should see all of the Power View dashboards and reports that you have created. Just select the one that you would like to add to the Role Center and click on **OK**:

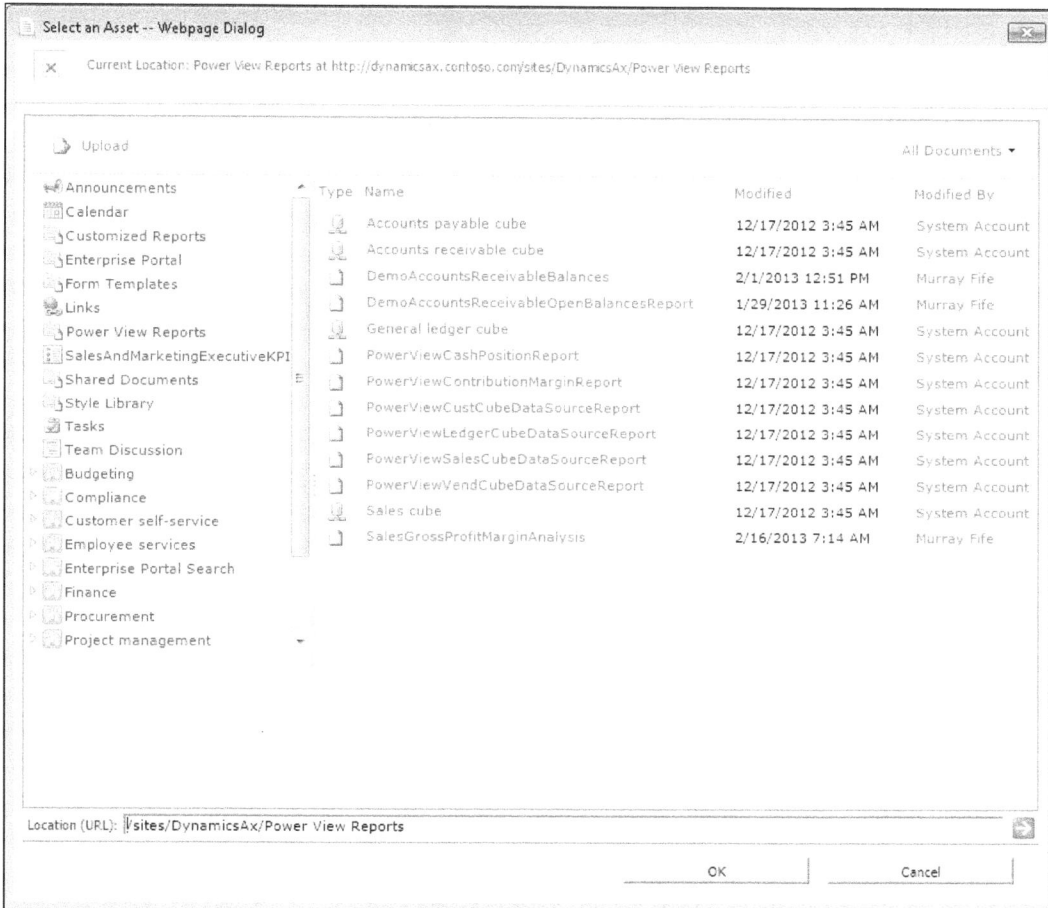

8. Now click on **OK** on the web part properties to save the changes, and then click on the **Stop Editing** button on the ribbon bar to return to view mode.

How it works...

Now when you see your Role Center, the Power View report will be displayed. The data that shows up will also be filtered based on the company that you are in, making the report context sensitive:

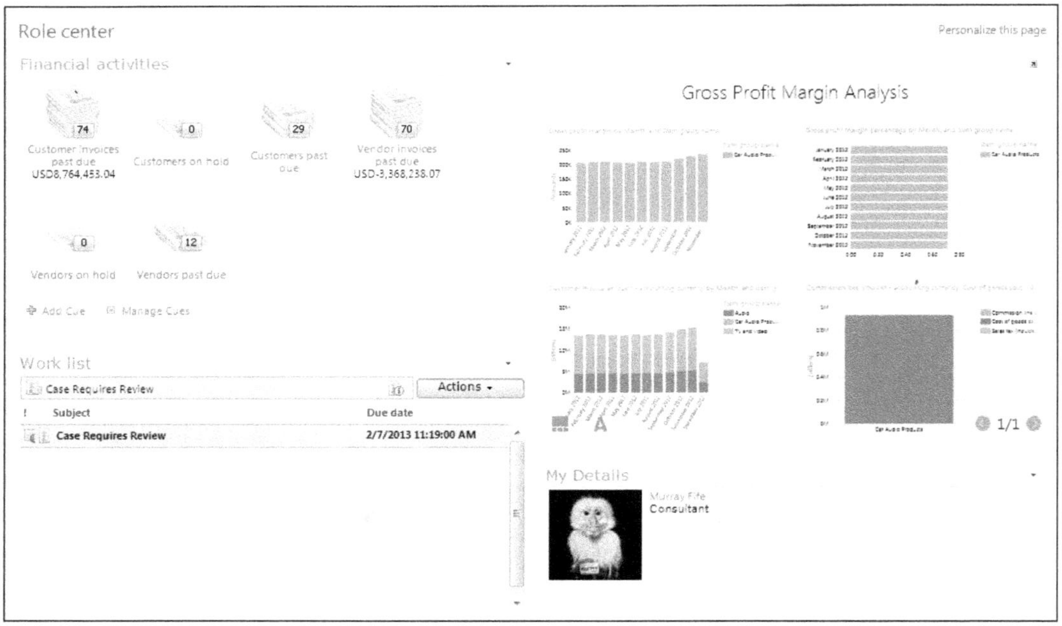

Additionally, if you click on the pop-out icon in the top-right of the Power View report in the Role Center, then the report will open in a new explorer window, allowing you to also enter edit mode and change the report:

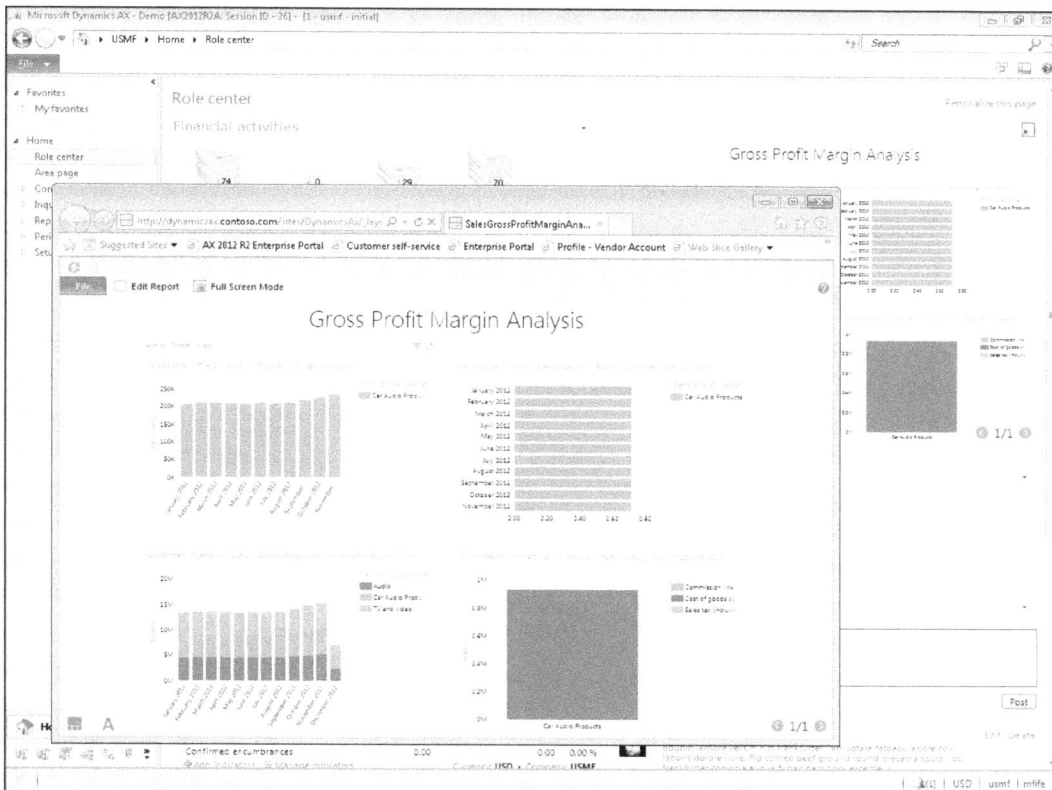

Exporting a Power View report to PowerPoint

If you spend your days recreating the same presentation, by refreshing the data in reports from Dynamics AX and then reformatting the information, then Power View has a very cool feature that you will be able to take advantage of that allows you to export any of the dashboards that you create to PowerPoint.

This is not your ordinary export that just takes a screen capture of your current view and then pastes it into your presentation, instead Power View is embedded into your presentation. If you have security to access the data, then your PowerPoint becomes an interactive dashboard whenever you enter into presentation mode. If you deliver the presentation to someone who does not have access to the source data, then the reports look just as they did when you last updated the data.

You can use this to create internal review presentations, or even start with a template and then filter the data individually to be delivered to customers or vendors for performance analysis.

In this quick recipe, we will show how you can easily use the **Export to PowerPoint** feature in Power View to create PowerPoint views.

How to do it...

To export a Power View report to PowerPoint, follow these steps:

1. Open up the Power View report that you want to export, and from the **File** menu, select the **Export to PowerPoint** option:

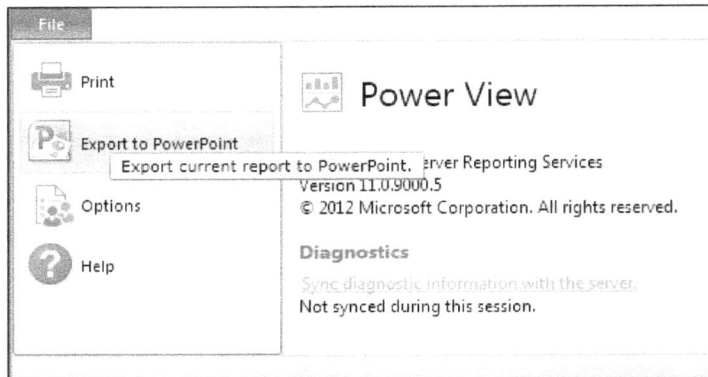

2. When the **Save As** dialog box shows up, give your PowerPoint a name and click on **Save**.

How it works...

When you open up your PowerPoint presentation, your report will be embedded in the slides:

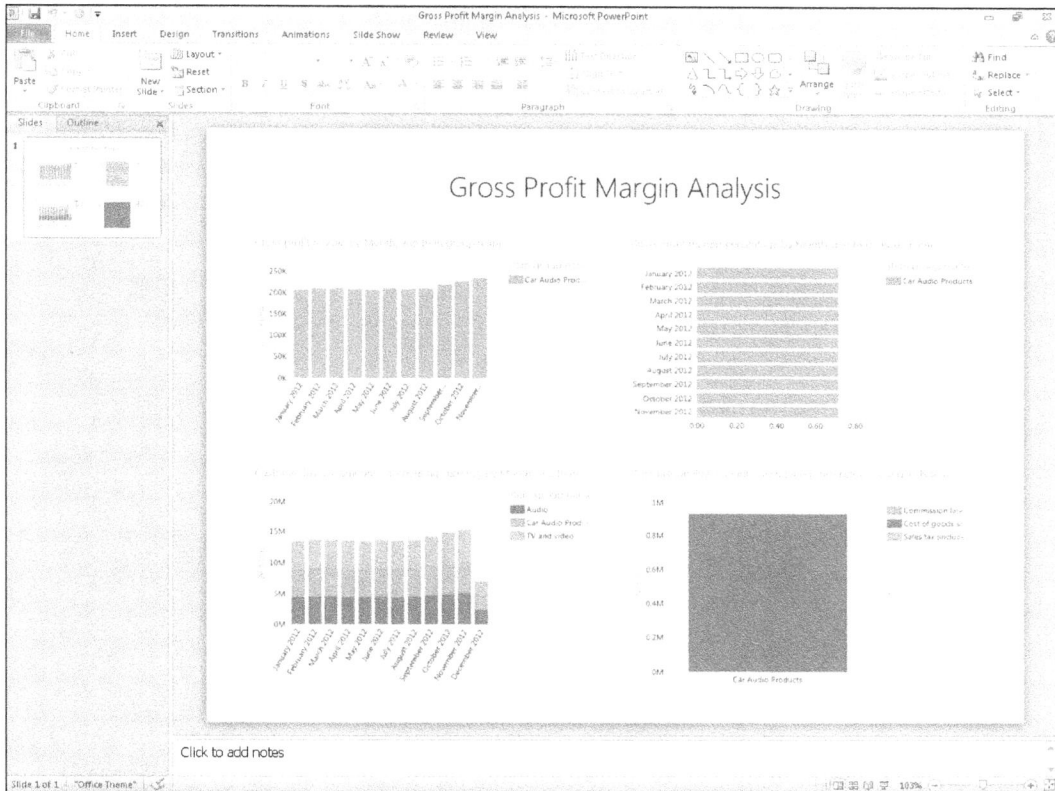

What makes this special though is that when you go into presentation mode, there will be an **Interact** button on the bottom-right of the dashboard:

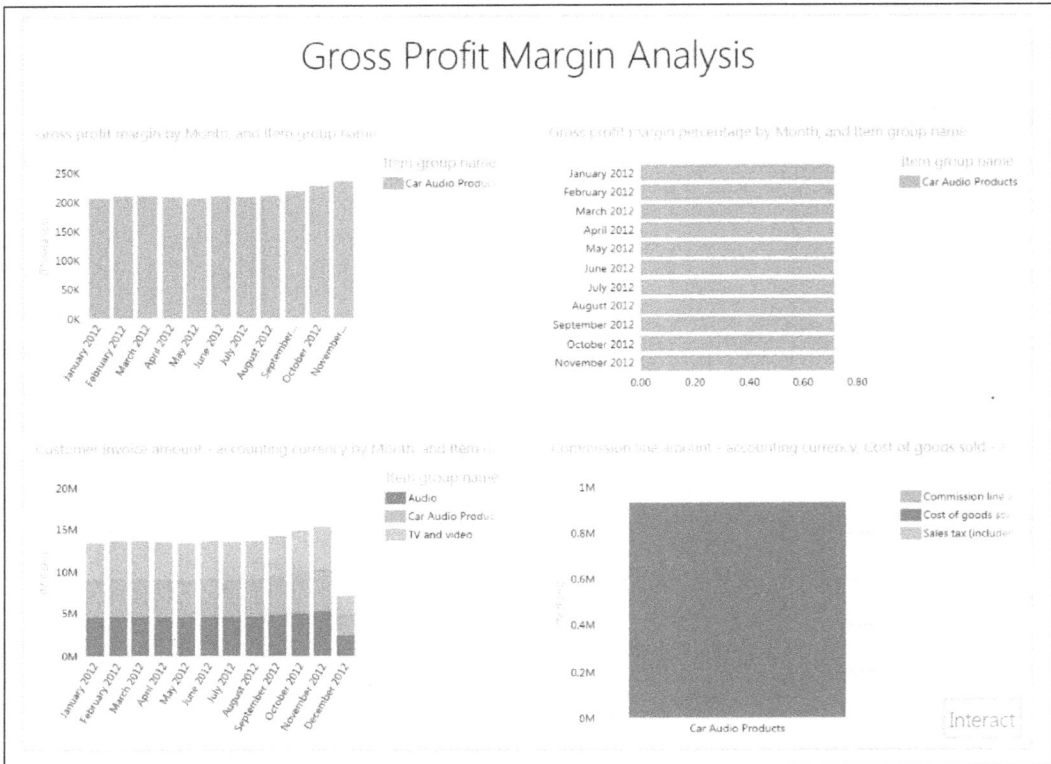

Clicking on the **Interact** button will turn the slide into a live dashboard that you are able to drill around just like you can do with all of the original dashboards.

Creating a PowerPivot gallery in SharePoint

Up until now, we have just been creating dashboards and reports within Power View from the pre-defined cubes that are delivered with Dynamics AX 2012 R2 or later. You are not limited to those data sources for reporting though, and you can use Excel and PowerPivot for Excel to create your own data sources that you can report off. This is also an option that is available to all versions of Dynamics AX, so if you have not yet upgraded to the R2 or higher releases, then you can still take advantage of all the benefits of Power View for user reporting.

In order to use Power View in this way you need to have a **PowerPivot Gallery** site configured in SharePoint. This is where you will store your data sources, dashboards, and reports that you create.

If you do not currently have a **PowerPivot Gallery** site configured, then the following recipe will step through the process of creating the site in SharePoint.

Getting ready

Before you start on this example, you will need to make sure that you have access to the **SharePoint Central Administration** console. To check this carry out the following steps:

1. Access your server that has SharePoint installed on it.

2. From the program menu, you should be able to find the **SharePoint Central Administration** console in the **Microsoft SharePoint Products** group.

3. If you cannot access this feature, then you may need to get help from your SharePoint administrator for this recipe.

How to do it...

To create a **PowerPivot Gallery** site in SharePoint, follow these steps:

1. From the **SharePoint Central Administration** console, access the **Application Management** area, and click on **Manage web applications**.

2. From the **Web Applications** tab, create a new SharePoint site by clicking on the **New** button on the ribbon bar:

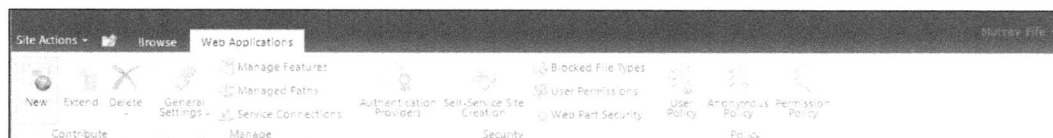

3. To create a new site, select the **Create a new IIS web site** option on the **IIS Web Site** group. Give the website a name, port, and host header, and then click on **OK**:

Create New Web Application

Warning: this page is not encrypted for secure communication. User names, passwords, and any other information will be sent in clear text. For more information, contact your administrator.

OK	Cancel

Authentication

Select the authentication for this web application.

Learn about authentication.

○ Claims Based Authentication
◉ Classic Mode Authentication

IIS Web Site

Choose between using an existing IIS web site or create a new one to serve the Microsoft SharePoint Foundation application.

If you select an existing IIS web site, that web site must exist on all servers in the farm and have the same name, or this action will not succeed.

If you opt to create a new IIS web site, it will be automatically created on all servers in the farm. If an IIS setting that you wish to change is not shown here, you can use this option to create the basic site, then update it using the standard IIS tools.

○ Use an existing IIS web site

Default Web Site

◉ Create a new IIS web site
Name
PowerView

Port
80

Host Header
powerview.contoso.com

Path
C:\inetpub\wwwroot\wss\VirtualDirectoi

Security Configuration

Kerberos is the recommended security configuration to use with Integrated Windows authentication. Kerberos requires the application pool account to be Network Service or special configuration by the domain administrator. NTLM authentication will work with any application pool account and the default domain configuration.

If you choose to use Secure Sockets Layer (SSL), you must add the certificate on each server using the IIS administration tools. Until this is done, the web application will be inaccessible from this IIS web site.

Authentication provider:

○ Negotiate (Kerberos)
◉ NTLM
Allow Anonymous

○ Yes
◉ No
Use Secure Sockets Layer (SSL)

○ Yes
◉ No

4. After the web application has been created we need to create a **PowerPivot Gallery** site. To do this return to the **Application Management** area of the **SharePoint Administration** console and click on the **Create site collection** link in the **Site Collections** group.

5. Select the Power View web application that we just created, give your site a title, enter a subfolder for the **Web Site Address**, select the **PowerPivot Site** template from the **Collaboration** templates, and then click on **OK** to create the site:

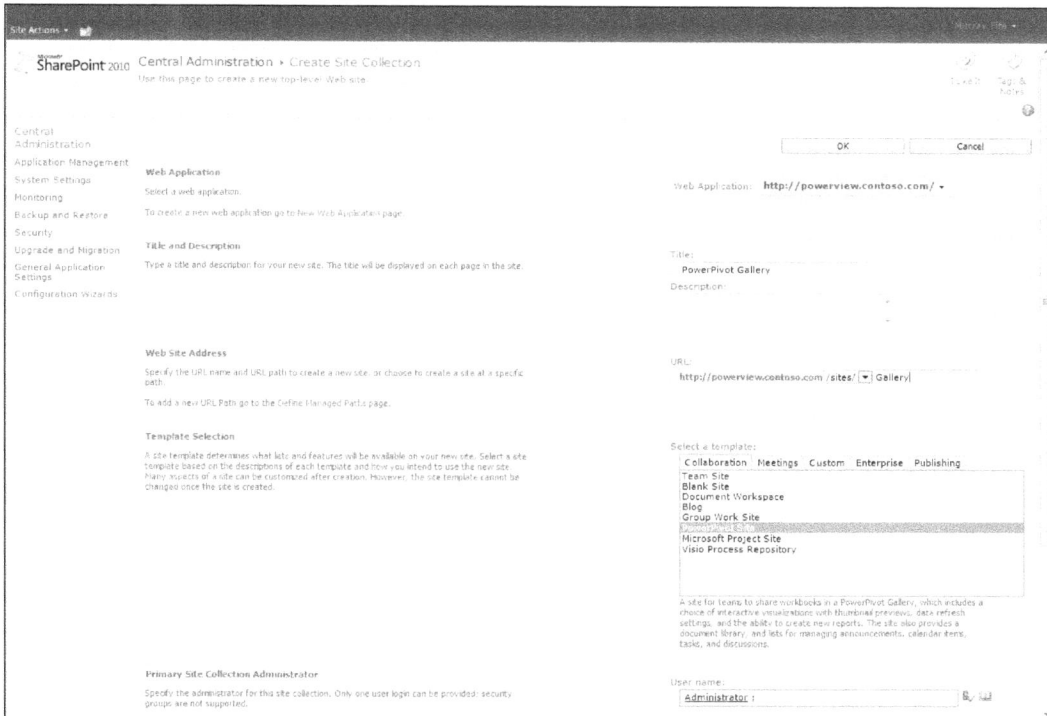

How it works...

Once you have created the site, you will be able to access the gallery. Right now it will look a little empty, but in the next set of recipes, we will start adding content to the site:

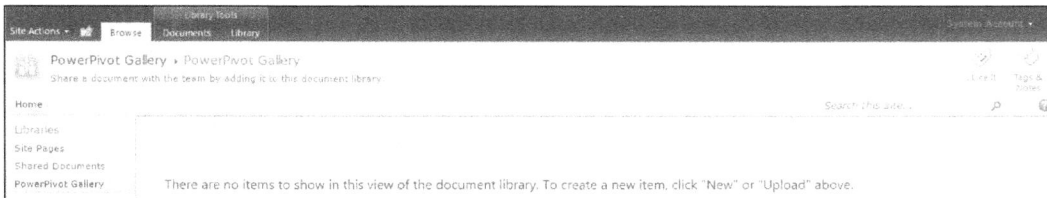

Creating a PowerPivot data source for Power View

You can create Power View reports directly off the data within Dynamics AX by building your own personal data sources through Excel and saving them to a PowerPivot gallery in SharePoint. This gives you the flexibility of accessing data that may not be in the existing Power View cubes, including custom tables and fields that you have added, without having to become a DBA and tweak the reporting cubes themselves.

In the following recipe we will work through a simple example of how you can use the PowerPivot add-on for Excel to access inventory information from Dynamics AX, and then save it to a PowerPivot gallery in SharePoint so that we can report off it.

Getting ready

Before you are able to create a PowerPivot data source, you need to make sure that you have the PowerPivot add-on configured in Excel. If you have it installed, then when you open up Excel, there should be a **PowerPivot** tab in the ribbon bar:

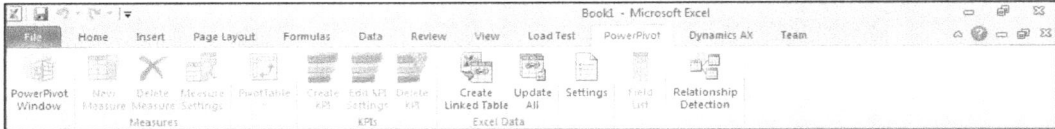

If you don't have it installed, then follow these steps to download the add-in before starting this recipe:

1. Download and install the **Microsoft SQL Server 2012 PowerPivot** for Microsoft Excel from the **Microsoft Download Center**:

   ```
   http://www.microsoft.com/en-us/download/details.aspx?id=29074
   ```

How to do it...

To create a PowerPivot data source against Dynamics AX for reporting through Power View, follow these steps:

1. Open Excel, and go to the **PowerPivot** tab. Click on the **PowerPivot Window** button:

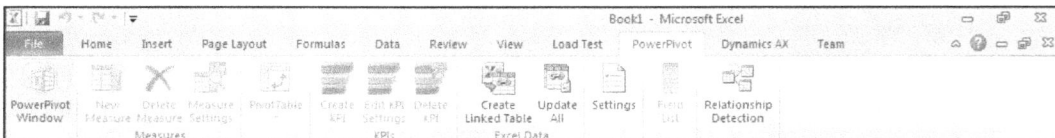

2. This will open up a new window that allows us to create our reporting data source. To add data from Dynamics AX, navigate to the **From Datasource** button on the ribbon bar, and then select the **From SQL Server** option:

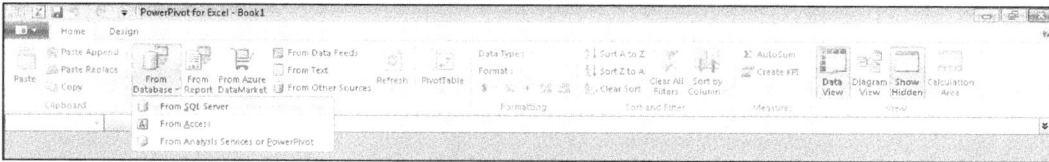

3. In the **Table Import Wizard** form, specify the server where your Dynamics AX database is stored, and then select the database name from the drop-down list:

4. The next option allows us to either select data directly from the tables within Dynamics AX, or write an SQL query to grab the data. For this example, navigate to the **table list** option.

5. The next form will allow you to select any table(s) from the database to use in your data source. In this example, select the `InventSum` table so that we will be able to report off all of the inventory levels:

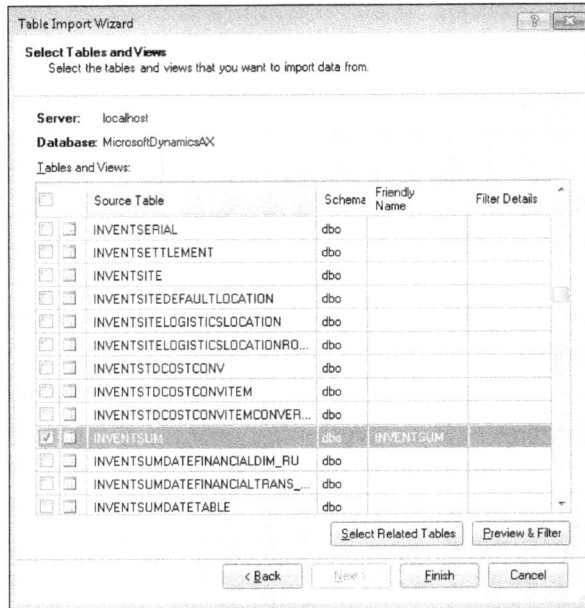

6. Once this is finished, Excel will retrieve the data from Dynamics AX and create a spreadsheet for us.

7. There are only a few columns in the table that we are interested in, so we can hide every column except for the `ItemID`, `AvailPhysical`, `PhysicalValue`, `PhysicalInvent`, and `DataAreaID` by right-clicking on these other columns and selecting **Hide from Client Tools**:

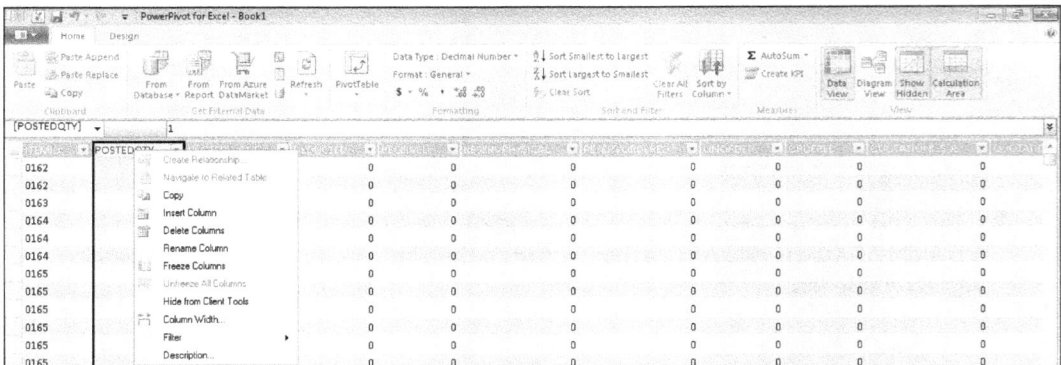

8. Rather than use the default field names for the columns, double-click on the column headings, and rename the visible fields to `Item ID`, `Available Qty`, `Available Value`, `Physical Qty`, and `Company`:

9. Finally, change the tab name for the data from **INVENTSUM** to **Inventory Summary**.

10. Now that we have defined the data for our data source, close the PowerPivot window and return to Excel. From the **File** menu, select the **Save & Send** option so that we are able to save the data source to your PowerPivot gallery in SharePoint. If you have done this already, then your PowerPivot gallery location will be remembered by Excel, if this is the first time that you publish the data, then you need to click on the **Browse for a location** option:

11. In the address bar of the **Save As** dialog box, enter the URL for your PowerPivot gallery, give the data source a name, and then click on the **Save** button.

How it works...

By saving your PowerPivot view to the PowerPivot gallery, it is stored away and available to be reused:

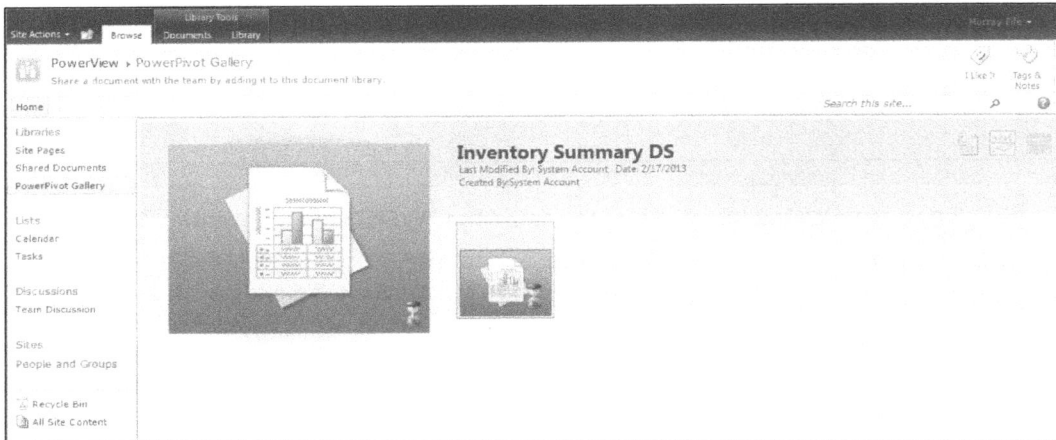

Creating a Power View report via the PowerPivot gallery

Once you have PowerPivot data sources published to your PowerPivot gallery in SharePoint, they become linked to Power View, and you are able to create dashboards and reports from them. Users can be given access to the PowerPivot gallery directly, or they can be given links to the Power View report designer so that they are able to create their own ad-hoc reports at any time.

In the following recipe we will show how you can create Power View reports directly from the PowerPivot gallery.

How to do it...

To create a Power View report from the PowerPivot gallery, follow these steps:

1. Open the PowerPivot gallery and find the data source that you want to report off:

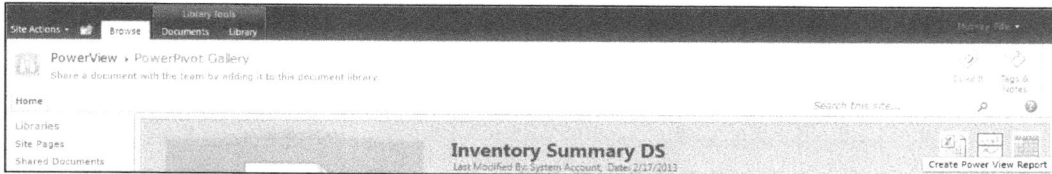

2. There are three icons on the top-right of the data source. The first will open up the data source in Excel, the second will allow you to create a Power View report from the data source, and the third allows you to define the refresh schedule of the data. For this example, click on the second icon labeled **Create Power View Report**.

3. This will open up the Power View report canvas, and the fields that are available for reporting will be the visible fields from our data source that we created. Select the `Item ID`, `Company`, and `Available Qty` fields, turn the report into a **Column** style chart, and then add a filter to the report to just show a single Company:

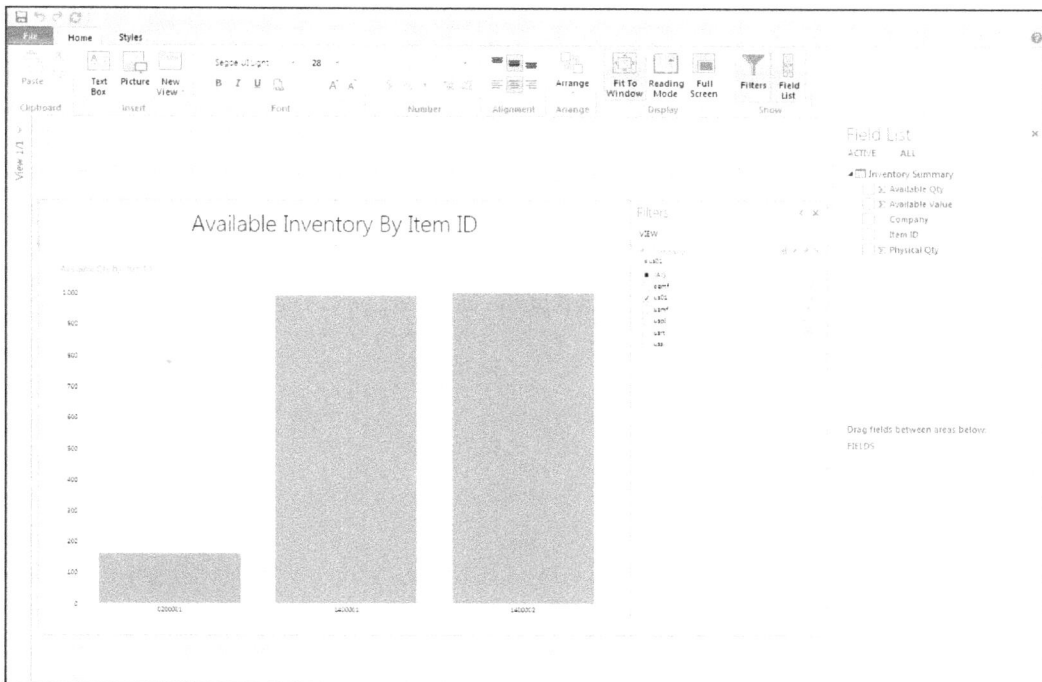

4. After you have created the report, select the **Save As** option from the **File** menu. You can save the Power View report to the PowerPivot gallery, or if you navigate through the site explorer in the address bar of the dialog then you are also able to save it to any other Power View folder, including the Power View library in the Dynamics AX Role Center:

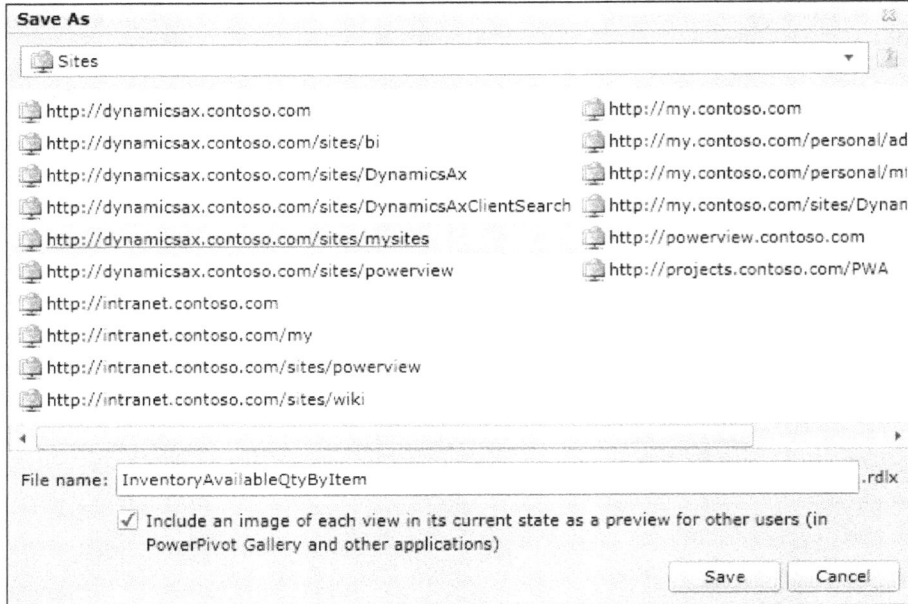

How it works...

The Power View reports from PowerPivot data sources work almost exactly the same way as the others that we created earlier on in the chapter, except, when you add them to the Role Center, in the **Microsoft Dynamics AX** group of the web part properties, make sure that you check the **IgnoreAxFilters** option:

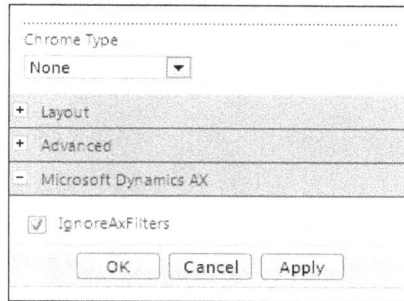

If you do not do this, the Role Center will try to pass through filters for Company and so on, into the dashboard.

Linking Power View reports to Dynamics AX forms

If you want to make your Power View dashboards and reports even more useful to the users, then you may want to add links to them directly within your Dynamics AX forms. This does require a little bit of X++ code, and a little bit of configuration in the AOT.

In this recipe we will show how you can easily add a button to the ribbon bar of an existing form that will link directly to a Power View report that you have, and even filter out the data so that you are just seeing the data that is related to the current record that you are in.

Getting ready

This example requires that you access the development environment and make changes to forms. Before you start on this example, make sure that you have developer rights on your installation of Dynamics AX.

How to do it...

To add links to Power View reports directly into Dynamics AX forms, follow these steps:

1. Create a new development project in AOT and call it **CustomerPowerViewButton**.

2. Find the **CustTable** form in the AOT forms and add it to your new project.

3. Expand the **CustTable** structure and open up the **ActionPanelTab** for the form **Design**.

4. Right-click on the **ActionPanelTab** and select the **ButtonGroup** control in the **New Control** menu to add a new button group to your form:

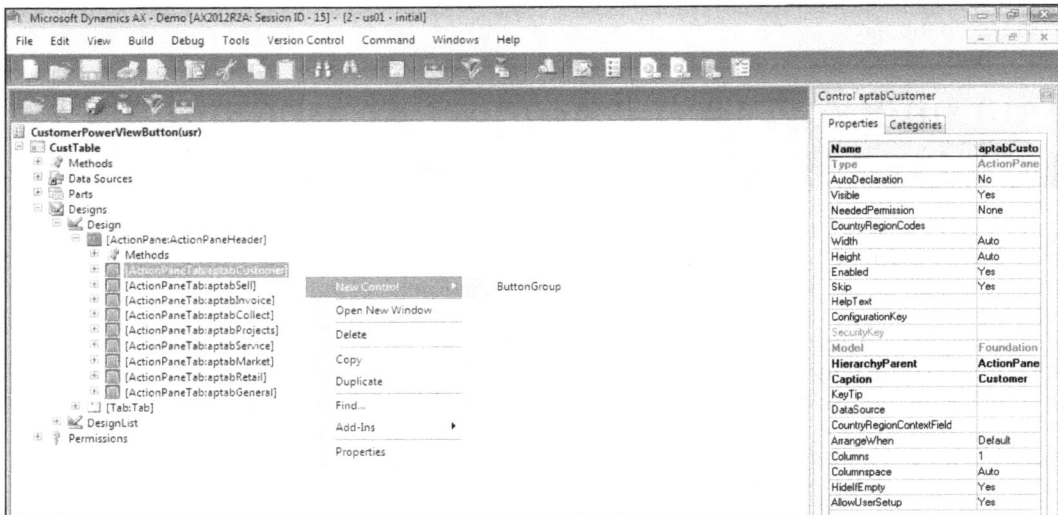

5. Move the button group to the bottom of the form by holding down the *Alt* key and using the down arrow.

6. Rename the button group to be **ReportingGroup** and change the caption to **Reporting**.

7. Right-click on the **ReportingGroup** tab and select the **Button from the New Control** menu item to add a new button to the form.

8. Rename the button to be **GrossProfitMarginAnalysis** and set the **Text** property to Gross Profit Margin Analysis:

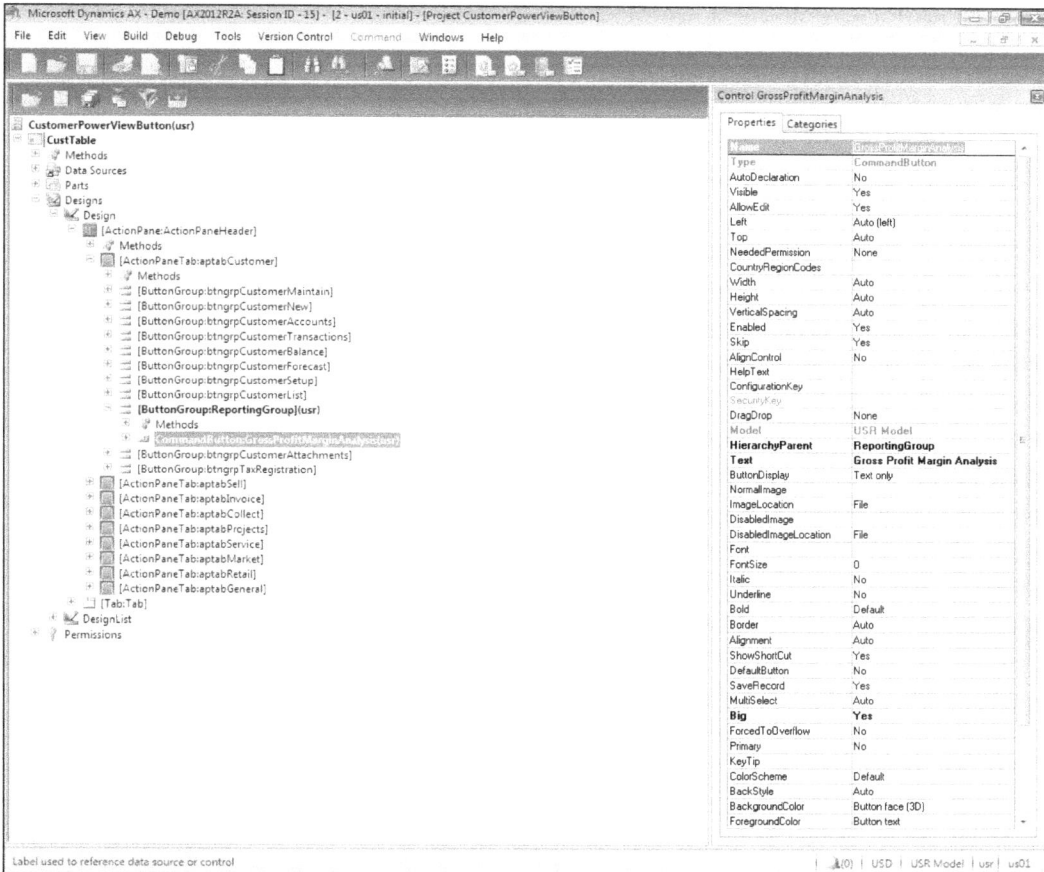

9. If you want to, you can assign an image to the button by linking an image file to the `NormalImage` property of the command button:

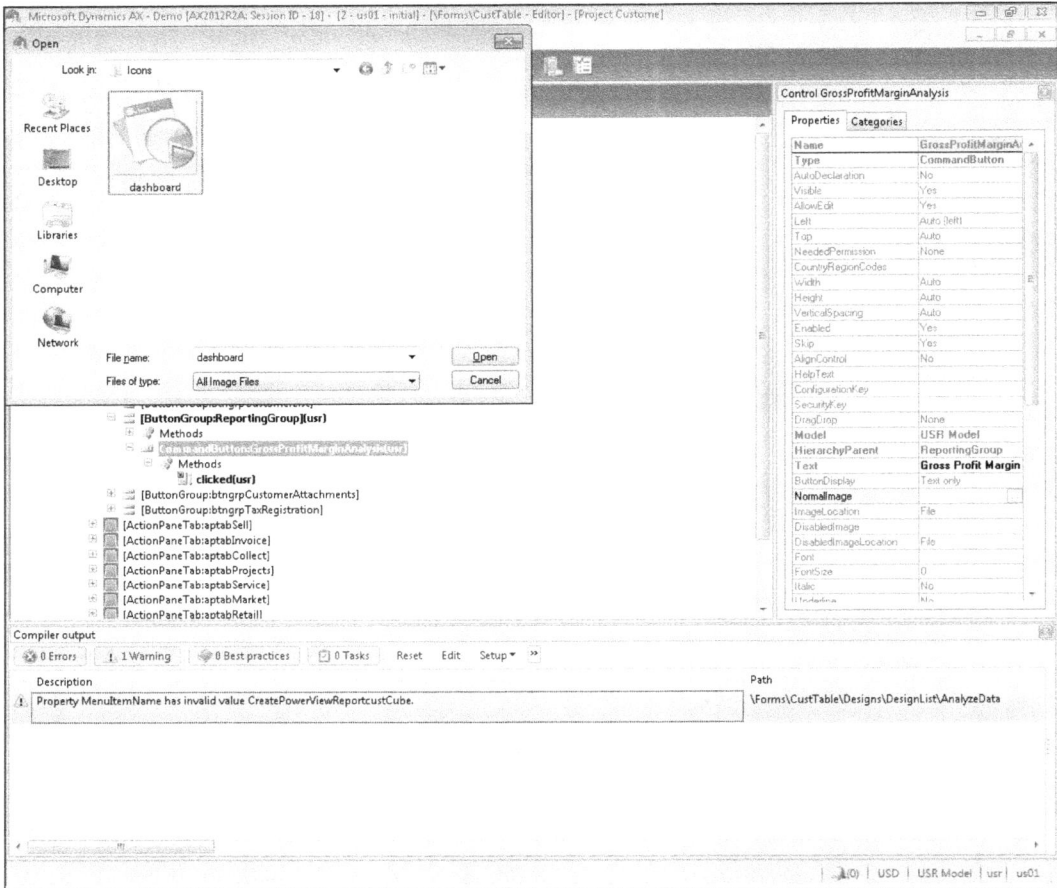

10. Expand out the button that you added so that you can see the button methods, right-click on the methods icon, and select the **Override** method menu item, and then the **clicked** method.

11. Change the code for the **clicked** method to be the following:

```
void clicked()
{
    str url = "";

    url = url + "http://dynamicsax.contoso.com/sites/DynamicsAx/_
layouts/ReportServer/AdHocReportDesigner.aspx";
```

```
    url = url + "?RelativeReportUrl=/sites/DynamicsAx/Power View
Reports/SalesGrossProfitMarginAnalysis.rdlx";
    url = url + "&ViewMode=Presentation";
    url = url + "&rf=[Customer].[Customer] eq '" + CustTable.
AccountNum + "'";

    infolog.urllookup(url);

    super();
}
```

Code Snippet 1

12. Save your project and you are done.

How it works...

Now when you open up the customer form, there is a new menu group in the **Customers** tab for reporting:

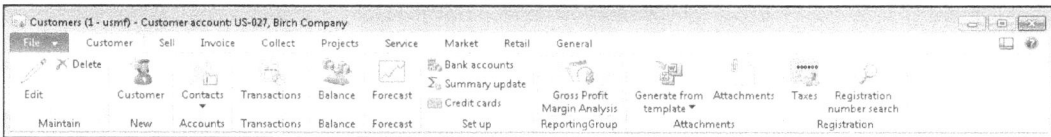

When you click on this link it will open up the Power View dashboard in another window, filtered out by the current customer record.

This example works by using some of the URL qualifiers that are available to be used with the Power View viewer. Inside the X++ code for this example, there are three qualifiers that we used to make this linked report dynamic.

RelativeReportURL allows you to define the default report that will be opened when the report viewer opens. In our case, we opened up the **Gross Margin** report.

We used the **ViewMode** qualifier to put the report in presentation mode, so that the users didn't immediately see fields from the report.

And to filter out the data that is returned in the report, you can use the **rf** qualifier, along with the field name, and the filter value.

Summary

Power View and PowerPivot are tools that are simple enough for almost everyone to use, and allow you to quickly build reports and dashboards that are useful. It becomes even more useful to the power users since they can also create their own data sources within Excel, a tool that everyone is familiar with using.

Once you start creating dashboards, you will discover that there are a lot of cool features that you can take advantage of. You may want to try:

- Adding external Azure services, XML feeds, and Dynamics AX ODataQueries to your PowerPivot data sources. This allows you to blend in dynamic reference data, such as weather, currency rates, or Twitter searches to make your dashboards more informative.
- Turning URL columns into pictures to allow your users to filter out the information visually rather than having lo look at codes.
- Using geographic information, such as city, state, and country to create geo-mapped reports.

Also, you don't just have to use Power View within Dynamics AX. Since you can publish the dashboards that you create to your SharePoint as a gallery, then everybody could access them directly. You may want to take advantage of this and use it to do some of the following:

- Show daily company metrics such as shift productivity metrics or real time sales volume on public monitors
- Use PowerPivot dashboards within presentations while working with customers and vendors
- Access Power View dashboards from tablets or surface devices

You don't have to be a reporting guru any more to create dashboards and reports with Power View and PowerPivot, but people will probably think that you are if you use them.

3

Dashboards, Charts, and Scorecards

In this chapter, we will focus on how you can use the **Business Intelligence** (**BI**) capabilities that are delivered with SharePoint and PerformancePoint to create your own charts and reports, and then share these with the users through the Dynamics AX Role Centers, and also to others through SharePoint dashboards. This chapter will cover:

- ► Creating a Business Intelligence site
- ► Configuring a PerformancePoint workspace to connect to the Dynamics AX cubes
- ► Creating a scorecard in PerformancePoint
- ► Adding scorecards to a user's Role Center
- ► Creating an analytical chart in PerformancePoint
- ► Adding an analytical chart to a user's Role Center
- ► Using Decomposition Trees to drill into the analytical charts
- ► Creating PerformancePoint dashboards in SharePoint

Introduction

For more advanced dashboards, charts, and scorecards for Dynamics AX, you don't have to go much further than your existing SharePoint portal. SharePoint 2010 has default template sites for BI, and also has a dashboard designer called PerformancePoint embedded in the system that allows you to build dashboards, KPIs, scorecards, and reports. When you combine this with the inbuilt reporting cubes, default charts, and reports that are delivered with the standard Dynamics AX 2012 installation, you end up with a great BI platform.

In this chapter, we will show how you can configure SharePoint to become a BI platform for Dynamics AX by setting up a BI site, and then how to attach PerformancePoint to the Dynamics AX default reporting cubes.

We will then show how you can use the **PerformancePoint Dashboard Designer** to create new charts and reports that can then be turned into dashboards that all users are able to access in order to view metrics directly from Dynamics AX.

Finally, we will show how you can embed the charts, scorecards, and reports created through PerformancePoint directly within the user's Role Centers, allowing them to view and drill into information without having to exit from Dynamics AX.

The PerformancePoint Dashboard Designer is a more powerful reporting tool than Power View, but that comes at the price of being a little more intimidating to general users. As a result, this is probably something that is of more use to the power users, or the technical users within an organization. But if you want to take the plunge and learn it, then it's well worth it, because you will be able to create much better reporting views on Dynamics AX.

Creating a Business Intelligence site

In order to use the PerformancePoint Dashboard Designer to create reports and scorecards, you first need to have a Business Intelligence site configured on your SharePoint server. Once you have this, you will be able to access the PerformancePoint Dashboard Designer, and you will also have a place that you can store all of your custom charts, scorecards, and reports.

In this recipe, we will show how you can set up a Business Intelligence site if you don't have one already configured.

Getting ready

Before you start on this example, you will need to make sure that you have access to the SharePoint Central Administration console. To check this carry out the following steps:

1. Access your server that has SharePoint installed on it.

2. From the program menu, you should be able to find the **SharePoint Central Administration** console in the **Microsoft SharePoint Products** group.

3. If you cannot access this feature, then you may need to get help from your SharePoint administrator for this recipe.

How to do it...

To create a Business Intelligence site in SharePoint, follow these steps:

1. For this recipe, it is a good idea to create your BI site in the same web application as your Dynamics AX Role Centers, so that it's easier for the Role Centers to access the charts and scorecards that you will build. So, from the **SharePoint Central Administration** console, access the **Application Management** area, and then click on the **Create Site Collection** page.

2. On the **Create Site Collection** page, select your Dynamics AX Role Center web application, give your site a name of `Business Intelligence`, give the **Web Site Address** a subfolder of `bi`, and from the **Enterprise** tab of the **Template Selection** box, navigate to the **Business Intelligence Center** template.

3. Click on **OK**, and SharePoint will create the site for you.

How it works...

The Business Intelligence center that is created will become the location where you can store all of your charts and scorecards that you create, but more importantly, if you click on the **Create Dashboards** option on the main page, there will be a link shown that says **Start using PerformancePoint Services** that will take you to the Dashboard Designer installation page.

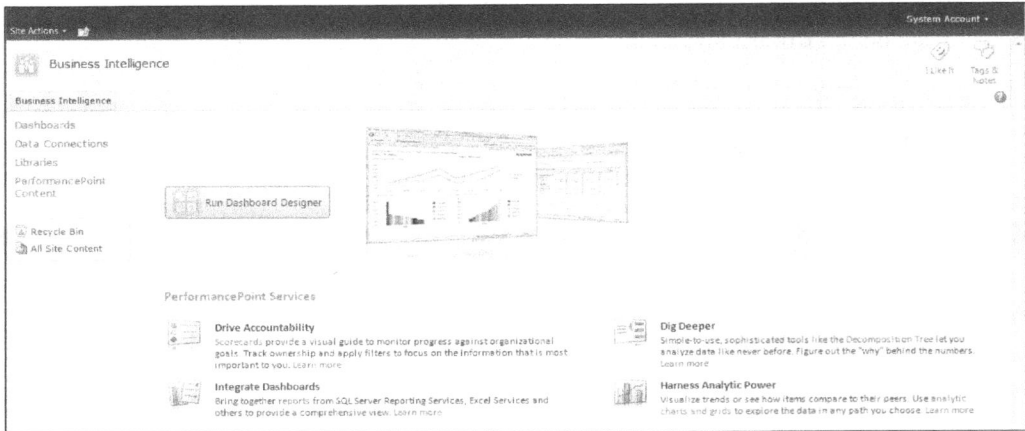

If you click on the **Run Dashboard Designer** button on this form, it will download and install **Dashboard Designer**, and start up the application.

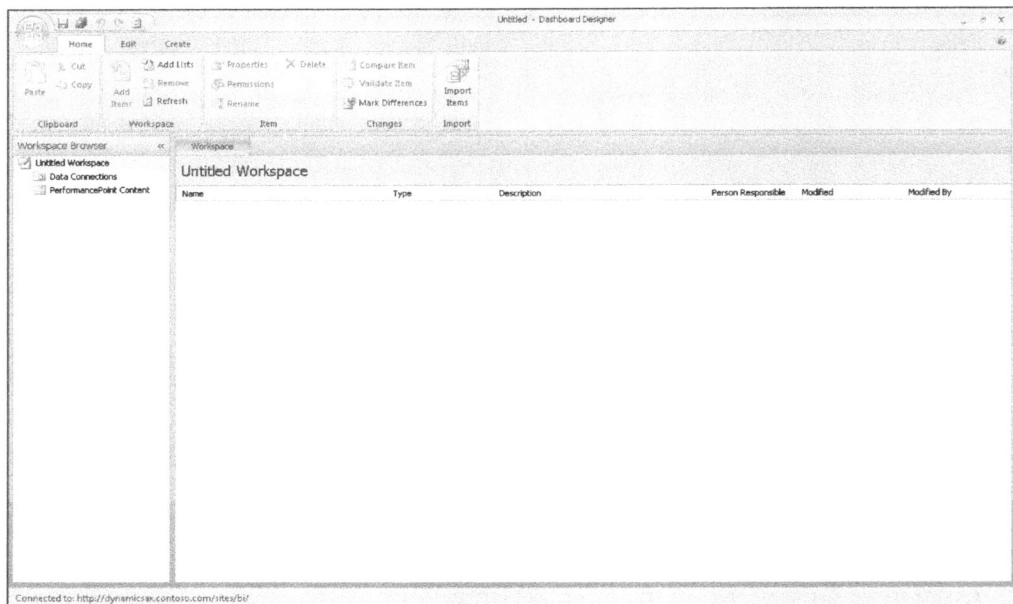

Now you are ready to start using PerformancePoint.

Configuring a PerformancePoint workspace to connect to the Dynamics AX cubes

Once you have access to the PerformancePoint Dashboard Designer you can then connect it to the default cubes that are delivered with Dynamics AX. Dynamics AX 2012 is delivered with 10 standard cubes for reporting, and Dynamics AX 2012 R2 increases the number of cubes available to 16. The cubes that are available, as of writing this book, are:

- Accounts payable
- Accounts receivable
- Budget control
- Budget plan
- Environmental sustainability
- Expense management
- General ledger
- Inventory valuation
- Production
- Profit tax totals
- Project accounting
- Purchasing
- Retail
- Sales
- Sales and marketing (also known as, Customer Relationship Management before R2)
- Workflow

In this recipe, we will show you how you can connect these cubes to a PerformancePoint workspace so that you can start creating charts and scorecards against the data.

Getting ready

Before you start on this example, you will need to make sure that you have deployed your analysis services cubes for Dynamics AX, and have fully processed them with your Dynamics AX data. If you are not sure if this has been done, you may need to check with your system administrator.

How to do it...

To connect a cube to a PerformancePoint workspace, follow these steps:

1. First, open up the **PerformancePoint Dashboard Designer** in a new blank workspace.

2. From the **Create** tab, select **Data Source** from the **Dashboard Items** group.

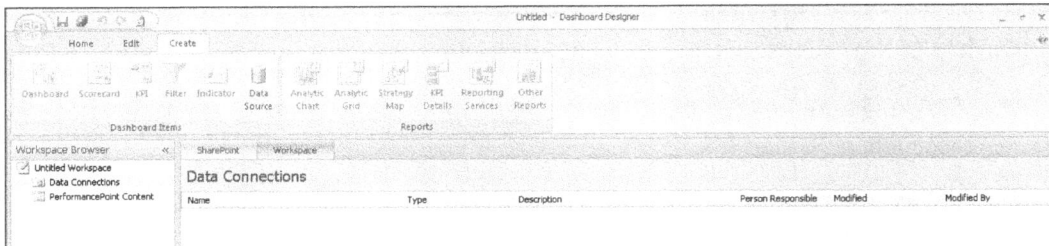

3. To connect to the default cubes that are delivered with Microsoft Dynamics AX, select the **Analysis Services** template data source.

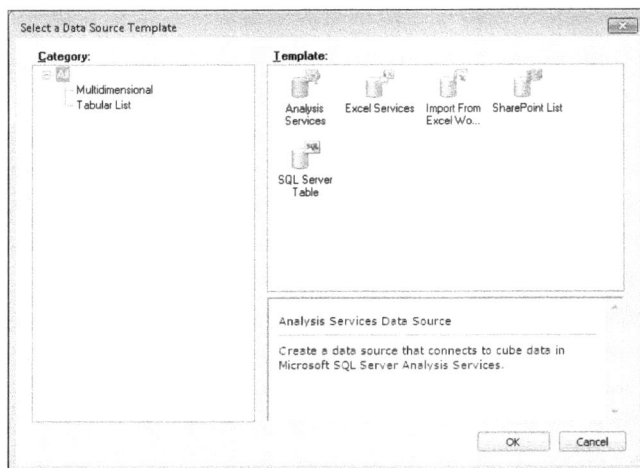

4. Rename the new data source that is created in the workspace browser.

5. In the **Editor** section of the data connection properties, enter the **Server** name where your SQL Analysis Services are running.

6. In the **Database** field, select the **Analysis Services** database that you would like to report off.

7. This will allow you to see all of the available reporting cubes for Dynamics AX. In this example, select the **Sales** cube.

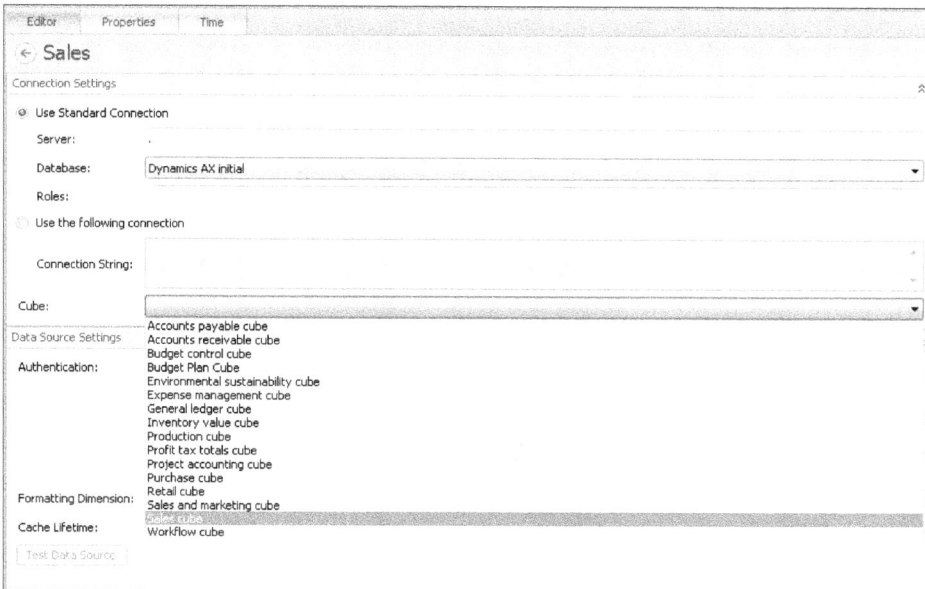

8. You can repeat the previous steps for all of the other cubes that you will want to report off.

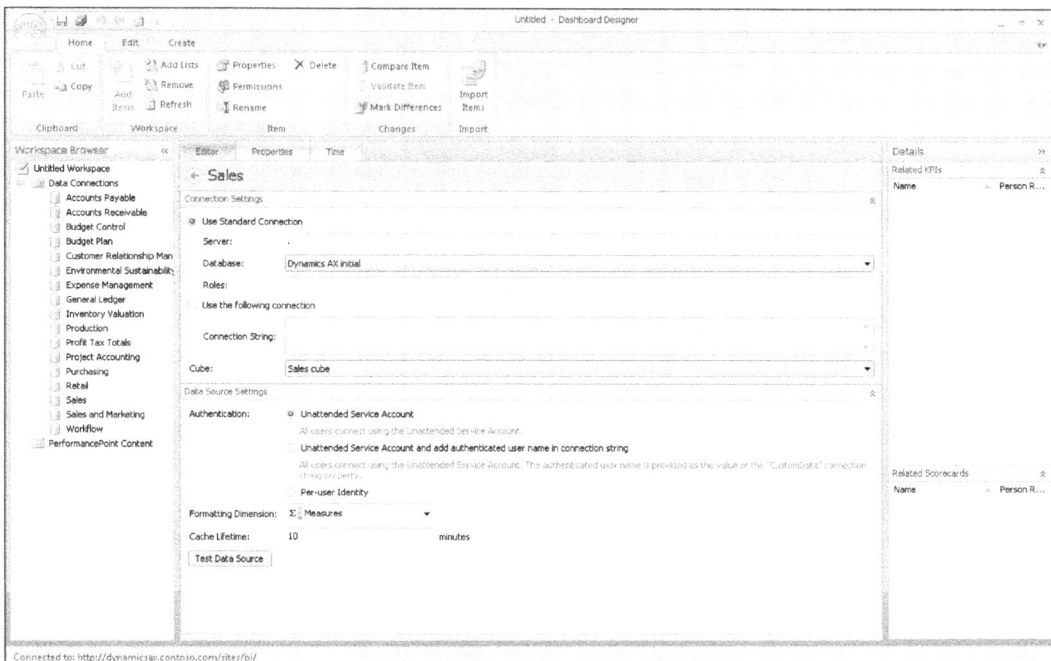

9. Once you have all of your cubes defined in your workspace, then save your workspace so that you are able to reuse this setup later on.

How it works...

Defining the data connections in the workspace not only creates connections in your workspace that you saved, but also saves the connections to SharePoint. This is useful because if someone else wants to create their own workspace, then they can add the connection information by selecting the SharePoint connection, and then clicking on the **Add Items** buttons from the **Workspace** group on the ribbon bar.

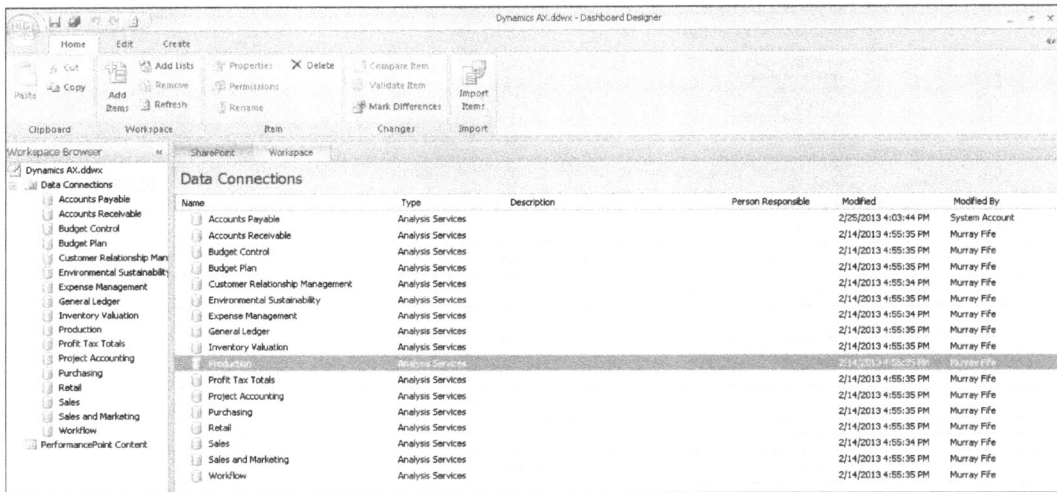

Creating a scorecard in PerformancePoint

The standard cubes that are delivered with Dynamics AX include a number of predefined **Key Performance Indicators** (**KPIs**) that you can start using right away. An easy way to display KPIs is through a scorecard, which you can easily create through the PerformancePoint Dashboard Designer.

In this recipe, we will show you how you can connect to the default cubes to find the KPIs that have already been defined, and use these within a scorecard Dashboard Item to create your own personal scorecard.

How to do it...

To create a new scorecard through PerformancePoint Dashboard Designer, follow these steps:

1. Open up the PerformancePoint Dashboard Designer, and then open up the workspace created in the last recipe that has the Dynamics AX cubes already defined.

2. From the **Create** tab, click on the **Scorecard** icon in the **Dashboard Items** group to start creating a new scorecard.

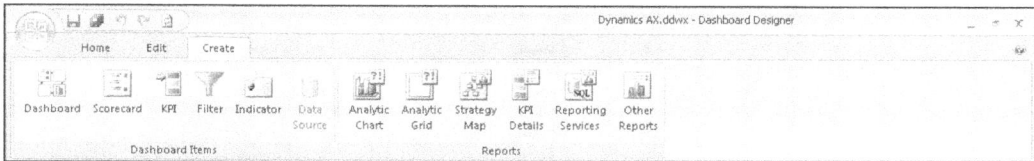

3. When asked to select the **Scorecard** template, choose the **Analysis Services** template.

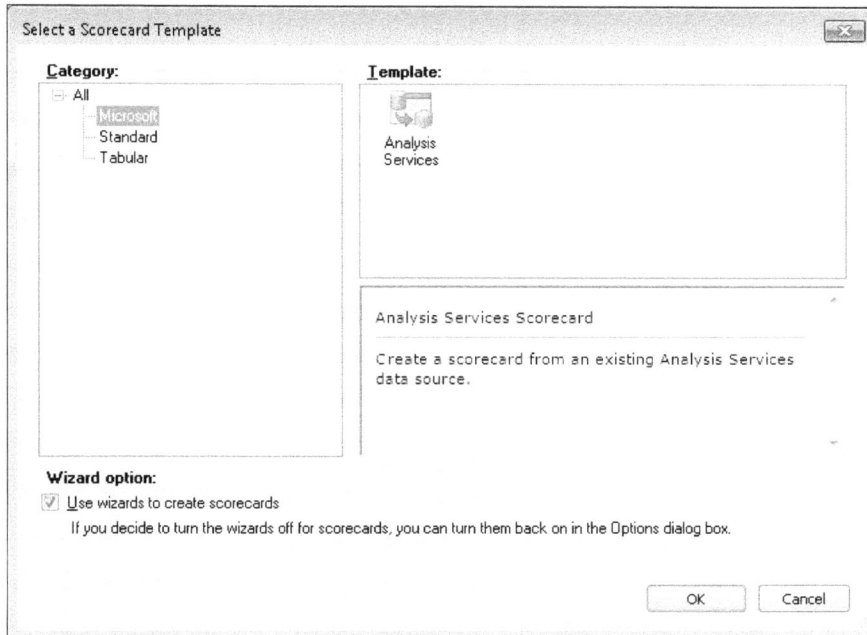

4. This will start the wizard process for configuring the scorecard. The first step is to select a cube that you want to show KPIs from. In this case we will navigate to the **Sales** cube.

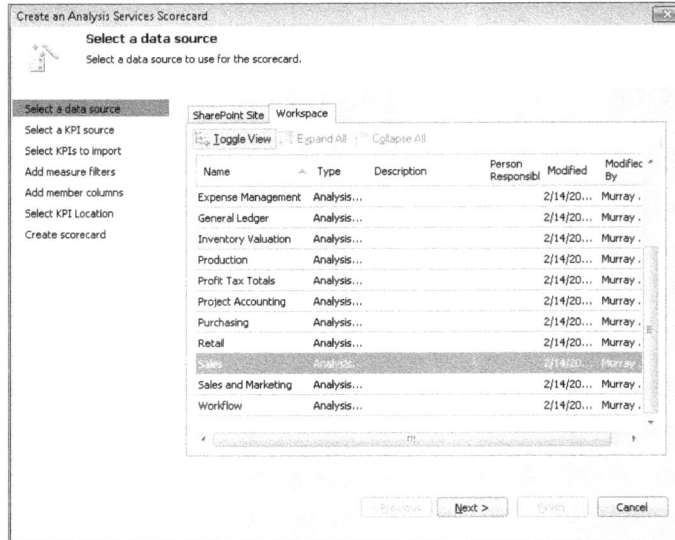

5. You can either create the KPIs individually, or import all of the KPIs from the **Analysis Services** cubes. For this example, select the **Create** option.

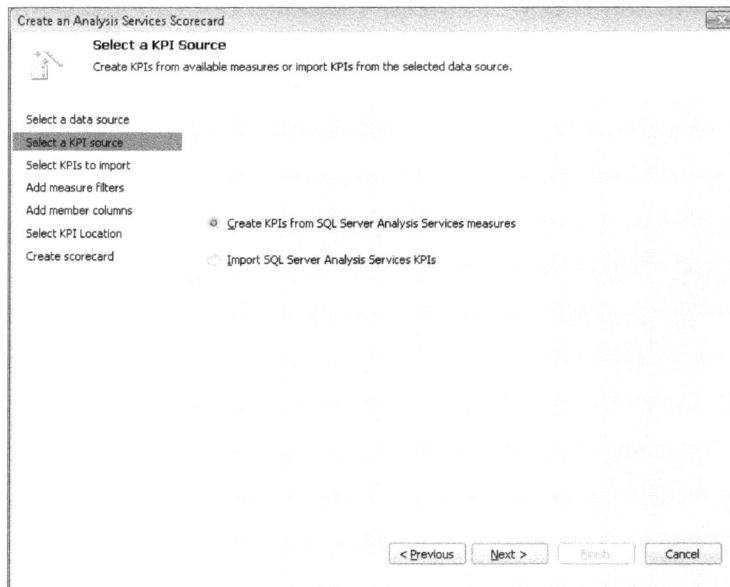

6. This will open up the KPI selection option. You can add KPIs individually by clicking on the **Add KPI** button, but for this example, we will select multiple KPIs by clicking on the **Select KPI** button.

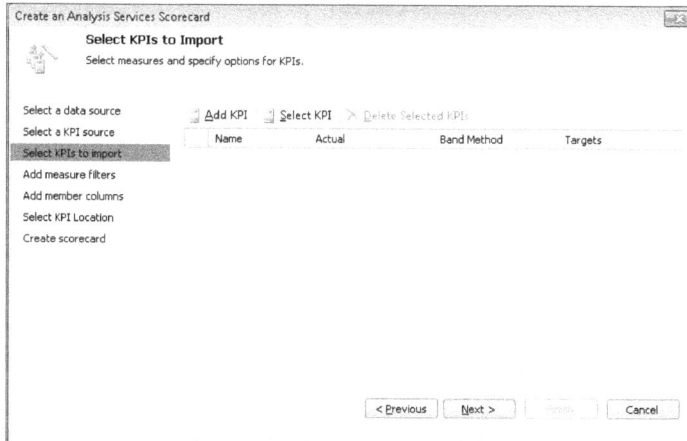

7. PerformancePoint will show you all of the KPIs that are available for you to add to your scorecard. Select **Gross Profit**, **Gross Profit Margin**, **Sales**, and **Total Revenue** from the KPIs and click on **OK**.

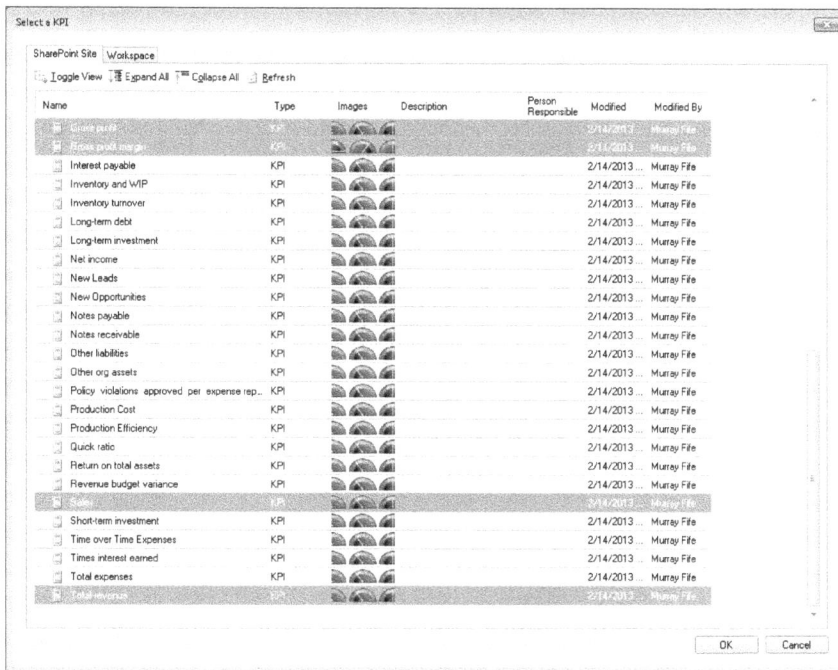

8. After selecting the KPIs, click on **Next** through the rest of the dialog boxes to accept the defaults, and you will see the new scorecard that you just created.

9. The final step is to give your scorecard a name and save it.

| Editor | Properties | | | | |

Sales Manager Scorecard

	Value	Goal and Status		Trend	
Total revenue	586258551.000017	0	-58,625,855,100%	1	58,625,855,000%
Sales	1906762895.60022			1	190,676,289,460%
Gross profit margin	96.001648369543	0	-9,600%	1	9,500%
Gross profit	562817628.180017	0	-56,281,762,818%	1	56,281,762,718%

How it works...

By creating the scorecard through PerformancePoint, the definition is saved to the Business Intelligence site. Once it is there, it becomes a Template Dashboard Item that you are able to use on dashboards, and also embed in user's Role Centers.

Adding scorecards to a user's Role Center

Once you have created scorecards through PerformancePoint, they can be added to any user's Role Center so that they can quickly see the KPIs that they are interested in and also track trends. In the following recipe we will show you how to easily do that.

How to do it...

To add a PerformancePoint scorecard to a user's Role Center, follow these steps:

1. Through the Dynamics AX client, go to the home page so that you are able to see the user's Role Center, and click on the **Personalize this page** link in the top-right of the page.

2. When the page goes into edit mode, click on the **Add a Web Part** link in the area that you would like to add the scorecard to.

3. From the **Web Parts** browser, navigate to the **PerformancePoint** category, and then the **PerformancePoint Scorecard** web part and click on the **Add** button.

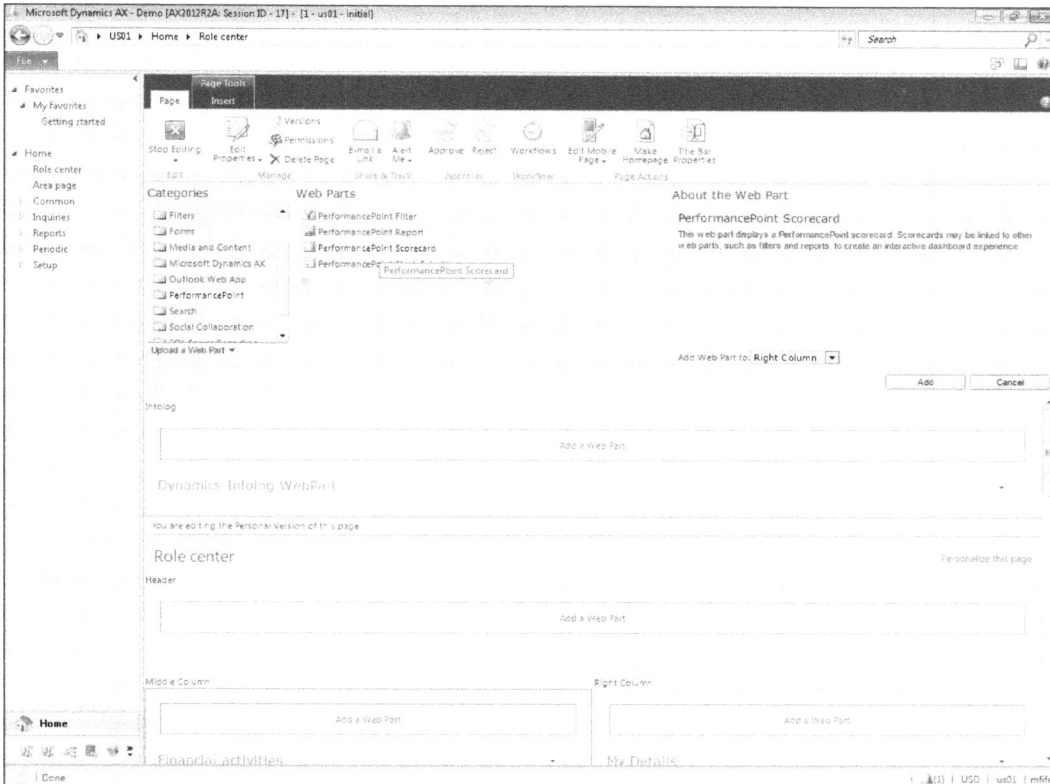

4. This will add a PerformancePoint panel to your page. Click on the **Click here to open the tool pane** link to open up the web part properties so that we can configure the scorecard.

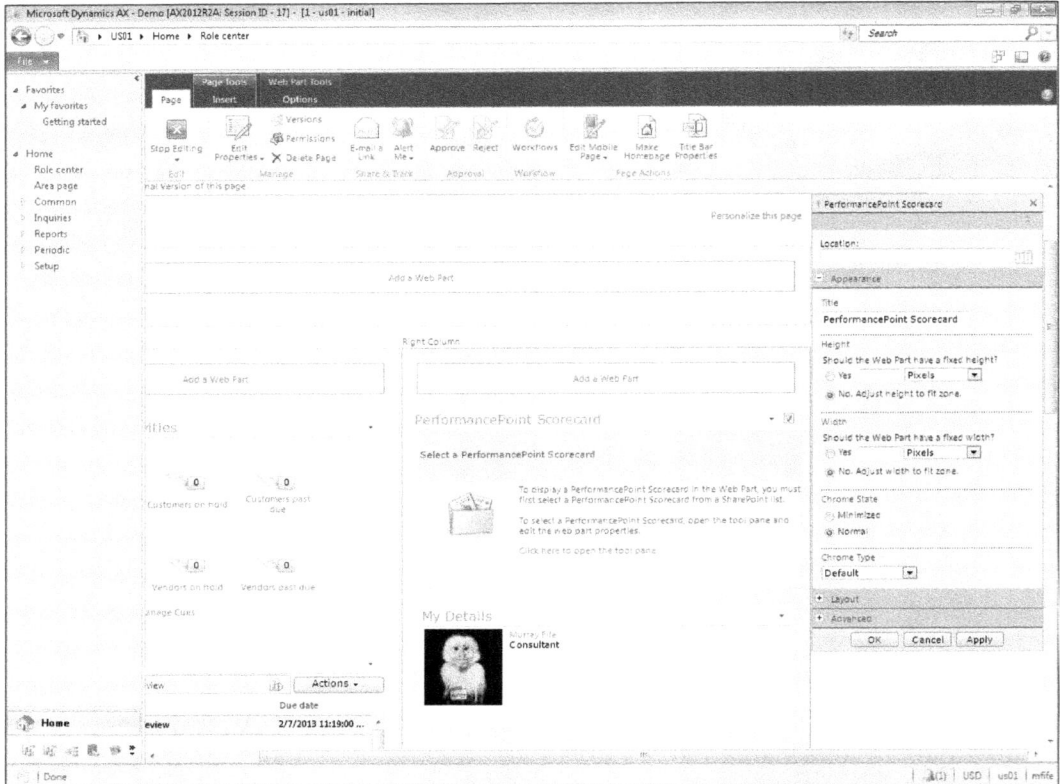

5. Click on the list search icon to the right of the **Location** property to search SharePoint for your scorecard.

6. When you first open up the search, it will probably be pointing to the wrong location for the scorecard. In the **Location** URL field, change the path to point to your Business Intelligence center. There will be a subfolder there called `PerformancePoint Content` where all of the Dashboard Items are stored. After selecting that folder, you should be able to find your scorecards. Select the scorecard that you want to add, and then click on **OK**.

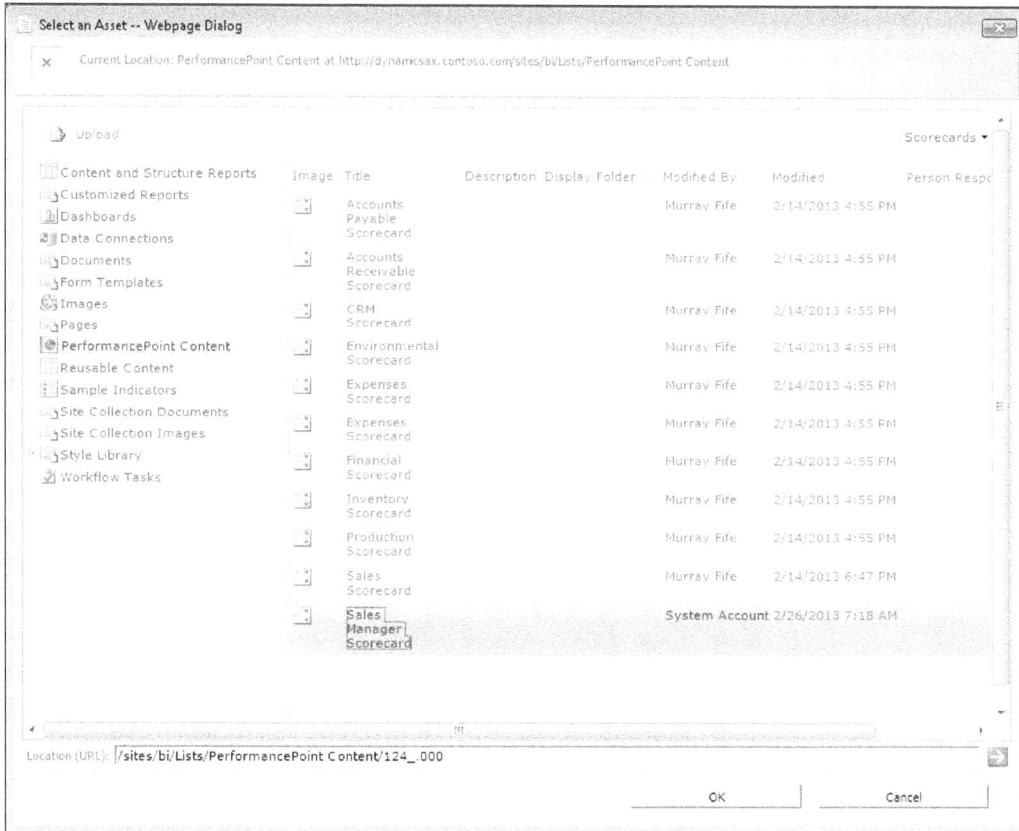

7. Give the web part a title, and then click on the **OK** button to save your scorecard.

8. Finally, click on the **Stop Editing** button to return to the view mode in the Role Center.

How it works...

By linking the PerformancePoint scorecard to the user's Role Center, the user is able to see the KPI details from their home page. Also, if you make a change to the scorecard itself through the Dashboard Designer then that changes on every user's Role Center page automatically.

Creating an analytical chart in PerformancePoint

Another type of Dashboard Item that you can create through PerformancePoint is called an analytical chart and allows you to create dashboard charts from any data source that you have defined through the Dashboard Designer. Since there are 17 predefined cubes available with Dynamics AX 2012 R2, the number of different ways that you can use this to slice and dice the information is virtually unlimited.

In this recipe, we will show how you can create a simple sales dashboard chart through the PerformancePoint Dashboard Designer.

How to do it...

To create a new analytical chart through PerformancePoint Dashboard Designer, follow these steps:

1. Open **PerformancePoint Dashboard Designer**, and then open up the workspace created in the last recipe that has the Dynamics AX cubes already defined.

2. From the **Create** tab, click on the **Analytic Chart** icon in the **Reports** group to start creating a chart.

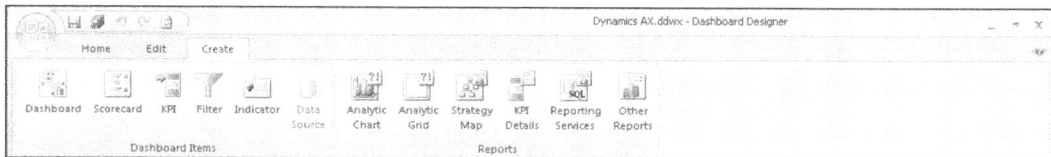

3. When the data source selection dialog box pops up, select the cube that you want to create your chart from. In this recipe we will select the **Sales** cube.

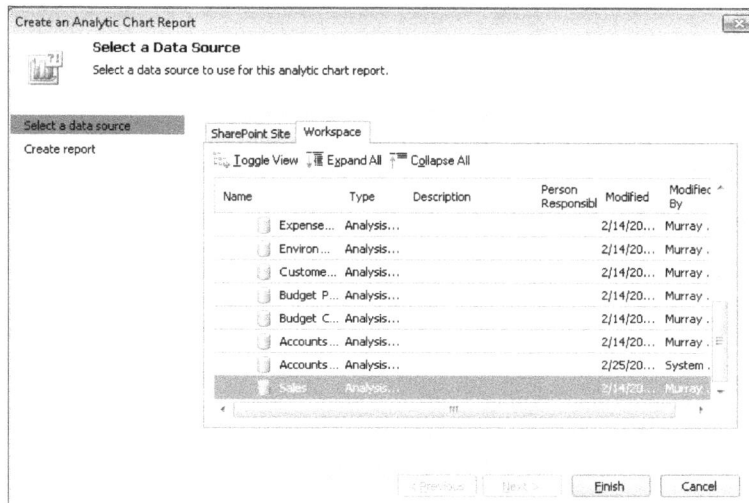

4. This will now open up the chart designer. On the right-hand side of the form will be all of the dimensions and measures that are available in the cube that you selected. At the bottom of the page will be drop areas for the Series, Axis, and also Background filters. From the measures group, find the **Customer invoice line amount – accounting currency** measure and drag it down into the **Series** drop area.

5. From the dimensions group, find the **Customer** dimension group, expand it out, and you will be able to find the **Customer – name** dimension. Drag that into the **Bottom Axis** drop box. You will now be able to see the chart.

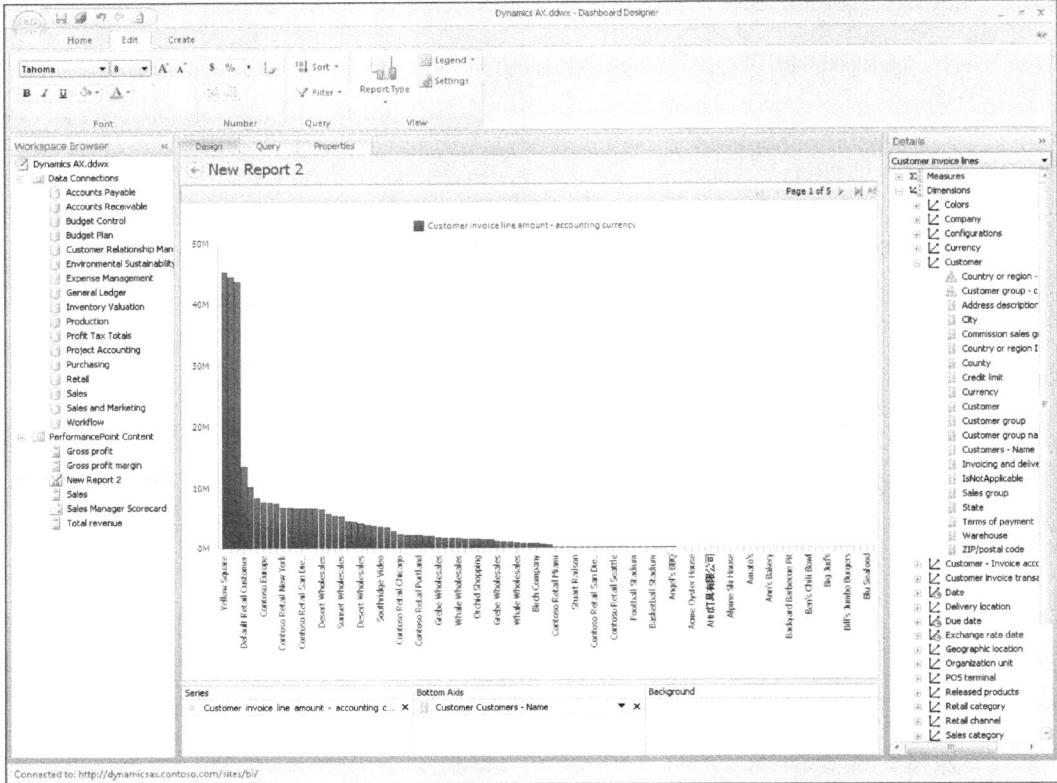

6. In this example, there is too much data, so by right-clicking on the canvas of the report you can open the pop-up menu. From there select the **Filter** menu, and choose the **Top 10** (Bottom Axis) menu item to open up the filter window.

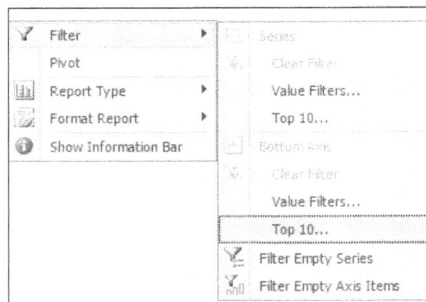

7. From here we will accept the defaults to filter out the customers to the top 10 highest grossing customers.

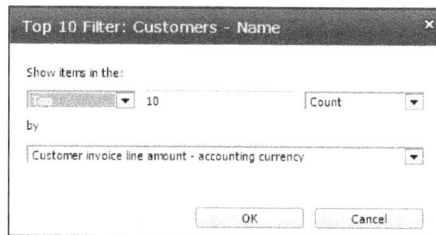

8. Now that you have the report completed, give it a more appropriate name, and save the chart to your `PerformancePoint Content`.

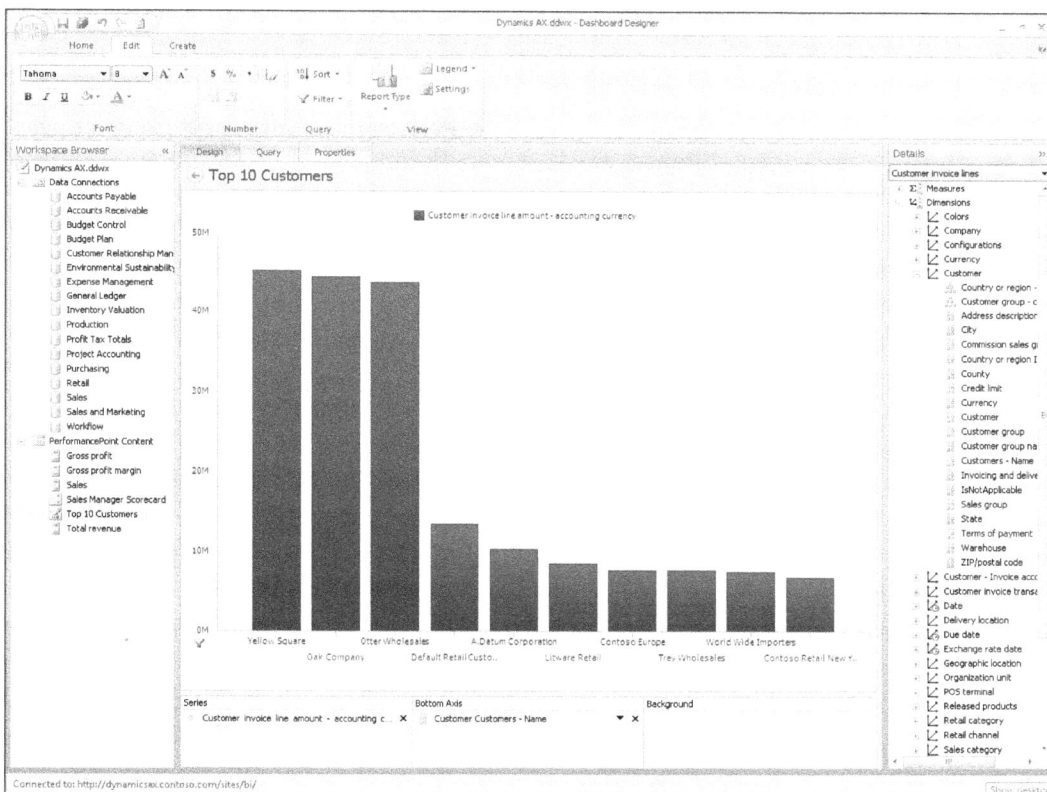

Adding an analytical chart to a user's Role Center

Once you have created your charts through PerformancePoint, they can be added to any user's Role Center in almost the exact same way as we did with the scorecards. In the following recipe we will show you how.

How to do it...

To add a PerformancePoint analytical chart to a user's Role Center, follow these steps:

1. Through the Dynamics AX client, go to the home page so that you are able to see the user's Role Center, and click on the **Personalize this page** link in the top-right of the page.

2. When the page goes into edit mode, click on the **Add a Web Part** link in the area that you would like to add the chart to.

3. From the **Web Parts** browser, navigate to the **PerformancePoint** category, and then the **PerformancePoint Report** web part, and then click on the **Add** button.

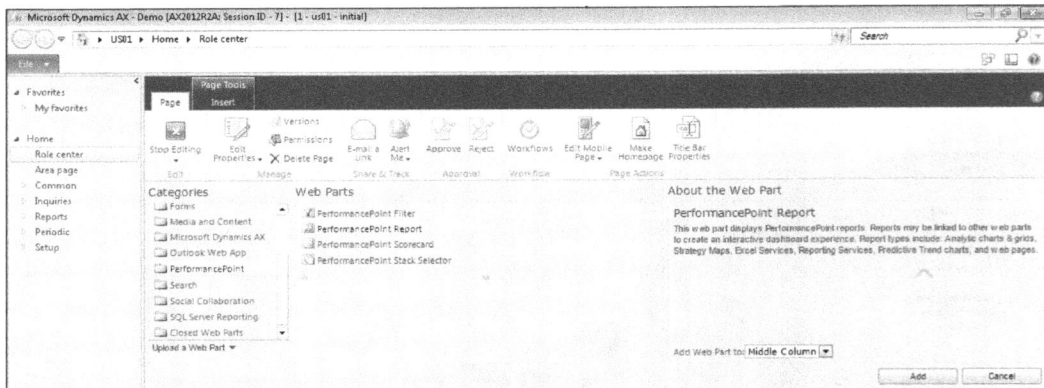

4. This will add a PerformancePoint panel to your page. Click on the **Click here to open the tool pane** link to open up the web part properties so that we can configure the chart.

5. Click on the list search icon to the right of the **Location** property to search SharePoint for your chart.

6. When you first open up the search, it will probably be pointing to the wrong location for the chart. In the **Location** URL field, change the path to point to your Business Intelligence center. There will be a subfolder there called **PerformancePoint Content** where all of the Dashboard Items are stored. After selecting that folder, you should be able to find your charts. Select the chart that you want to add, and then click on **OK**.

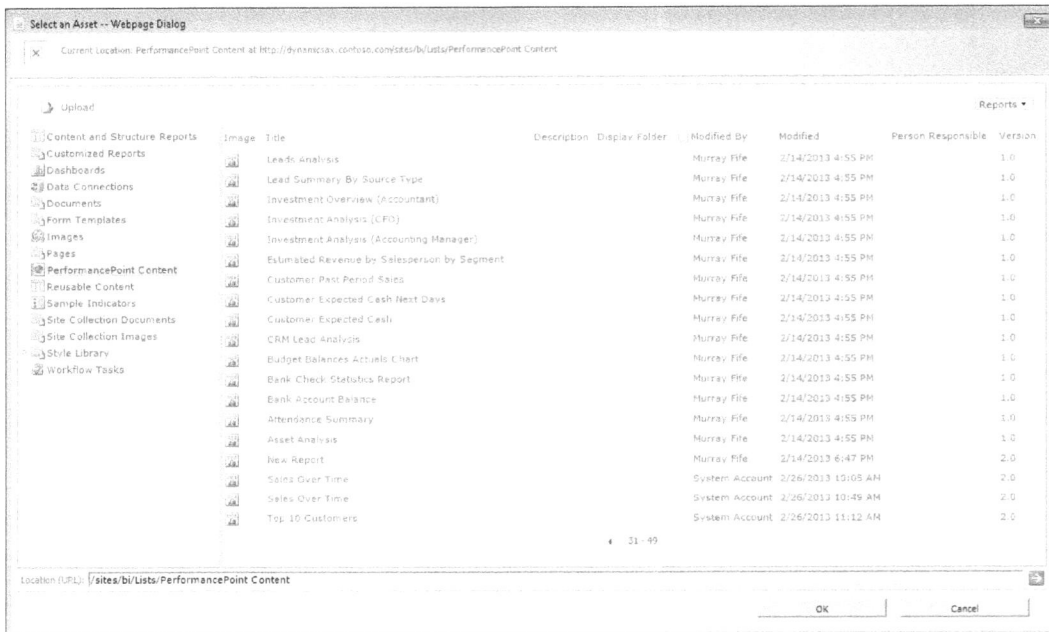

7. Give the web part a title.

8. Sometimes charts render a little on the large size in the Role Center. To make sure this doesn't happen on this example, set the **Width** to 500, and the **Height** to 300 within the web part properties.

9. Now click on the **OK** button to save your chart.

10. Finally, click on the **Stop Editing** button to return to the view mode in the Role Center.

How it works...

By linking the PerformancePoint analytical chart to the user's Role Center, the user is able to see it from their home page, but changes may be made globally through the Dashboard Designer.

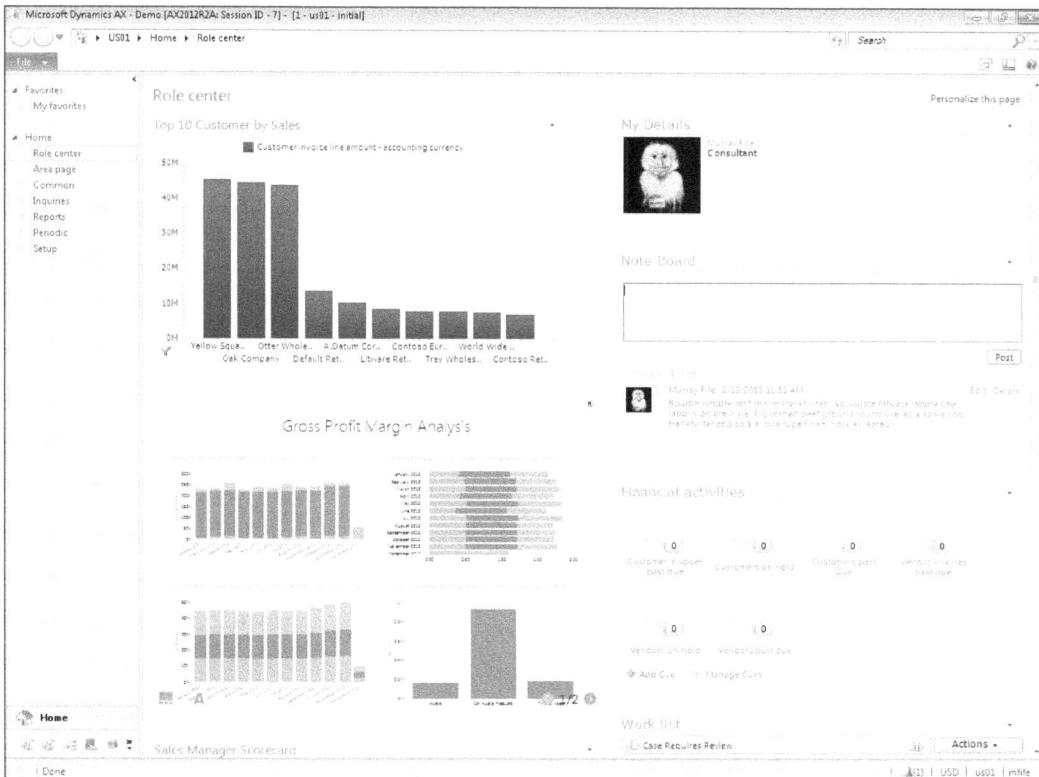

Using Decomposition Trees to drill into the analytical charts

The analytical charts have a feature enabled that allows you to drill into any piece of data that you see and then explore it using any of the available dimensions in your cube. This is useful if you see data such as a large spike in sales, and then want to look at that data to see who the customer was that purchased the largest amount of product, and then maybe what the products were. All this is possible through the Decomposition Tree function, without leaving the dashboard chart.

In this quick recipe we will show how you can use the Decomposition Tree feature to explore the chart that we created in the previous recipe.

How to do it...

To drill into a PerformancePoint chart using the Decomposition Tree function, follow these steps:

1. Right-click on the data element on the analytical chart that you want to explore to open up the pop-up menu, and navigate to the **Decomposition Tree** menu item.

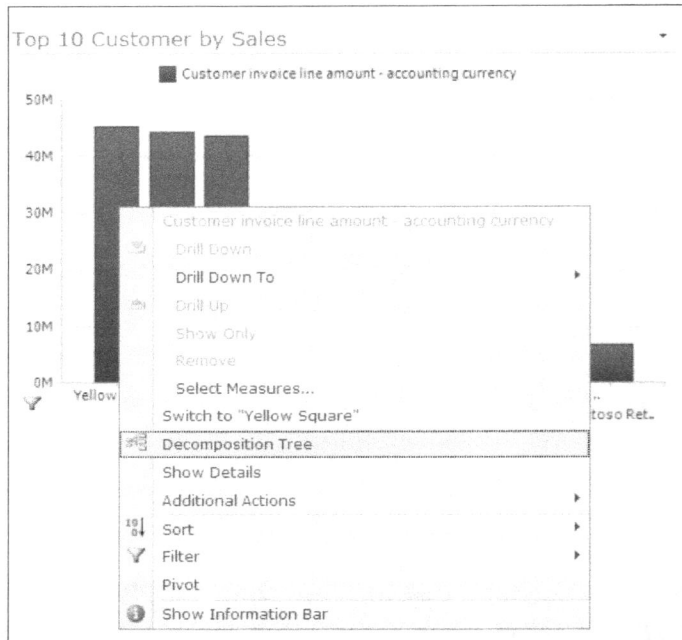

2. This will open up a new window allowing you to slice and dice the data based on any of the dimensions in the cube. In this example we will drill into the sales for the Yellow Square Co., navigate to the **Released products** field group, and then select the **Product name** dimension to see the products that this customer purchased.

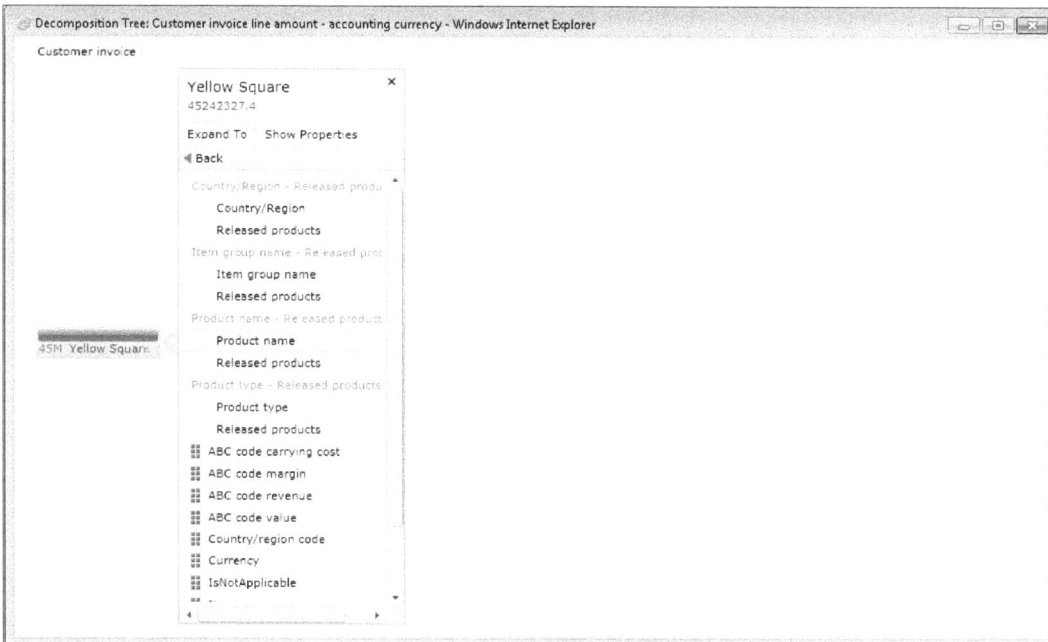

3. We can continue slicing by selecting different dimensions to further explore the data. If you click on the field name at the top of the page you get additional functions allowing you to change the sort options of the data, and also convert the data back to a bar chart.

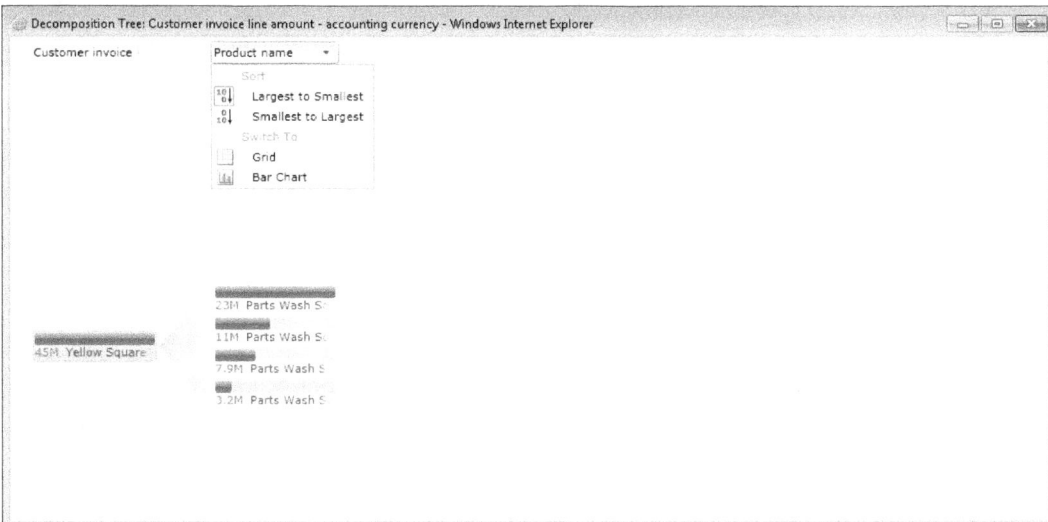

4. Once the data is converted back to a chart, you can select any type of chart that you like for presentation purposes.

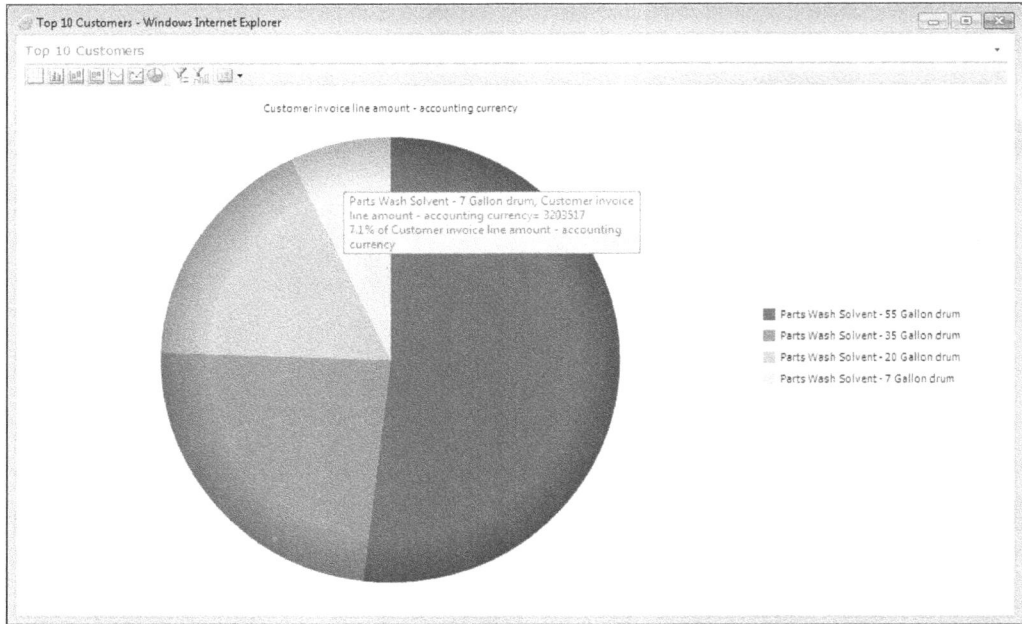

Creating PerformancePoint dashboards in SharePoint

The scorecards and charts that you create through the PerformancePoint Dashboard Designer do not have to just be shown through the Dynamics AX Role Centers. They can be combined together and deployed out to SharePoint as standalone dashboard pages, allowing you to create analytical pages that everyone in the organization is able to view.

In this recipe we will show how you can use the dashboard capabilities to easily publish this data to SharePoint.

How to do it...

To create a dashboard using PerformancePoint Dashboard Designer, follow these steps:

1. Open up the PerformancePoint Dashboard Designer, and then open up the workspace with the charts and scorecards that you have built.

2. From the **Create** tab, click on the **Dashboard** icon in the **Dashboard Items** group to start creating a new **Dashboard Page**.

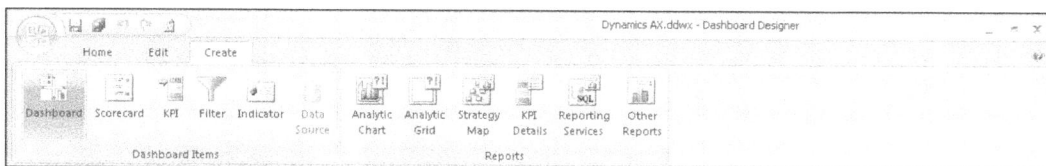

3. The Dashboard Designer will then ask you to select a template for the dashboard.

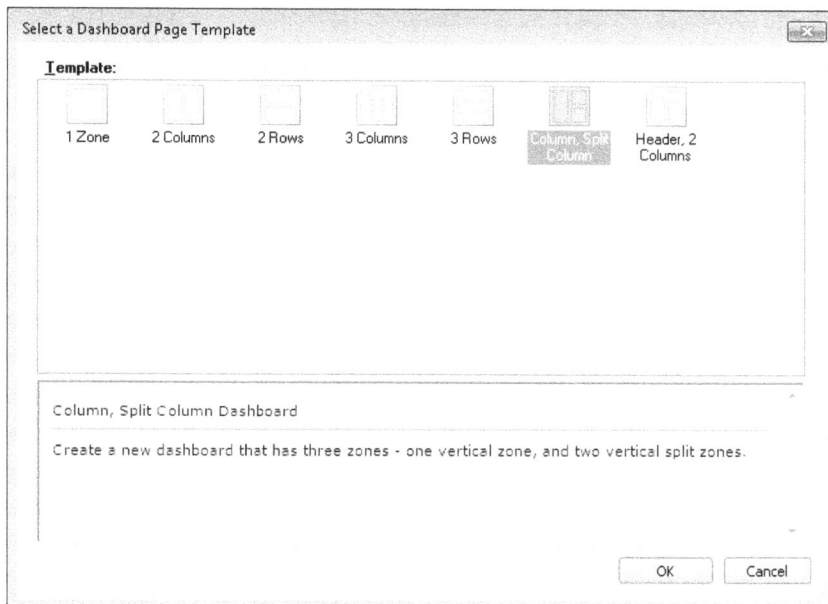

4. When the dashboard template is displayed, change to the **Properties** tab and give your dashboard a name. In this example it will be the **Sales Manager Dashboard**.

5. Return back to the **Editor** tab of the dashboard template, and you will see the **Pages** section at the top of the template form. A dashboard may have a number of pages associated with it. Change the page name from **Page 1** to something a little more descriptive. This example will be called **Sales Manager Overview**.

6. From the right-hand panel you will be able to explore through the scorecards and reports that you have created and saved to your Business Intelligence site. Open up the **Scorecards** group, and add a few scorecards to the left column of the dashboard.

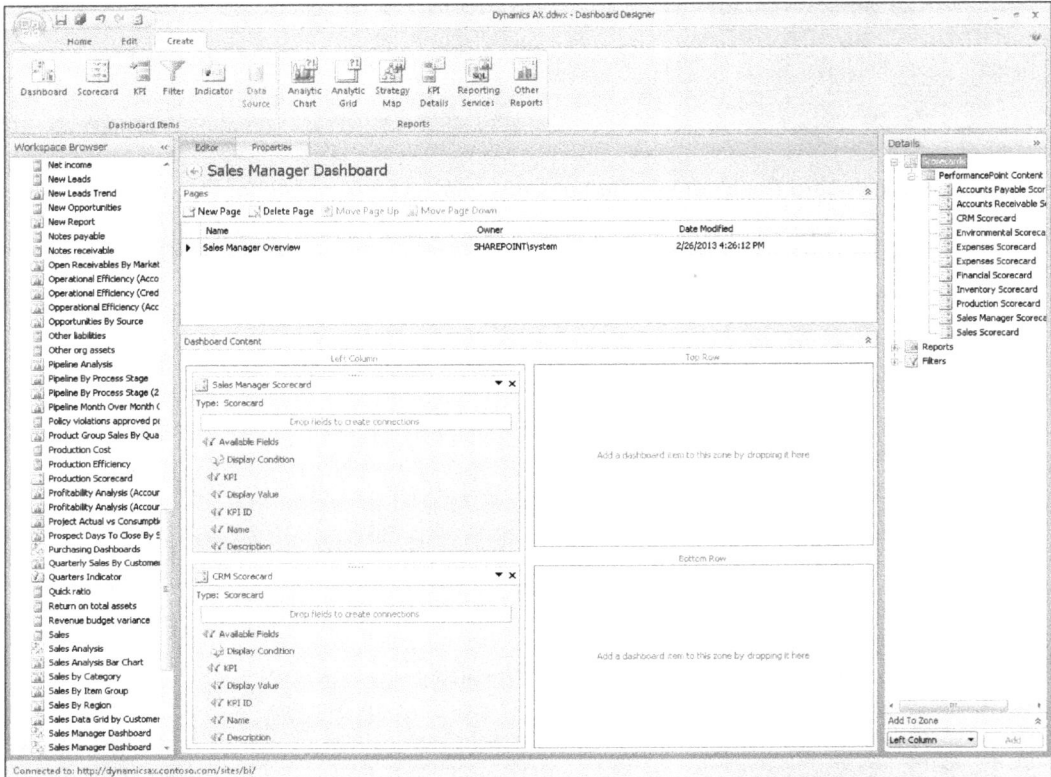

7. Explore through the **Reports** group and add some of the sales reports to the right column sections of the dashboard.

8. Once you have built your **Dashboard Page**, you need to save the dashboard and deploy it to SharePoint. To do this, select the **Deploy** option from the file menu on the Dashboard Designer.

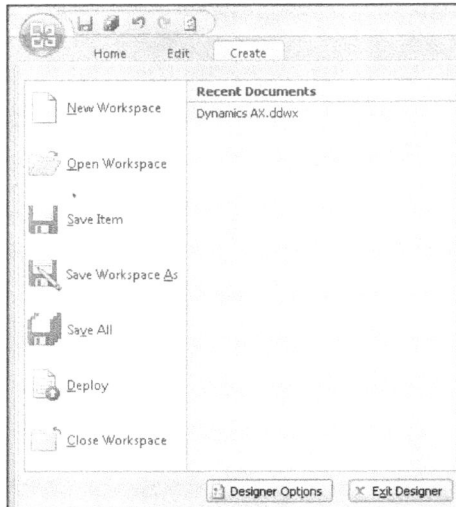

9. The first time that you deploy the dashboard, you may be asked where you want to send it to. If you have multiple BI repositories, then you will need to select the portal that you want to save it to.

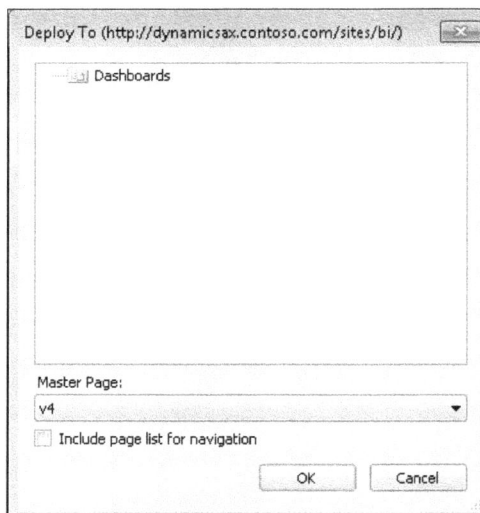

10. Now you will be able to see your dashboard within SharePoint.

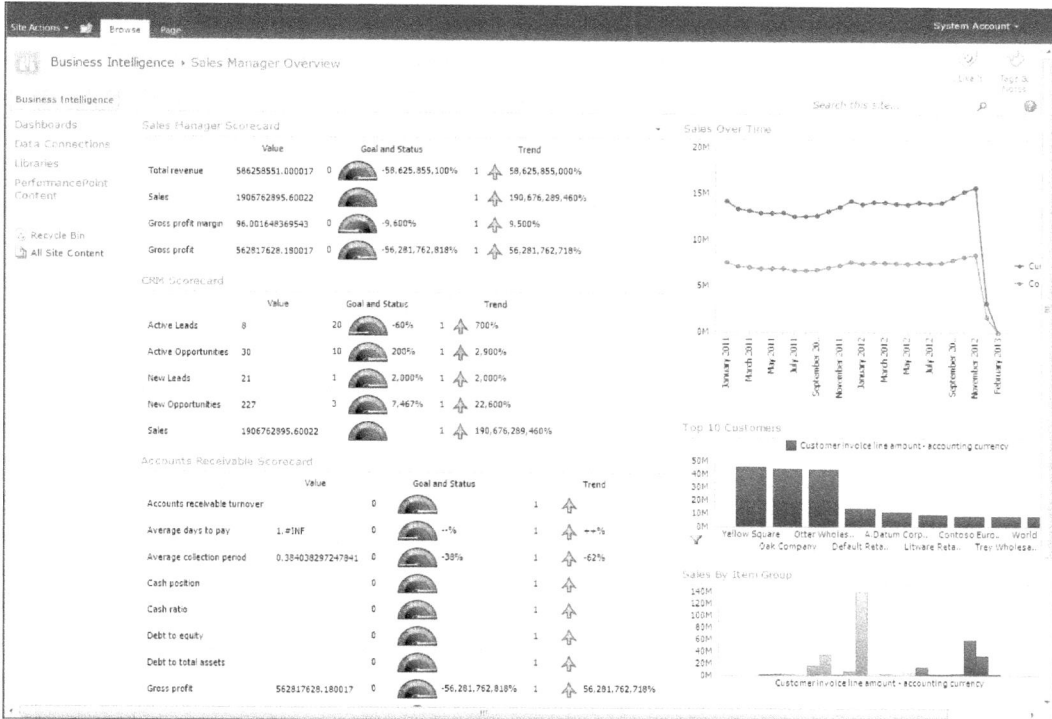

How it works...

Anyone who has access to the SharePoint site where the dashboard is deployed will be able to view the dashboard. If you add a **IsDlg=1** qualifier to the end of the URL, then the dashboard will become even more sleek by removing the navigation and title bars, making it perfect for displaying company metrics on public systems.

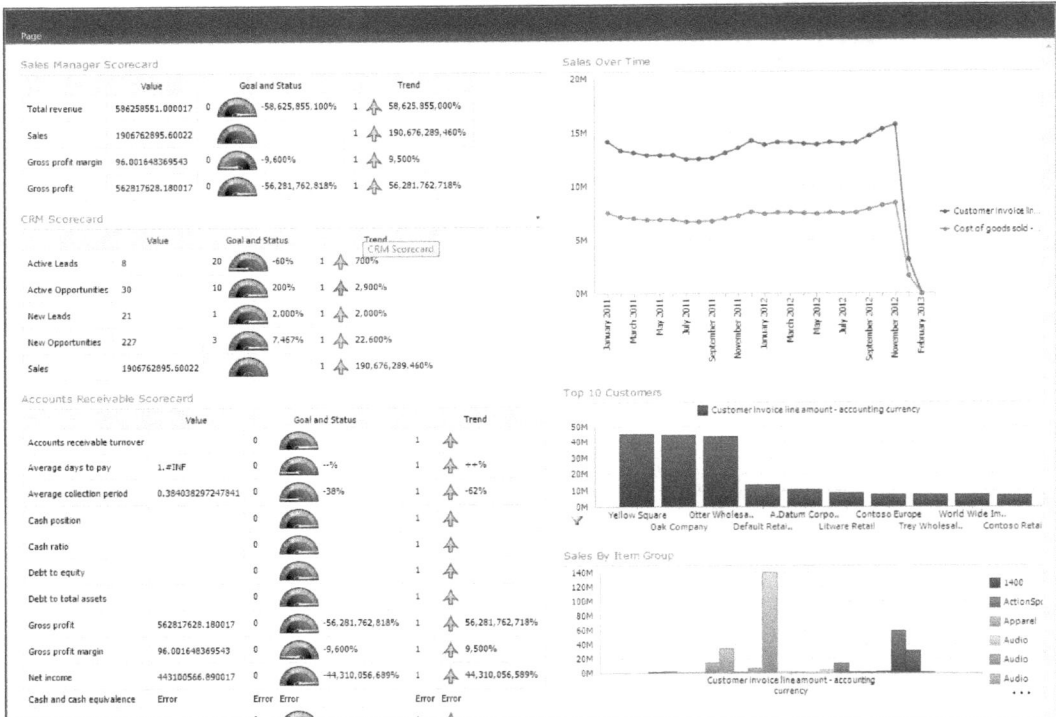

Also, the form factors of the dashboards are perfect for deployment to tablet devices for users who just need to check information on the run.

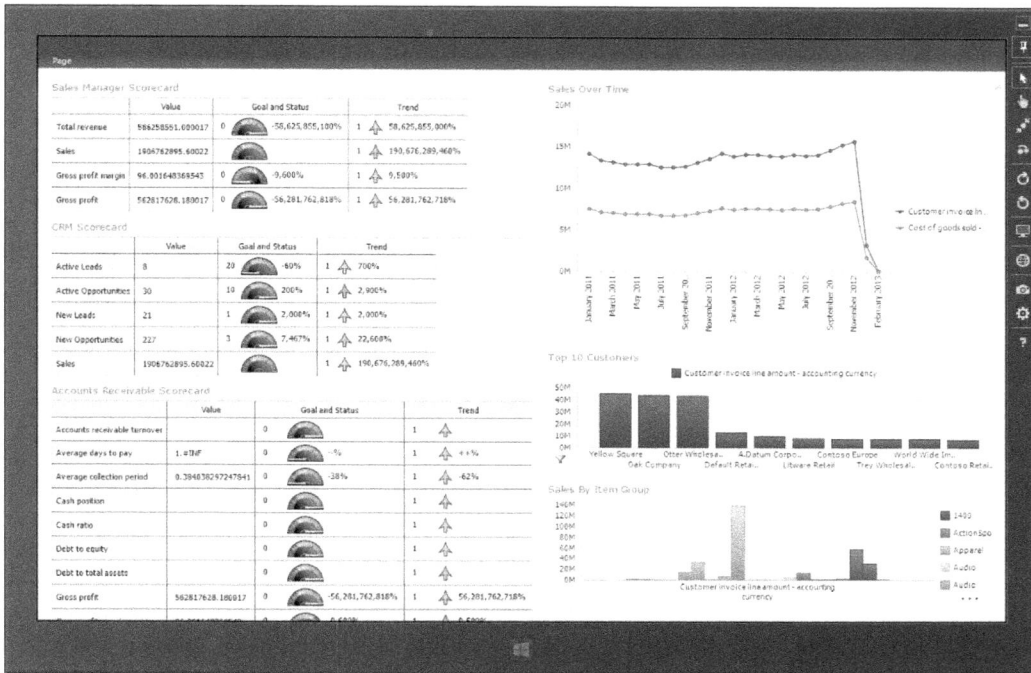

Summary

PerformancePoint is a very flexible reporting and dashboarding tool that allows you to quickly get information out to the users. However, in this chapter we have just scratched the surface of what you are able to do when it is paired up with Dynamics AX.

Once you have mastered these examples, you might also want to try:

▶ Creating filters that can be used to further refine your results

▶ Linking dashboard elements together so that selecting one item also filters others

▶ Using Reporting Services reports as dashboard elements, allowing you to use the Reporting Services controls, such as gauges and maps within your dashboards, and to also use hyperlinks to link to the Dynamics AX forms

▶ Attaching secondary databases that you may be using in conjunction with Dynamics AX, including other MSSQL databases, MS Access data sources, Excel worksheets, and more

Once you have your dashboards, charts, and views built, you can also re-use them in other ways such as:

▶ Embedding them in your companies' intranet portal so that users who normally don't use Dynamics AX are able to see business metrics and measures

▶ Using them within your customer and vendor portals to allow other companies to see how you are tracking their performance

That's not too bad for a tool that is included in your current SharePoint environment.

4
Communication and Collaboration

In this chapter, we will show how to configure and use tools such as Outlook and Lync to keep up-to-date with all your tasks and appointments, and also to contact others inside and outside your organization. This chapter will cover:

- Linking Outlook with Dynamics AX
- Flagging Dynamics AX contacts for synchronization
- Synchronizing Dynamics AX contacts with Outlook
- Using the Outlook Social Connector to research Dynamics AX contacts
- Communicating with contacts from within Dynamics AX
- Using Lync to collaborate with other users directly from Dynamics AX

Introduction

Chances are you are already using Microsoft Outlook for your e-mail and contact management, and hopefully you are also using Lync within the organization for messaging and communication. So why not configure Dynamics AX to use them as well so that you can be even more productive?

Dynamics AX allows you to link your user account with your Outlook client. Once you have done this, you are able to synchronize Dynamics AX contacts, tasks, and appointments with Outlook. This means that all this information will now be available on your desktop, tablet, and also your smartphone for the times that you are disconnected from Dynamics AX. You can then take advantage of tools such as the **Outlook Social Connector** to see what your Dynamics AX contacts are up to on Facebook, LinkedIn, and Microsoft Live. And if you want to send your contacts an e-mail through Outlook, then you can initiate it directly from the Dynamics AX client.

The Lync integration connects you as well, but this time with the other people in your organization. If you have Lync installed and have all of the users registered with their Lync IM account, Dynamics AX will turn on presence and messaging directly from the forms, allowing you to text, call, video chat, and share desktops directly from the their username. Because Lync has clients that run on the desktop, on tablets, and also on smartphones, if you have a question about something within Dynamics AX, you can get your answer right away, and then continue on, rather than having to track down people by foot. Lync is very cool, and I use it every day to do just that.

None of the recipes that are described in this chapter require you to have system administrator privileges to configure, so as long as you have Outlook/Exchange and Lync running, then you are ready to test these out.

Linking Outlook with Dynamics AX

The first step in using Outlook with Dynamics AX is to set up the connection through Dynamics AX. In this recipe we will show the steps required to do this.

Getting ready

Before we start on this example, you will need to make sure that your user profile in Dynamics AX is associated with your e-mail account. This will ensure that Dynamics AX will be able to share information with your Outlook profile. To do this carry out the following steps:

1. From the **File** drop-down menu on the Dynamics AX client, navigate to the **Tools** menu, and then the **Options** submenu.

2. Within the **Options** dialog box, check that you have the e-mail address that is in the **E-mail:** field:

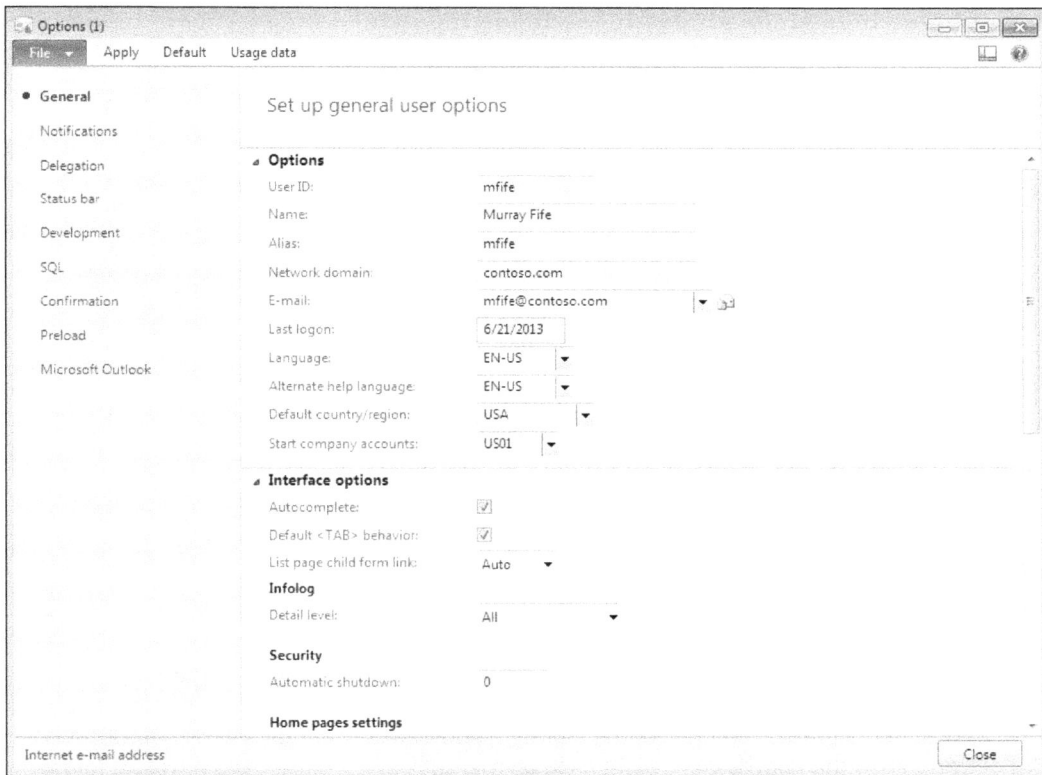

How to do it...

To set up the synchronization link between Dynamics AX and Microsoft Outlook, follow these steps:

1. From the **Home** Area Page, open up the **Microsoft Outlook setup wizard** from the **Setup** group.

2. Step through the wizard screens until you reach the page **Microsoft Outlook synchronization**. This may already be populated with your current username and folders to synchronize with. If not, click on the **Use current Microsoft Outlook profile** button to load the details:

3. You can mingle your Outlook contacts, appointments, and tasks with the ones that are synchronized from Dynamics AX, but in this recipe we will configure it so that items from Dynamics AX are stored in subfolders in Outlook. Open up Outlook, and go to the folders view. Right-click on the Calendar folder, and navigate to the **New Calendar** option to create a subcalendar folder. Name the Calendar folder, **Dynamics AX Calendar**.

4. Right-click on the Contacts folder, and navigate to the **New Folder** option to create a subcontacts folder. Name the Contacts folder, **Dynamics AX Contacts**.

5. Right-click on the `Tasks` folder, and navigate to the **New Folder** option to create a subtasks folder. Name the `Tasks` folder, **Dynamics AX Tasks**:

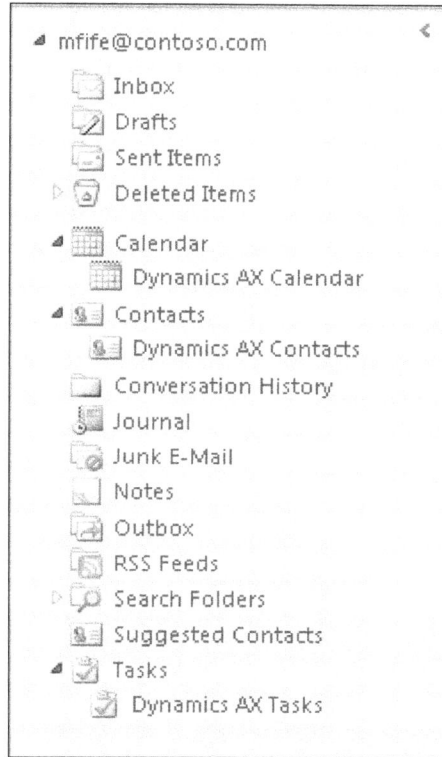

6. Return to the **Microsoft Outlook synchronization** form in Dynamics AX, and click on the **Pick contact Microsoft Outlook folder** button. This will open up a folder explorer from Outlook. Navigate to the `Dynamics AX Contacts` folder that you just created.

7. Click on the **Pick task Microsoft Outlook folder** button. This will open up a folder explorer from Outlook. Navigate to the `Dynamics AX Tasks` folder that you just created.

8. Click on the **Pick appointment Microsoft Outlook folder** button. This will open up a folder explorer from Outlook. Select the `Dynamics AX Calendar` folder that you just created.

9. Set the **Days before:** field for the appointment synchronization to 30, and the **Days after:** field to 90 to pull in the past month, and 3 months of future appointments:

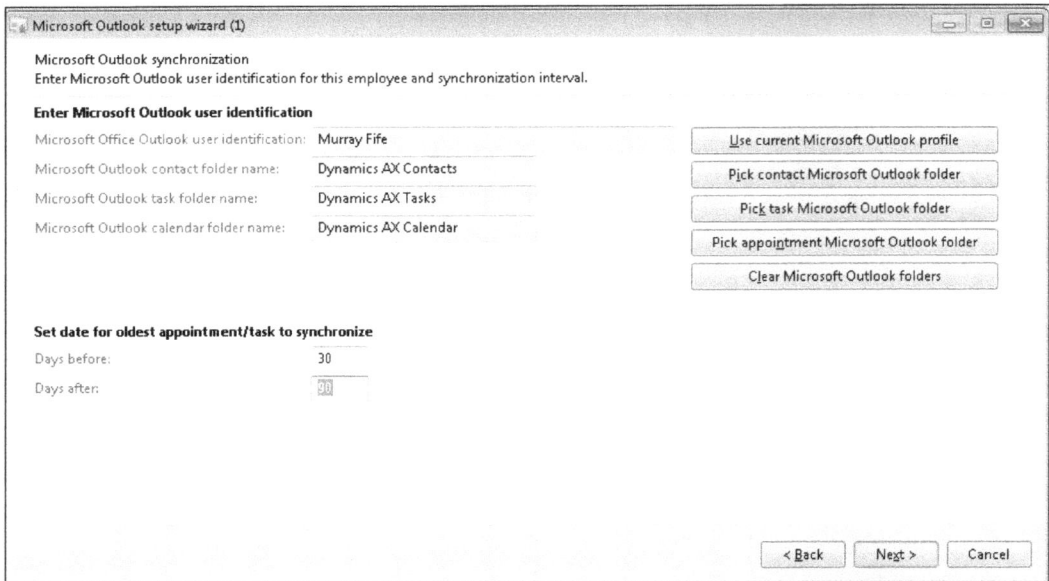

10. Click on the **Next** button and you should be able to finish the synchronization setup wizard.

Flagging Dynamics AX contacts for synchronization

You probably don't want all of the contacts from Dynamics AX to be moved over to Outlook, probably just the contacts that you are working with. Dynamics AX gives you the option to flag the contacts that you want to synchronize directly from the contact management screens. In this recipe we will show you how you can do this.

How to do it...

To flag your Dynamics AX contacts for synchronization to Outlook, follow these steps:

1. From the `Sales and Marketing` module, open up the **My contacts list** page from the `Contacts` folder in the **Common** group.

2. Select the contacts that you would like to synchronize:

3. Click on the **Add to Microsoft Outlook contacts** button in the **Include** group of the **Contact** ribbon bar tab. You should get a dialog box showing how many new contacts have been flagged for synchronization:

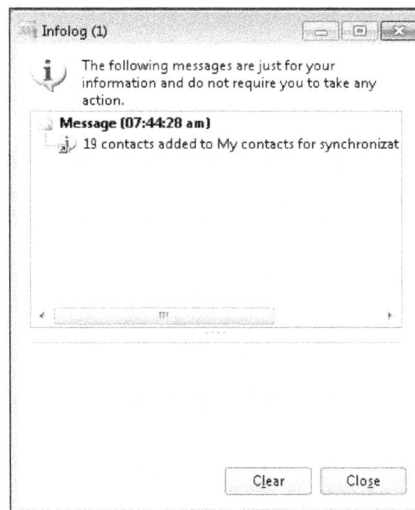

Synchronizing Dynamics AX contacts with Outlook

After you have linked Dynamics AX with Outlook and then selected the contacts that you want to synchronize, getting the contacts over to Outlook is as simple as starting the synchronization process. This recipe will show how to start the synchronization task.

How to do it...

To synchronize Dynamics AX contacts with Outlook, follow these steps:

1. From the **Home** area page, open up the **Synchronize** menu item in the **Microsoft Outlook synchronization** folder of the **Periodic** group.

2. In the dialog box for synchronization, you can choose if you want to synchronize the contacts, tasks, and appointments. For this recipe we will synchronize everything:

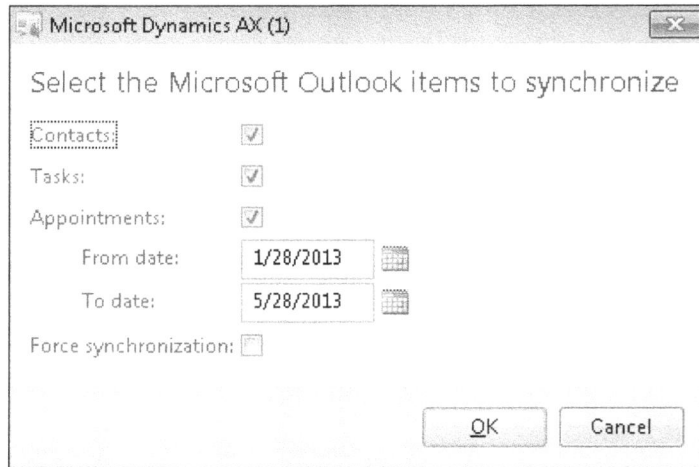

3. After clicking on the **OK** button, Dynamics AX will process the updates and then you will be done.

How it works...

After running the synchronization process, all of your flagged contacts, new appointments, and new tasks will be transferred to your profile in Outlook including name, company, physical addresses, e-mail addresses, and phone numbers:

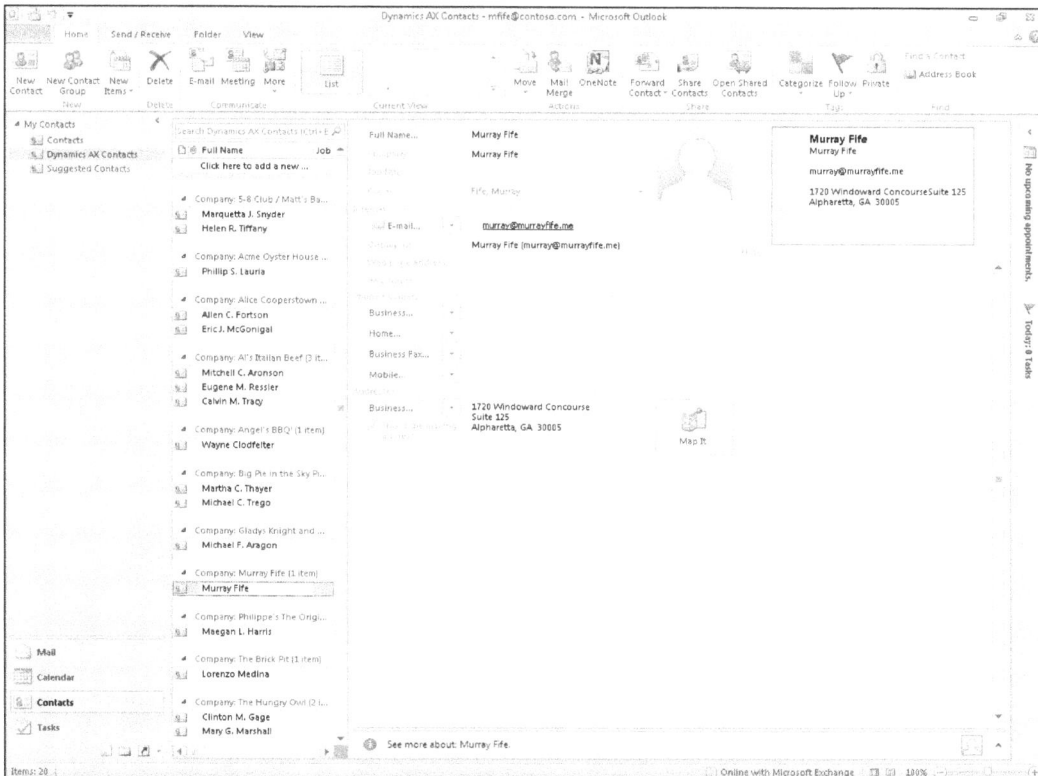

> Synchronization is only one way. Changing the contact information within Dynamics AX will update your contacts in Outlook, but if you change the contact in Outlook those changes will be overwritten the next time you synchronize with Dynamics.

Using the Outlook Social Connector to research Dynamics AX contacts

Since you now have your Dynamics AX contacts in Outlook, you can take advantage of some of the Outlook add-ons to automatically search online sources for additional information about them. In this recipe, we will show how you can configure one add-on called the **Outlook Social Connector** that will search the social networks to find out information about contacts based on their e-mail addresses. The Outlook Social Connector is available in Outlook 2010 and higher. All you need to do is link it to your social accounts.

Getting ready

Before you start walking through this recipe, you will need to make sure that you have the **People Pane** turned on within Outlook because it will display all of the social research on the contacts. To do this:

1. Go to the View tab on the Outlook ribbon bar.

2. Select the drop-down list for the **People Pane** in the **View** group and make sure that the **Normal** option is checked:

How to do it...

To configure the Outlook Social Connector in the Outlook client, follow these steps:

1. When you open up a contact on Outlook, at the bottom of the contact preview panel will be the **People Pane**. The first time that you see this, there will not be a lot of information showing, because no connectors will be configured:

2. Click on the preceding link on the profile picture for the contact, which says **Connect to social networks**, and Outlook will show you the available social connectors. Initially there will only be one, allowing you to connect to your SharePoint My Site:

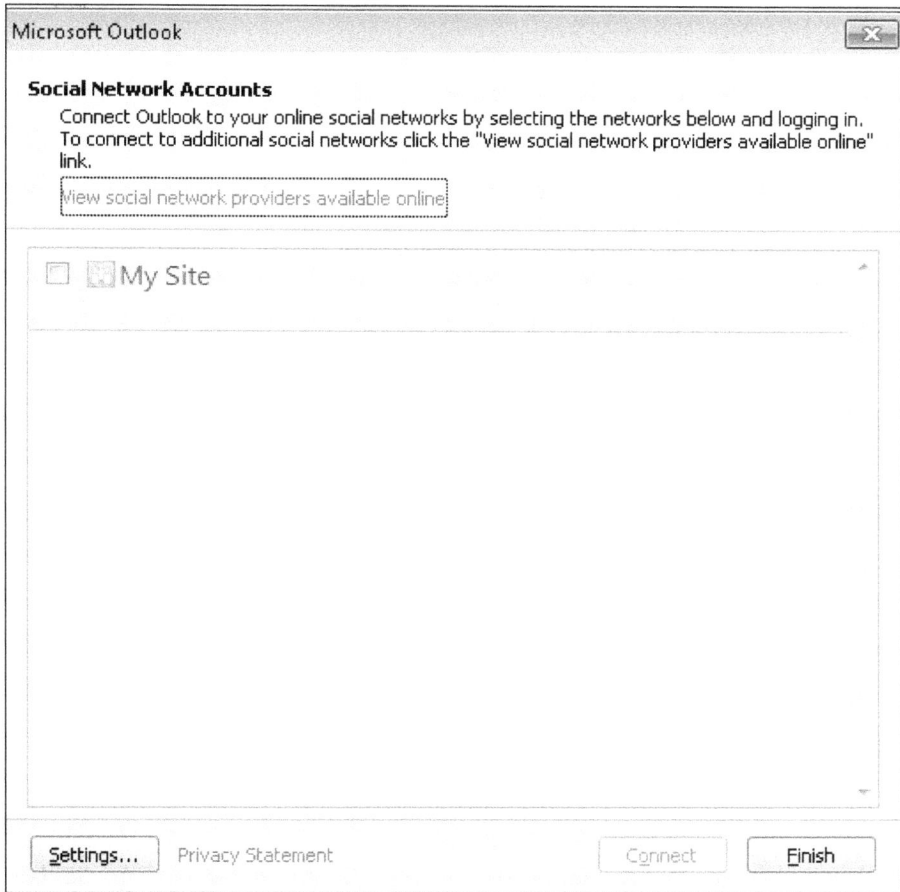

3. We will want to add some more social connector providers before we continue. So click on the link, that says **View social network providers available online**, and you will be taken to the Office download page for the social connectors:

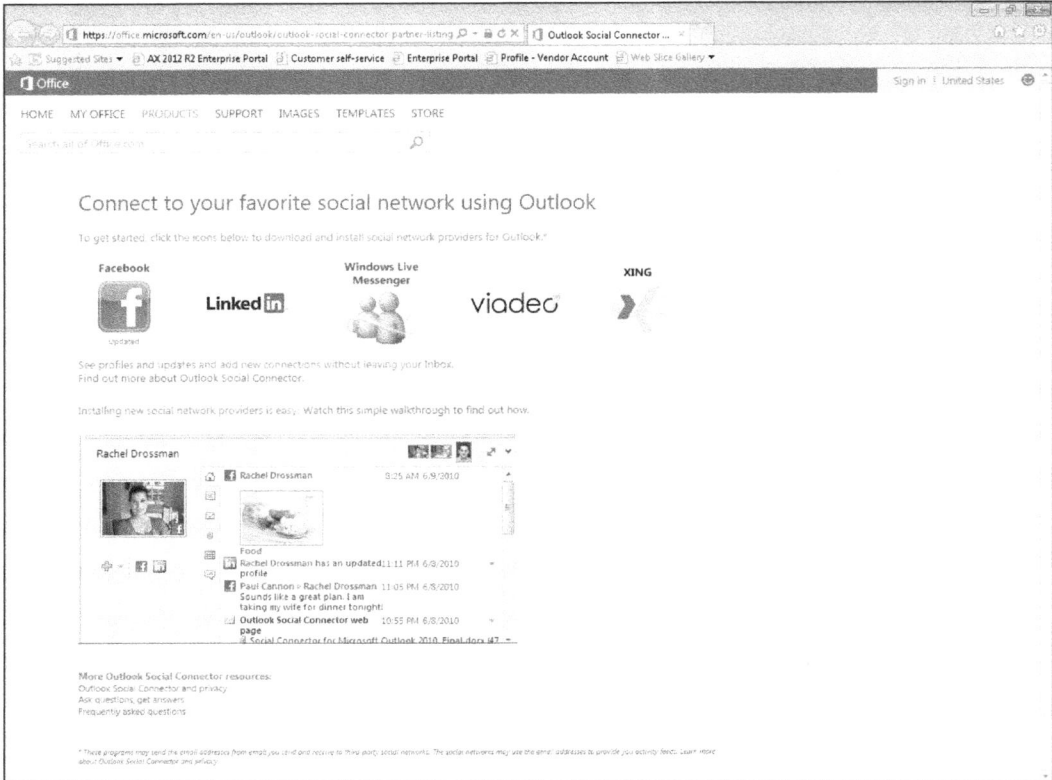

4. You can select any or all of the available connectors, which will then install the connector add-on for you. After you have finished, you can return to the **Social Network Accounts** dialog box and you will be able to enter in your credentials for the social networks:

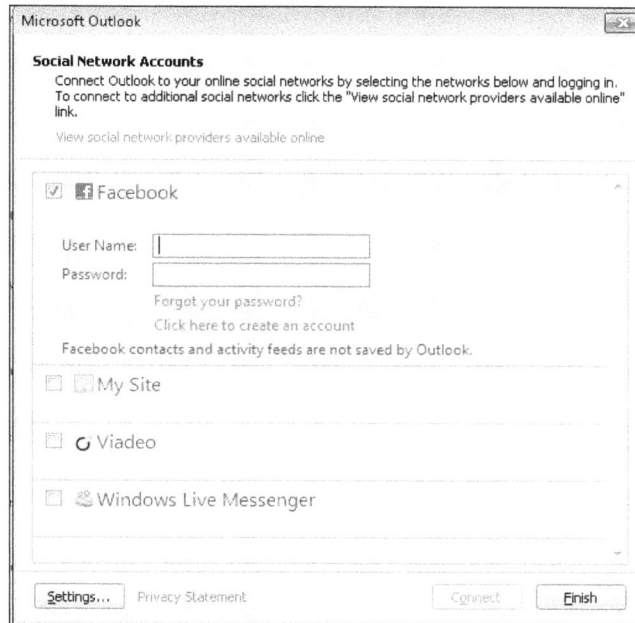

5. After you have configured the social networks that you want to use, you can just click on the **Finish** button and you are done:

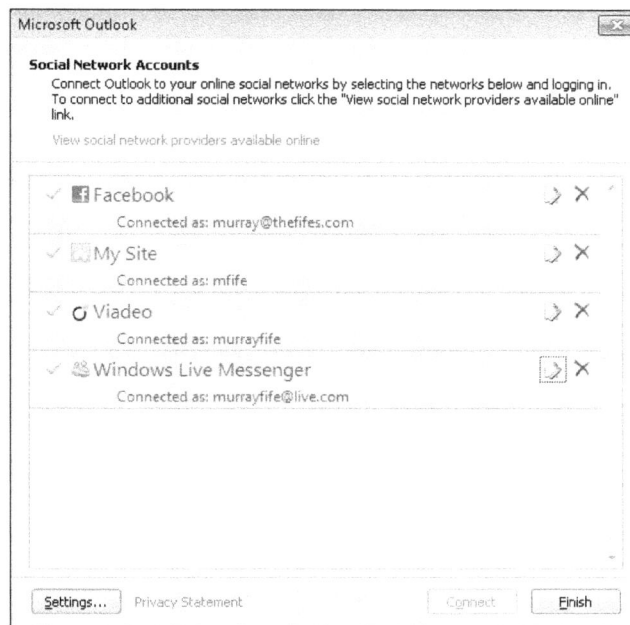

How it works...

Now when you open up a contact within Outlook, you will be able to see all of their social activity in the **People Pane**:

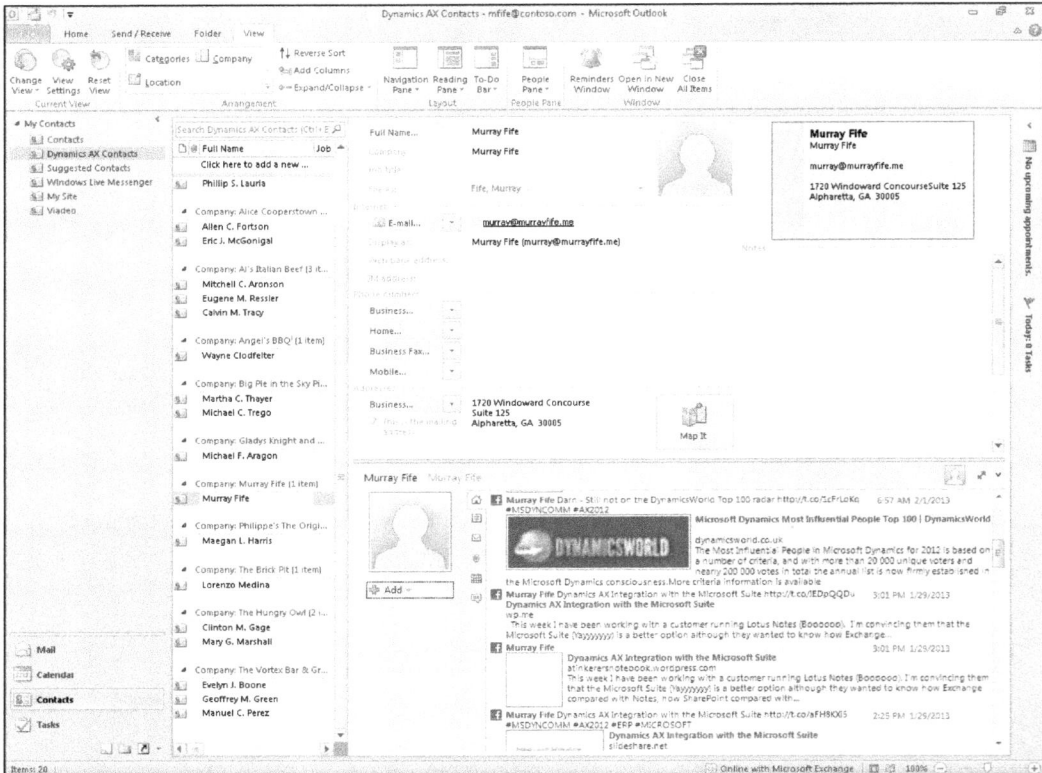

Communicating with contacts from within Dynamics AX

You don't have to leave Dynamics AX in order to start e-mailing and instant messaging with contacts. As long as your contacts have e-mail addresses defined against their record, you can start communicating with them directly from the application. This quick recipe will show you how to do this.

Getting ready

In order to e-mail and instant message from Dynamics AX to a contact, you just need to make sure that you have the e-mail addresses defined against the contact itself. To do this:

1. Open up the contact record and make sure that the **Contact Information** is populated:

How to do it...

To start e-mailing directly from the contact on the Dynamics AX form, follow these steps:

1. Anywhere that a **Contact ID** is shown in Dynamics AX, you should be able to see a presence indicator (a small round ball) before the ID. If you right-click on the ball, then a pop-up menu will show that will allow you to create e-mails using any of the contact information that is defined against the contact:

How it works...

Initiating an e-mail directly from Dynamics AX will open up your Outlook client and you can start e-mailing.

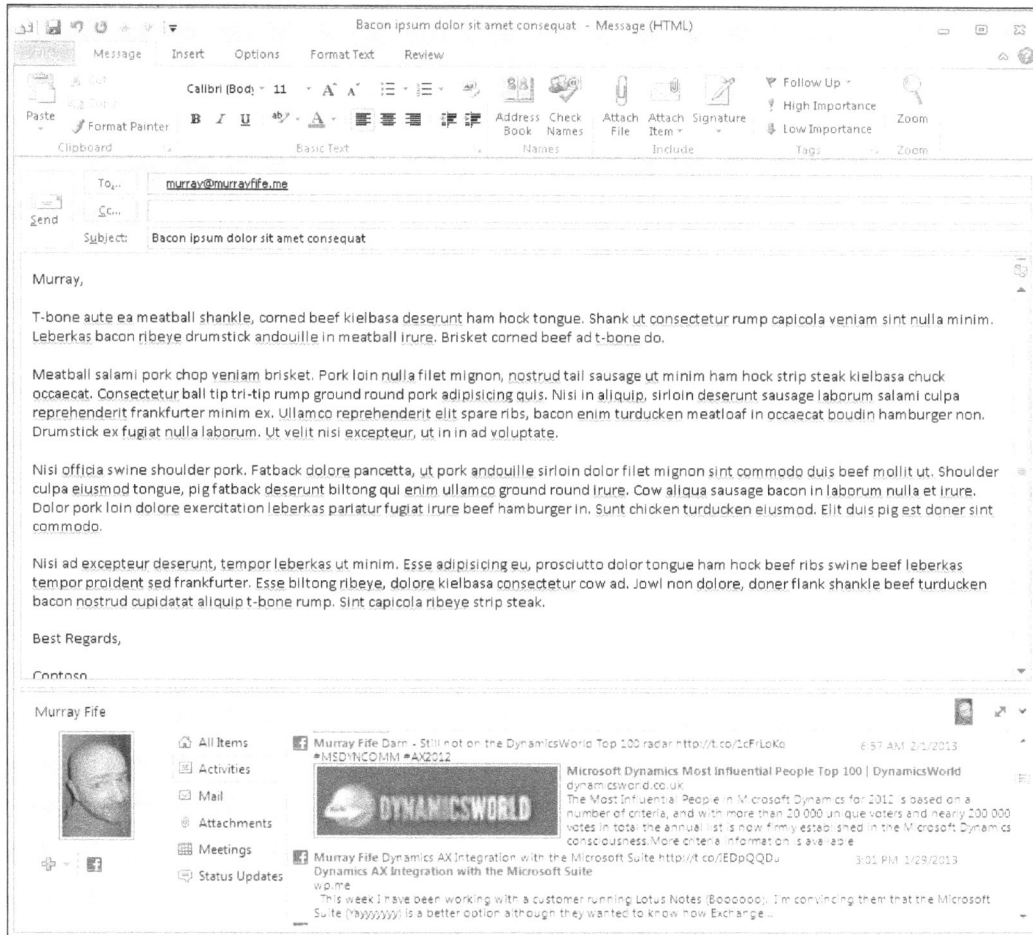

Using Lync to collaborate with other users directly from Dynamics AX

There may be times when you are looking at some information within Dynamics AX that someone else created, and you need to ask them a question about it. If you have Lync installed and configured, then Dynamics AX gives you a quick and easy way to contact other users, and usually you don't even have to leave the current form that you are in. Through the users name that is shown on the form, you are able to see if they are online, if they are available, and then **instant message** (**IM**) them, call them, video chat with them, and even share your desktop with them.

This quick recipe will show how to start a communication with other employees directly from a Dynamics AX form.

Getting ready

Before you are able to use Lync to contact other people in the organization, you need to make sure that there is an IM account associated with the users **Worker** profile. To do this, follow these steps:

1. From the **HR** area page, open up the **Workers** form from the **Common** group, and make sure that there is an e-mail address:

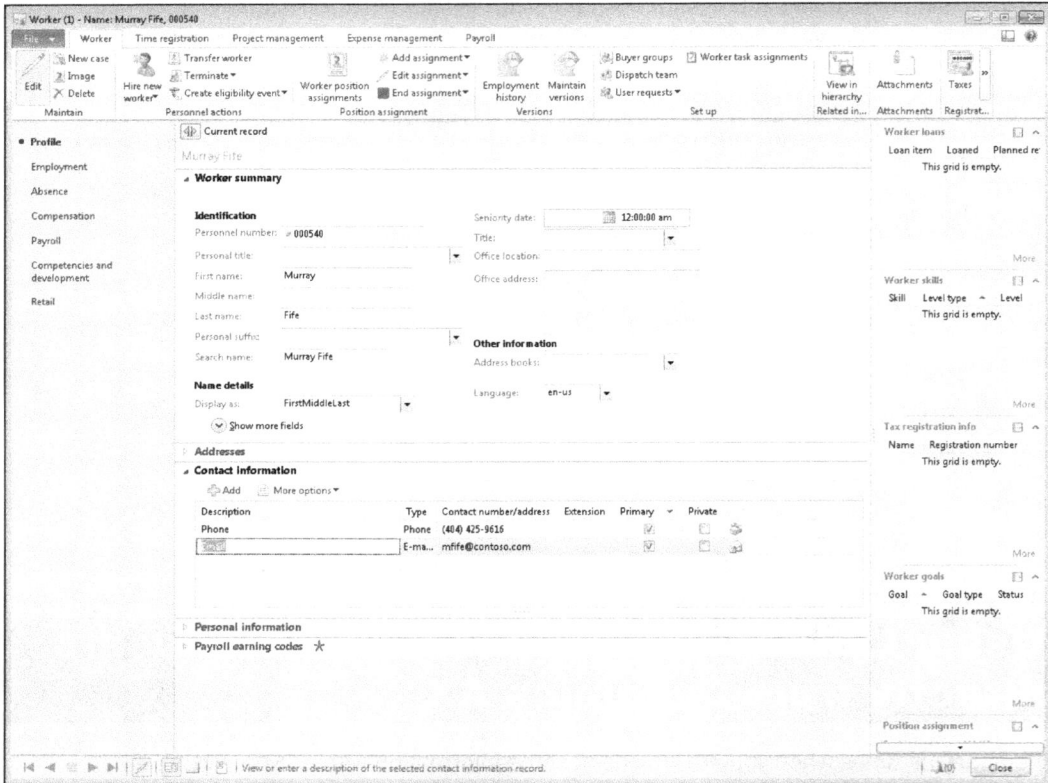

2. Select the e-mail address, and from the **More options** drop-down list in the **Contact Information** group, select the **Advanced** option to open up the detailed view of the contact information. For the e-mail address that is going to be used for Lync IM communication, make sure that the **Instant message** checkbox is selected:

Edit contact information (1) - Name: Murray Fife, 000540

File ▼ | ➕ Add | ✖ Remove

Description	Contact number/address
Phone	(404) 425-9616
Email	mfife@contoso.com

Location:	000002297
Description:	Email
Type:	E-mail address
E-mail address:	mfife@contoso.com
Purpose:	Home ▾
Instant message:	☑
Instant messenger sign-in:	☑
Primary:	☑
Private:	☐

Reference field in a different table

Close

How to do it...

To start an IM conversation in Lync directly from a Dynamics AX form, follow these steps:

1. When you are using Lync, if any of the users on any of the records are online with Lync as well, then the **Presence** icon will be colored in:

Personnel
Responsibility:
Responsible: ➚ Murray Fife

Reminder
Reminder: ☐
Reminder minutes:

Description
Notes:

Worker

Murray Fife

Status:	Employed
Personnel number:	000540
Position:	000493
Department:	Client Services
E-mail:	mfife@contoso.com
Telephone:	(404) 425-9616
Office location:	
Office address:	

2. To communicate with the users through Lync, just right-click on the icon and you will be shown all of the different ways that you can start communications:

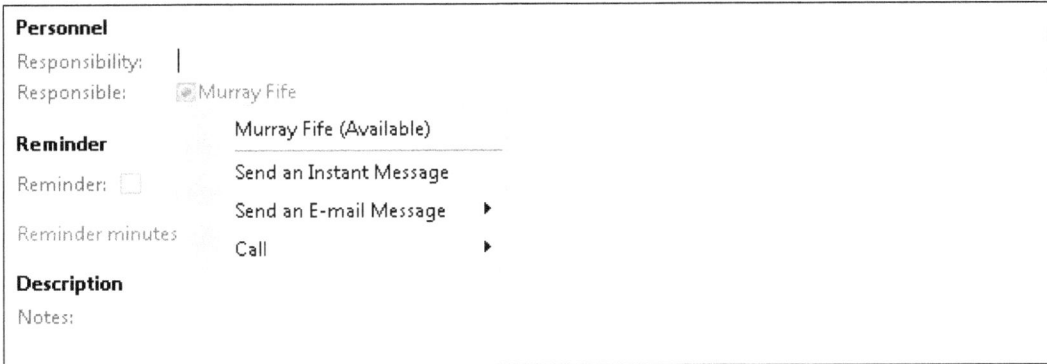

Personnel

Responsibility: |

Responsible: ☑ Murray Fife

Murray Fife (Available)

Reminder

Reminder: ☐   Send an Instant Message

Send an E-mail Message   ▶

Reminder minutes   Call   ▶

Description

Notes:

3. If you start a Lync IM, then all you have to do is start typing:

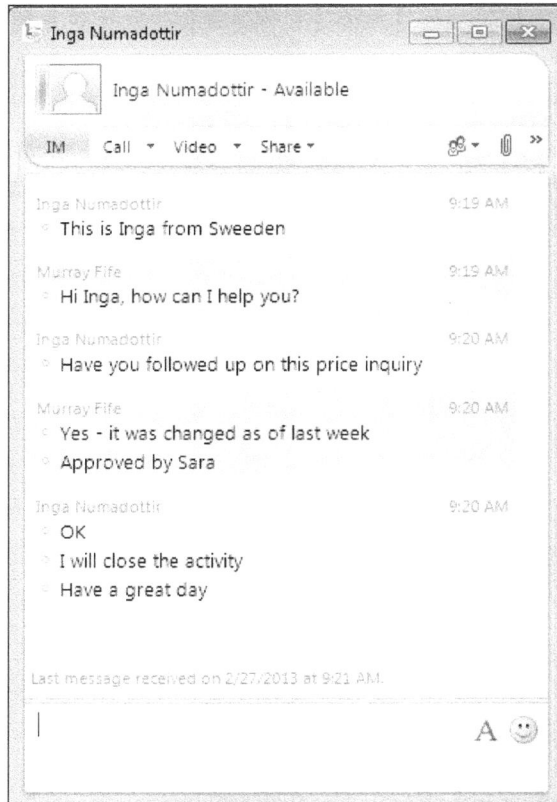

🗔 Inga Numadottir   ☐ ☐ ✖

Inga Numadottir - Available

IM   Call ▾ Video ▾ Share ▾   ☐▾ 〚 ⟫

Inga Numadottir   9:19 AM
  This is Inga from Sweeden

Murray Fife   9:19 AM
  Hi Inga, how can I help you?

Inga Numadottir   9:20 AM
  Have you followed up on this price inquiry

Murray Fife   9:20 AM
  Yes - it was changed as of last week
  Approved by Sara

Inga Numadottir   9:20 AM
  OK
  I will close the activity
  Have a great day

Last message received on 2/27/2013 at 9:21 AM.

| A ☺

How it works...

Apart from being able to IM others within the organization, Lync allows you to start voice and video calls from your chat session, invite other people to the session, and also share desktops if you need to show them something.

Lync is also integrated with Outlook and Exchange, and all of your conversations are saved in Outlook for you so that you can always reference back to them after the fact:

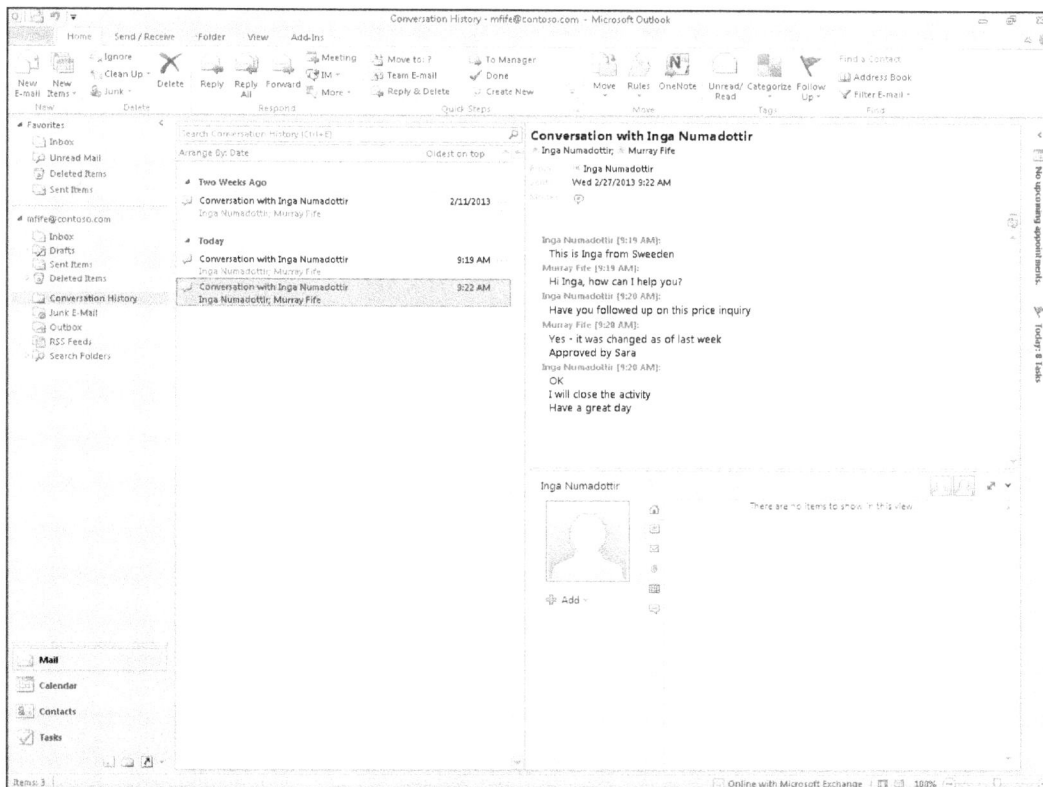

Summary

Not everyone will be in front of their computer all of the time and able to access Dynamics AX, but chances are they will have their tablet or smartphone within arm's reach almost all of the time, which makes them a great extension point for the Dynamics AX system.

Some other ways that you can use Outlook and Lync include:

- **Adding contact images to Outlook contacts**: The Outlook Social Connector will do this for you, but you may need to do this for some of the more camera-shy contacts. This gives you a personal reminder of who you are communicating with, and will be shared with your smartphone as well.

- **Creating Lync meetings directly from Outlook**: Even if the other people you are contacting do not use Lync, the web client includes voice, video, and desktop sharing.

- **Federating with other companies, Lync systems**: This allows two companies that use Lync to see each other's availability and presence, as well as contact each other directly, which is great for key vendors, customers, and business partners.

You're almost certainly using Outlook, and probably using Lync as well, so linking them to Dynamics AX is just the natural thing to do.

5
Using Cases to Manage Incidents and Requests

In this chapter, we will give examples of how you can use the new Case and project management capabilities within Dynamics AX 2012 to manage and streamline your business. This chapter will cover:

- ▸ Creating Case categories
- ▸ Assigning tasks through Cases
- ▸ Creating appointments through Cases
- ▸ Defining the standard processes for Case management
- ▸ Assigning Knowledge articles to Cases
- ▸ Associating additional business entities to Cases
- ▸ Creating projects from Cases
- ▸ Creating collaboration workspaces for Case projects

Introduction

Sometimes you don't have to leave Dynamics AX in order to extend out your business processes. With Dynamics AX 2012, a new feature was added called Cases that allows you to record interactions, issues, and incidents throughout the system, assign them to users for investigation or management, and then track all information collected along the way. It works like a traditional Case file, hence the name. Cases are not just a filing system though. Cases can be automatically routed to different people for review and investigation, and they can have standard processes assigned to them so that you can track their progress from creation to close, which may be different based on the Case category. The Case owners are able to assign tasks and create appointments linked to the Cases, or have the system automatically recommend them based on a suggested process.

By linking Knowledge Base articles with Case categories users are able to quickly access standard information in order to try to resolve issues. These can be rated by the users on their success or failure as they are being applied to the Cases, allowing you to retire the ones that are not successful.

When incidents or requests that are being managed through Cases start becoming more involved then there is the ability to create projects associated with them, managed through the project management module of Dynamics AX. This allows for project plans to be created, time and expenses to be applied, and also for collaboration workspaces to be created within SharePoint for collaboration.

In this chapter, we will show you how you can use Cases to manage the New Product Request and Development process within Dynamics AX.

Creating Case categories

All cases are assigned to a Case category within Dynamics AX, and separated by a category group which defines where within Dynamics AX the cases can be accessed from. These are the mechanisms that determine what processes the Case follows, allowing you to use the same functionality for different purposes, which is why Cases are such a useful feature within Dynamics AX.

In this recipe, we will show how you can create a Case category within Dynamics AX so that we can start creating **Cases**.

How to do it...

To create a new Case category, follow these steps:

1. From the **Organization administration** area page, open up the **Case categories** form from the Cases folder in the **Setup** group:

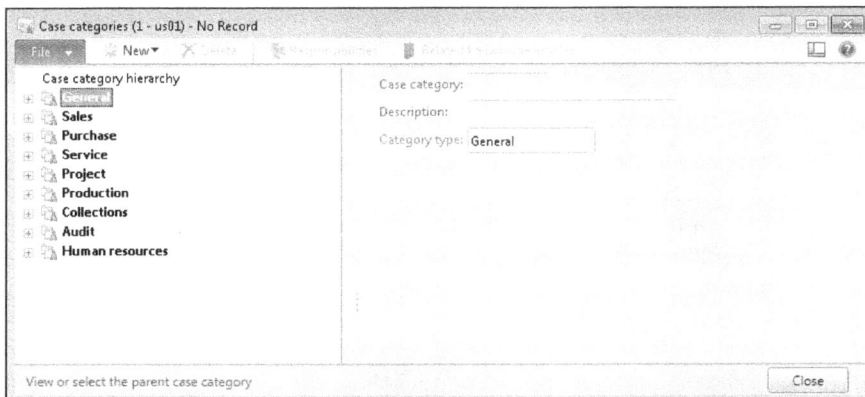

2. Click on the **New** menu, and navigate to the **Case category** option to create a new base category for our **New Product Request** cases.

3. When the **New Record** form is shown, set the **Case category** and **Description** both to Requests, and set the **Category type** to General. The **General Category** type is visible to all of the modules, which makes it useful for sharing Case categories over all modules. We are creating a base folder for all requests to make it easier to find them if we have different variations of requests later on.

4. Expand out the General folder on the left and select your new **Requests** Case category. Select the **Child** Case category function from the **New** menu to create a subcategory within the **Requests** group.

5. For this category, set the **Case category** to NewProd, and the **Description** to New Product Request. If you like, you can also assign a **Worker** as the **Default owner** of the Case category. This will be the user who is assigned to the case by default every time it is created:

How it works...

Once you have a **Case category** defined, you can create cases associated with it throughout Dynamics AX. With this recipe we created a Case with a **General category** type which means that it may be used throughout Dynamics AX, whereas if we had created it within one of the other category types then security would restrict who is able to access the case and where it is shown.

To use cases to record a **New Product Request** from a customer, we can just open up the **Customers** form, and go to the **General** tab in the ribbon bar. In the **New** group you will see a **Case** button that will allow you to create a new case:

When the **New** case form is shown, it will automatically be associated with the customer that we created the case for. This form also allows us to select the **NewProd Case category** that we just created.

While we are creating the Case, we can also record more information about the **New Product Request** from the customer, such as product specs, descriptions, and priorities:

Once you click on the **Create** button, you will have a request recorded in Dynamics AX.

Assigning tasks through Cases

Tasks can be created at any time through the Case allowing you to create reminders for yourself, or to assign tasks to others within the organization. The tasks will show up in the users' activity list, and also if you have the Outlook synchronization configured (see *Chapter 4, Communication and Collaboration*), then these will also show up within Outlook. These will also be associated with the Case, so you can always track the progress of these tasks from one single location.

In this recipe, we will show how you can create a new task from a case.

How to do it...

To create a new task from within the Case form, follow these steps:

1. Open up the **Case** that you want to create the task and from the **General** tab on the ribbon bar, click on the **Activities** button in the **Related Info** group. From the drop-down box, select the **New task** item:

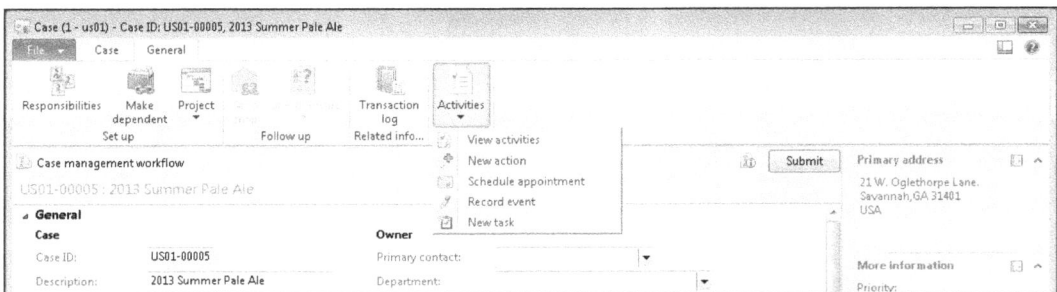

2. This will open up a form for recording the new task. You can give the task a title by filling in the **Purpose** field, set the **Start date** and **End date**, and also add additional information by using the **Notes** field. The **Responsible** field will default from the Case itself, but you can reassign the task to anyone within the organization if you like:

3. Click on the **Close** button to confirm the task and you will be done.

How it works...

Once the task is created, the user that is responsible for the task will see it on their activity list, which they could also turn into a Cue (see *Chapter 11, Role Center Personalization and Customization*):

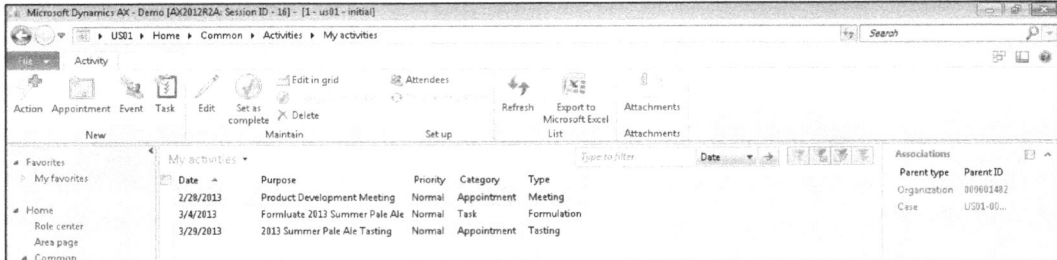

Also, if you have your **Work list** showing on your Role Center page, then you will be notified that a task has been assigned to you there as well:

From the **Work list** you are able to open up the Case from the **Actions** menu.

Creating appointments through Cases

Appointments can also be created and associated with the Case at any time via the ribbon bar. These will also show up in the users' activity list on Outlook (if you have Outlook synchronization configured).

In this recipe, we will show how you can create a new appointment from a Case.

How to do it...

To create a new appointment from within the Case form, follow these steps:

1. Open up the **Case** that you want to create the task and from the **General** tab on the ribbon bar, click on the **Activities** button in the **Related Info** group. From the drop-down box, select the **Scheduled appointment** item:

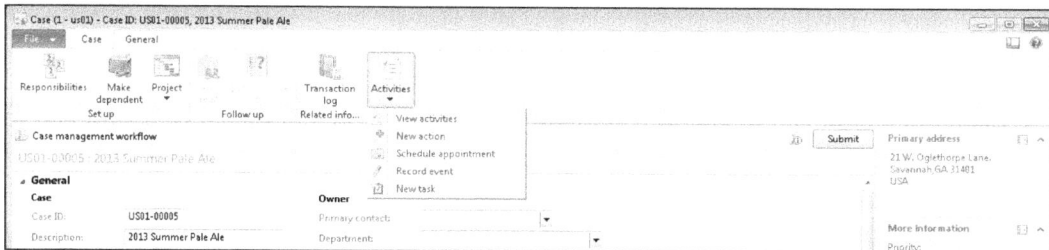

2. This will open up a form for creating the new appointment. You can give the task a title by filling in the **Purpose** field, set the **Start date** and **End date**, and also add additional information by using the **Notes** field:

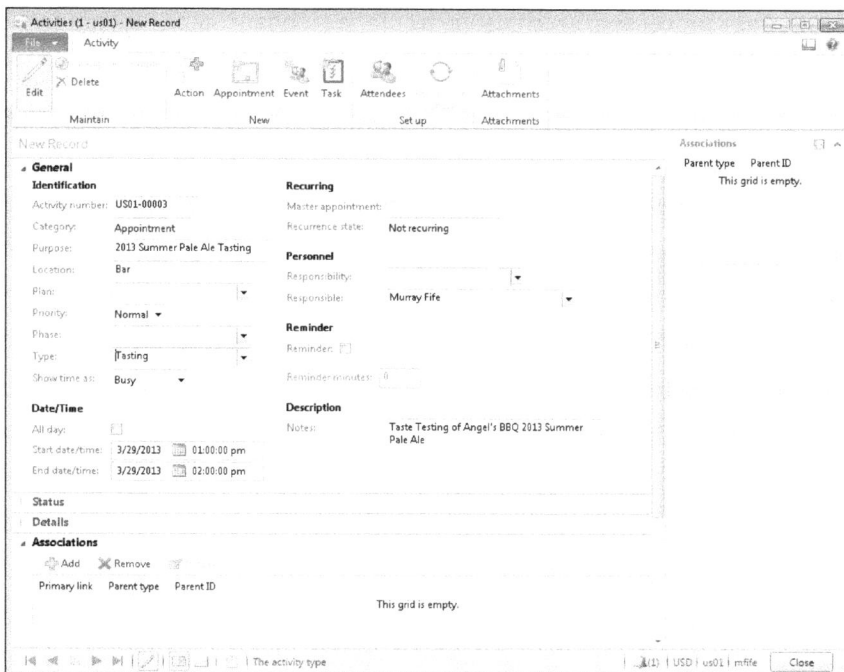

3. Click on the **Close** button to confirm the task and you will be done.

How it works...

Just as with the tasks, the user who is associated with the **Scheduled Appointment** will see it within their activity and work list:

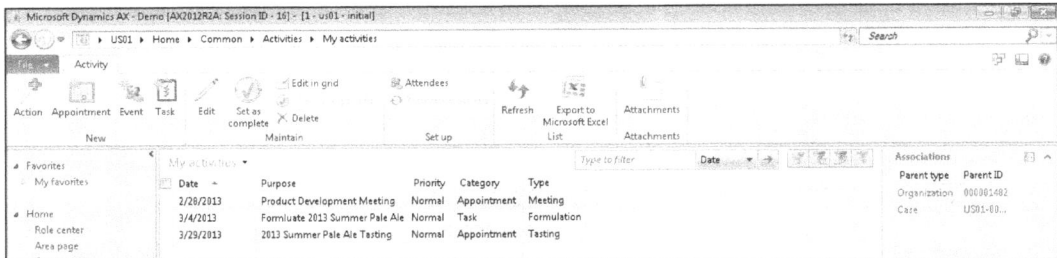

Defining the standard processes for Case management

Cases will typically have their own process or life cycle that you will want them to follow as a standard business procedure. Each type of case may be different though. Dynamics AX allows you do this with **Case processes**, which define all of the standard steps that are required to be performed. Through the Case processes you can also have tasks and appointments created automatically at particular steps in the process so that you don't have to manually create them. These template processes can then be associated with one or more Case categories.

In this recipe, we will show how you can use the **Case processes** feature to turn a generic case into a specialized process that you want users to follow.

How to do it...

To create a new Case process and use it within Cases, follow these steps:

1. From the **Organization administration** area page, open up the Case processes form from the `Cases` folder in the **Setup** group.

2. Click on the **New** button in the menu bar to create a new **Case process**.

3. Set the **Name** and the **Description** for the **Case process**.

4. In the body of the form, you will see an entry for **Stage 1** of the **Case process**. Change the **Purpose** of the stage to something a little more appropriate. In this case we will always start off our new product requests with a **Review** step:

5. To add additional stages, click on the **Activity** menu button above stages, or right-click on the parent folder and select the **Create level** item:

6. To create default tasks and appointments for the stages, just right-click on the stage that you want them to be associated with and select the **Create task** and **Create appointment** menu items:

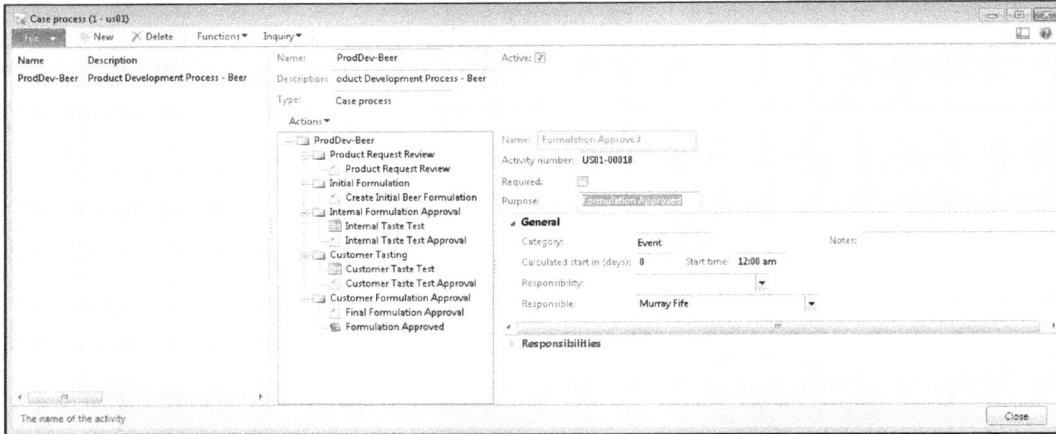

7. After you have finished, click on **Close** to save your **Case process**.

8. The final step in the setup is to open up your **Case categories** form and select the **Case category** that you would like to associate the process with. In the **General** tab, you will be able to select your Case process that you just defined within the **Case process** field:

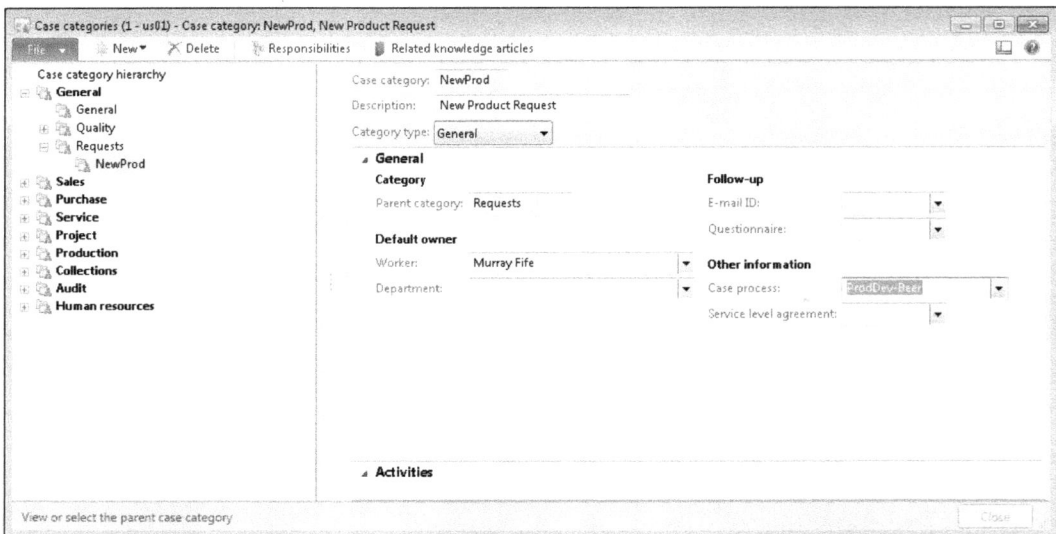

How it works...

Now, when you create a new Case, the **Process** fact box will show the standard stages that your case should step through. If there are tasks and appointments associated with the stages, then it will automatically show them to you, and also create them within Dynamics AX so that you don't have to create them manually. Also, if you select the **Change stage** option from the **Process** group on the **Case** ribbon bar, you will be able to move the case from one stage to the next:

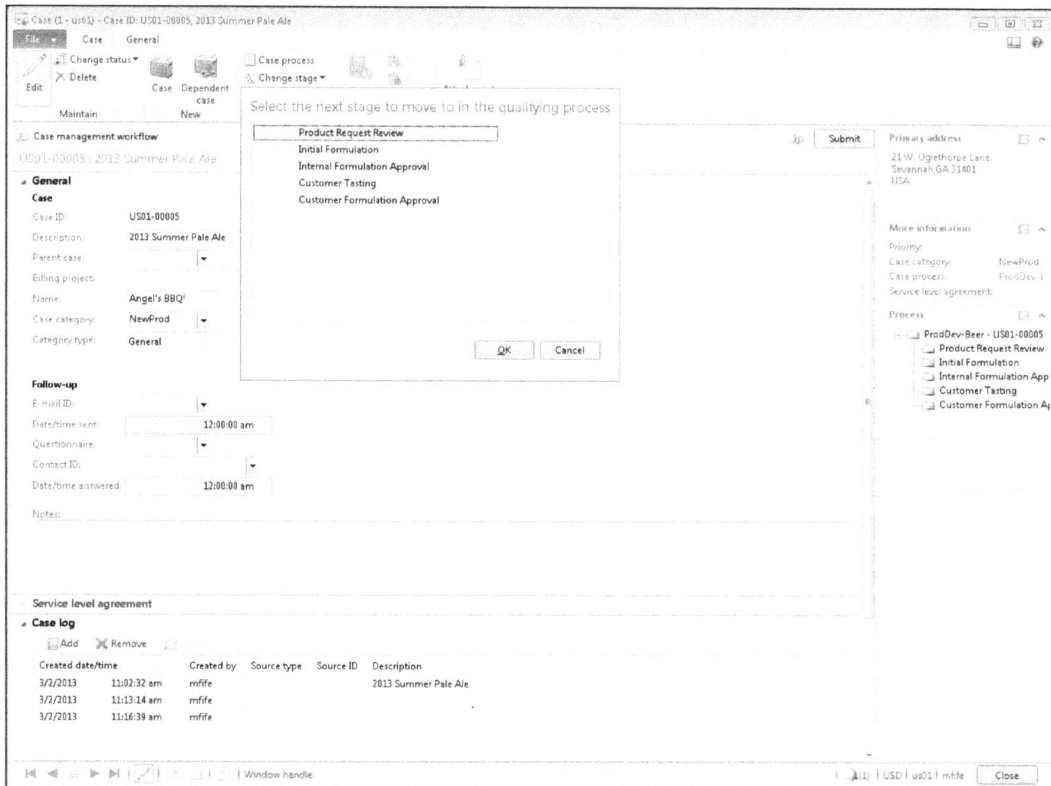

You can place constraints around the stages as well to ensure that all of the tasks and appointments have been completed, and that users are not skipping steps.

Assigning Knowledge articles to Cases

Many times, you will have Standard Operating Procedures or Knowledge Base articles that are useful when investigating or processing cases. These could be resolutions to common problems, standard procedures to be performed, or just information that may be useful to the person working through the case process.

Rather than making the user remember these documents and procedures, Dynamics AX allows you associate Knowledge articles that you have uploaded with the Case categories. Then when a case is accessed, these articles will be displayed automatically to the user and they can open them up directly from the Case itself.

In this recipe, we will show how you can create these associations within the cases.

Getting Ready

Before you start this recipe, make sure that you have your Knowledge articles uploaded into Dynamics AX. To do this:

1. From the **Home** area page, open up the **Knowledge articles** form from the `Document management` folder in the **Common** group.

2. If your articles are not uploaded, click on the **Knowledge article** menu item to add the file. You will be able to give your article a name and also upload the document from your local system:

Knowledge articles (1 - us01) - New Record		
Knowledge articles		
Knowledge article item ID:	US01-00064	
Parent ID:		
Knowledge article name:	SOP BT1 - Beer Tasting Guide	
Document:	C:\Users\Public\Documents\Standard Operati	
Type:	File ▼	
	OK	Cancel
File path and name.		

3. This will allow you to upload as many documents as you like:

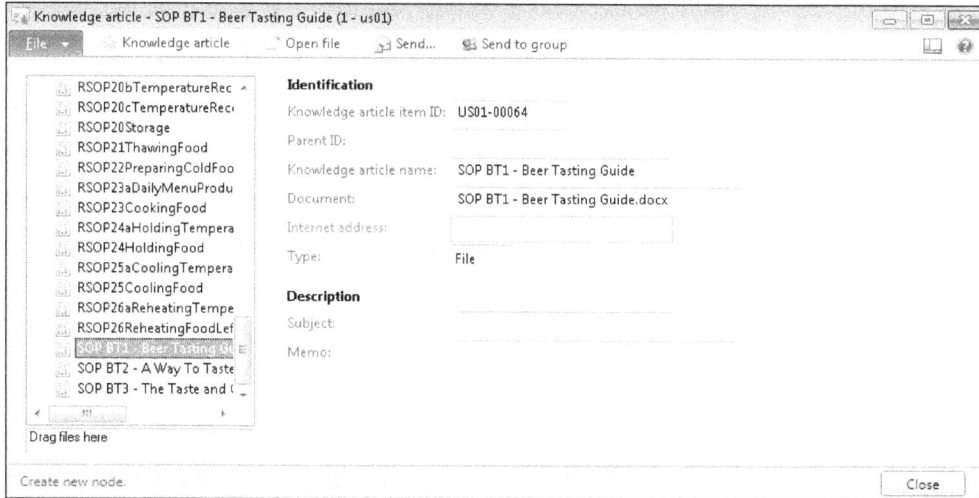

How to do it...

To associate Knowledge articles to your Case process, follow these steps:

1. From the **Organization administration** area page, open up the **Case categories** form from the `Cases` folder in the **Setup** group.

2. In the menu bar of the form, click on the **Related Knowledge articles** menu item.

3. Click on the **New** button on the menu bar to create a new **Related Knowledge article**. Within the **Identification** field you will be able to select any of the articles that have been uploaded:

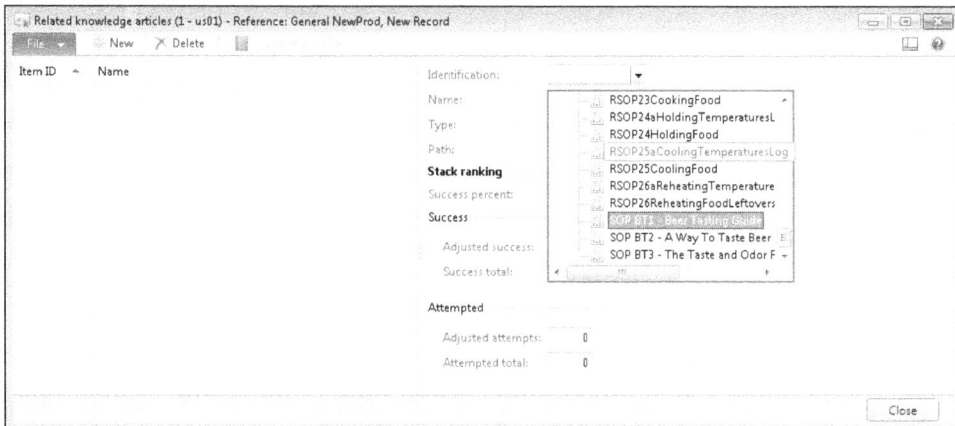

4. After adding all of the related articles, you will be able to close the form:

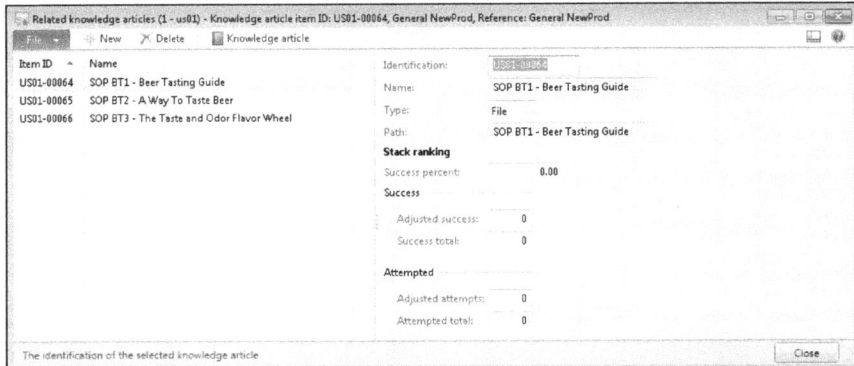

How it works...

Now, any time that you open up a **Case** that has **Knowledge articles** associated with the **Case category**, then the **Knowledge article** tab will be populated with links to those articles. The user is able to see the file just by clicking on the **Open** button for instant access:

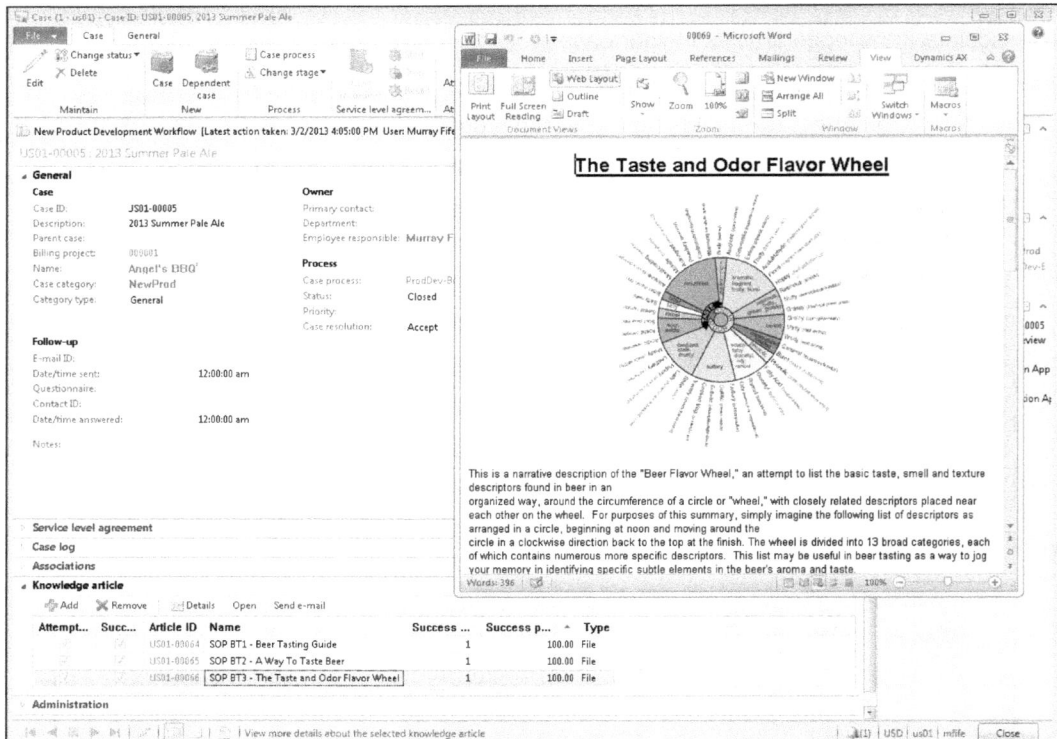

Also, the users are able to track if they attempted to use any of the articles, and if they were useful, giving you metrics on the usefulness of the articles that you are providing to them.

Associating additional business entities to Cases

Cases are linked to business entities (such as customers, products, and vendors) within Dynamics AX through associations. When the cases are initially created, they are automatically linked with that entity so that you can always link back to them. As a case is processed though, more entities within Dynamics AX may be associated to it making it visible within other areas of the system.

Examples of this may be that a customer creates a complaint. Initially the Case will be associated with the customer. When the defective product is identified, then this should be associated with the Case. If it is decided that this was caused by a vendor shipment issue, then the Case should be associated with that as well. Now, when looking at the customer, product, or vendor, the user will be able to track back to all of the Cases associated with them.

In this recipe, we will show how easy it is to create additional associations from a Case to other records in Dynamics AX.

How to do it...

To create a new association to a Case, follow these steps:

1. Open up the **Case** that you want to link to other records.
2. Open up the **Associations** tab within the form.
3. Click on the **Add** button to create a new association.
4. From the **Entity type** field, select the type of record that you would like to link to. In our recipe it will be an **Item**.
5. In the **ID** field, select the record that you want to link to:

Primary	Entity type	ID	Name
☐	Item	1400003	BEER, PALE ALE, SUMMER
☑	Customer	101004	Angel's BBQ

◢ **Associations**

⊕ Add ✖ Remove

How it works...

If you open up the record that you have just associated your case to, you will be able to see it by going to the **General** tab on the ribbon bar, and clicking on the **All cases** button in the **Maintain Cases** group:

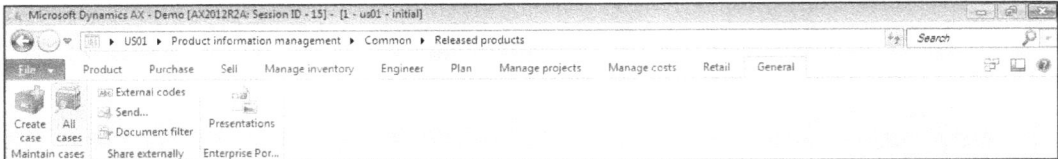

This will take you to the **All cases** view filtered just to that record:

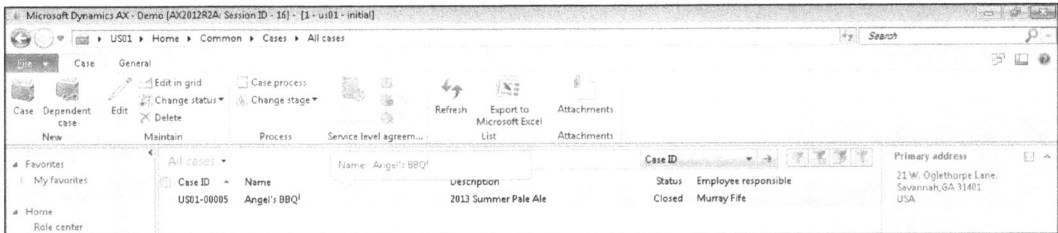

Creating projects from Cases

Sometimes issues and incidents grow to the point that they become a project and need a little more management and control than is provided through the Case process. You may want to start tracking time and materials, and link purchases to the process. In our example of the New Product Request, when the product is approved, and moved into the formulation stage, product development may want to track the profitability of the development by tracking their time.

To make this process easier, Dynamics AX Cases provide the ability to create new Billing Projects within Project Management directly from the Cases form, which we will show in this recipe.

How to do it...

To create a new billing project from a Case, follow these steps:

1. Open up the **Case** that you want to create the billing project.

2. From the **General** tab in the ribbon bar, click on the **Project** button in the **Set up** group. Select the **Create new billing project** option:

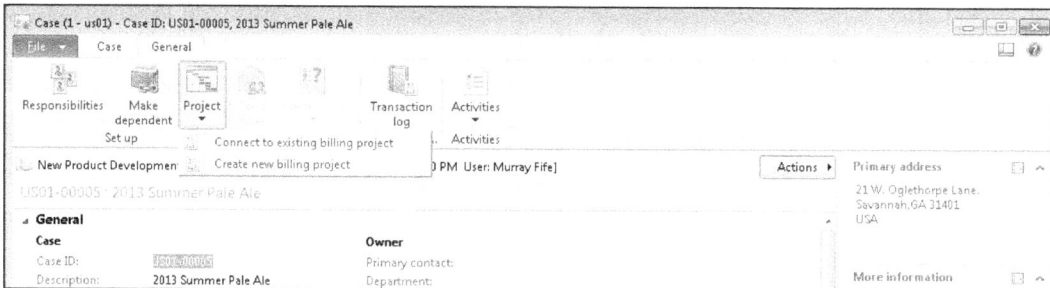

3. This will open up the **Create project** form where you can give the general details of the project and create it:

How it works...

After creating the billing project, you will be able to see it in the **Associations** tab on the **Case**:

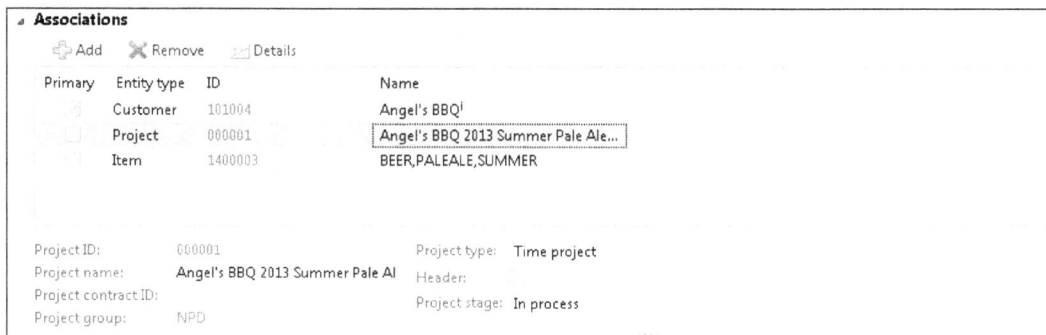

This will allow you to access the project, and track all of your time and materials, as well as create a more detailed work breakdown structure.

Creating collaboration workspaces for Case projects

Apart from giving you better tracking of time and materials, billing projects created from Cases provide the ability to create **Collaboration workspaces** within SharePoint that you can use to store files that could be accessed internally, and also accessed externally for collaboration with customers and vendors.

In this recipe, we will show you how to do this directly from the project form.

How to do it...

To create a new **Collaboration workspace** from a project, follow these steps:

1. Open up the billing project that is associated with your Case.

2. From the **Project** tab on the ribbon bar, click on the **Collaboration workspace** button in the **Set up** group, and select the **Create collaboration workspace** item:

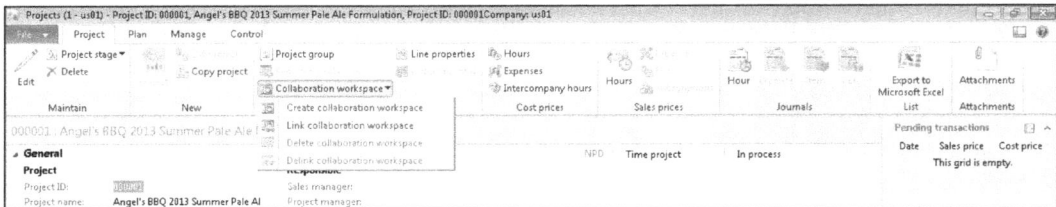

3. Give your workspace a title, and click on the **OK** button to create the workspace:

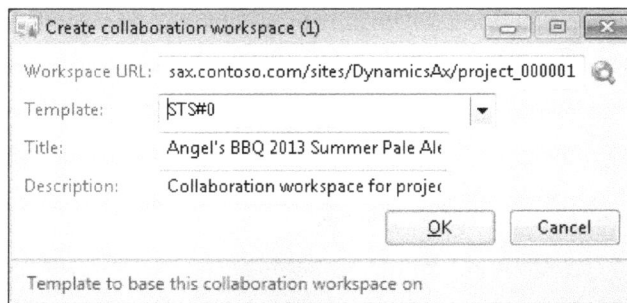

How it works...

If you now look at the bottom of the **Project** form, and open up the **Collaboration workspace** tab, you will see that the **Internal URL** and **External URL** fields are linked to SharePoint:

⊿ **Collaboration workspace**
Internal URL: sites/DynamicsAx/project_000001
External URL: http://dynamicsax.contoso.com/s

Clicking on these links will take you into the SharePoint site that has been created just for this project:

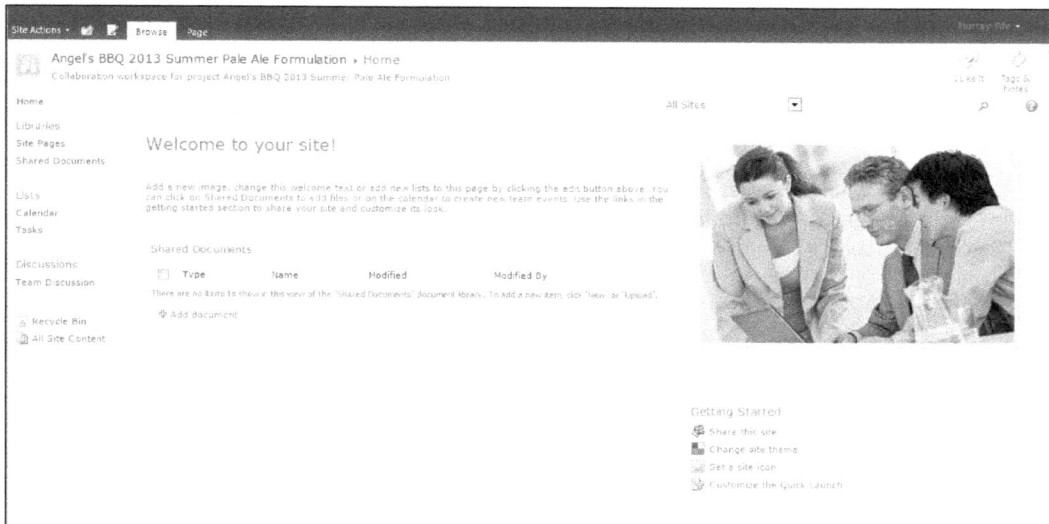

Summary

Within this chapter we have shown a number of the features that are available within Cases that you can use to help you to manage some incidents and requests. Using tools such as tasks, appointments, and standard processes for managing Cases will streamline your procedures. Also, using Knowledge Base articles and project collaboration workspaces will improve the management of information around the cases.

Once you have mastered the basics of how Cases can be used, you may want to try looking at some of the other capabilities that are enabled through the Case function within Dynamics AX. You may want to try:

- Creating workflows that add alerts and more elaborate routings of tasks within the organization
- Using questionnaires that are linked to the Case categories to gather more information as the Cases are being generated
- Creating PowerView dashboards to track the status and frequency of cases within the organization

Cases give you a great tool for creating tracking events and issues within Dynamics AX without having to write a single line of code. Some other areas that you could use Cases for include:

- Tracking customer and consumer complaints
- Reporting vendor quality and delivery issues
- Recording internal quality issues with products
- Tracking simple maintenance and service orders

6

Organizing Your Workflows

In this chapter, we will show you how to take advantage of the in built workflow capabilities in Dynamics AX 2012 to manage common business processes, and also how to develop your own workflows to manage the not so common processes. You will also learn the following:

- ▶ Creating a new workflow design from a template
- ▶ Adding task steps to workflows
- ▶ Saving and activating workflows
- ▶ Setting the default workflows
- ▶ Submitting and using workflows
- ▶ Adding conditional decisions to a workflow
- ▶ Adding manual decisions to a workflow
- ▶ Adding workflow status notifications
- ▶ Adding text placeholders to workflow messages

Introduction

There are two types of processes that you probably want to manage more effectively: business and people. The first one is the easiest because you can generally control how a program or system is going to work. Making sure that the people processes are working correctly is a little trickier.

You would want to:

- ▸ Assign the right people to tasks, some of whom may not use Dynamics AX on a daily basis

- ▸ Have different processes based on business rules

- ▸ Make sure that steps are not skipped

- ▸ Ensure that tasks are done within a reasonable amount of time

Fortunately, Dynamics AX 2012 comes preconfigured with a workflow engine and standard workflow templates that you can use to help wrangle people. All you need to do is create the workflow design and activate it. Don't worry if you are not a programmer, this will all be a zero coding experience.

In this chapter, we will show you how you can design workflows by adding a workflow to manage the case management process within Dynamics AX.

Creating a new workflow design from a template

If you look through the area pages of the different modules in AX, within the **Setup** group on most of these you will notice forms for designing and managing that module's workflows. But if you open these forms, there may not be a lot of workflows showing up. Don't worry, Dynamics AX 2012 comes preloaded with a number of standard workflow templates. All you need to do is create your workflow designs from them.

In this recipe, we will show you how you can create a new workflow design from the standard workflow templates that are delivered.

How to do it...

To create a new workflow template, follow these steps:

1. From the **Organization administration** area page, click on the **Case workflow** menu item in the Cases folder of the **Setup** group to view all the workflows associated with cases.

2. To start a new workflow design, click on the **New** button in the **New** group of the **Workflow** ribbon bar. This will open up a dialog box with all the available workflow templates that are available from that area of Dynamics AX.

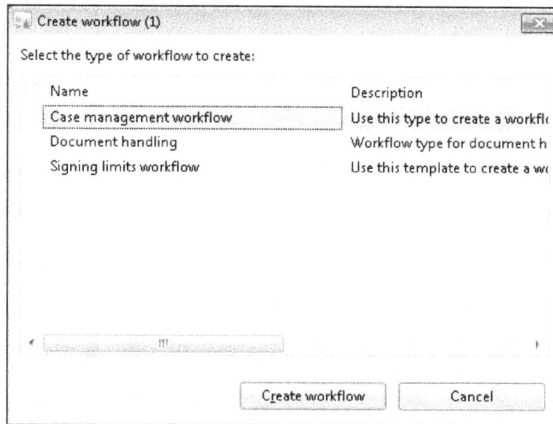

3. Click on the **Case management workflow** template to create a new instance of the workflow design.

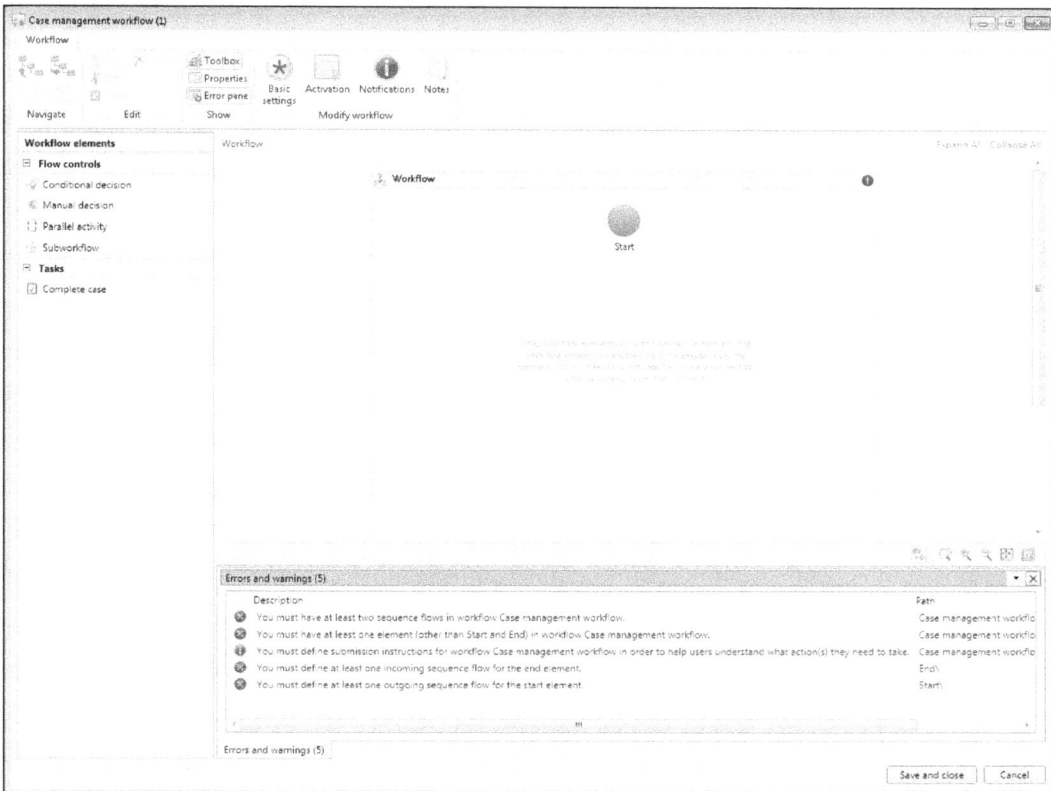

> Anywhere that a red exclamation bullet shows on the workflow designer is an indication that there is some information that needs to be added or configured on the workflow.
>
> If you click on the **Error pane** button on the **Show** group of the **Workflow** ribbon bar, the workflow designer will show you all the messages and warnings, and clicking on the messages will take you to the workflow element that needs to be fixed.

4. Click on the **Properties** button on the **Show** group of the **Workflow** ribbon bar to open up the general workflow properties. Here you can give your workflow design a name, and also instructions that will show up when the users ask for information about this workflow.

Properties	▾ ☒

Case management workflow - new workflow

Instructions: Submitting this workflow will initiate a case approval process.

★ Basic Settings
▢ Activation
ⓘ Notifications
▢ Notes

Enter the following information

Name: Case management workflow

Owner: mfife ▾

Email template for workflow notifications: CaseMail ▾

Submission instructions: 📋 Insert placeholder 🔍 Translations (0)

Submitting this workflow will initiate a case approval process.

Close

Adding task steps to workflows

Once you have a design started, you can add steps in the workflow that will allow you to assign tasks to users, which we will show in the following recipe.

How to do it...

To add a new task step in a workflow, follow these steps:

1. On the left-hand side of the workflow designer form, you will see all the workflow elements that you are able to use within your workflow. These will differ slightly depending on the workflow template you choose.

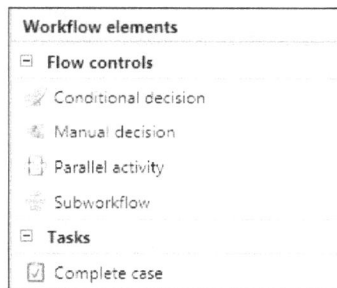

2. Click on the **Complete case** task and drag it onto your workflow canvas.

3. Hover your mouse over the **Start** node, and you will see connector points appearing around the node. Click on one of them and drag the connector line that appears down to the **Complete case** node that you just added to the form. This will link the two workflow steps.

4. Do the same for the **Complete case** and **End** nodes as well to make a continuous workflow.

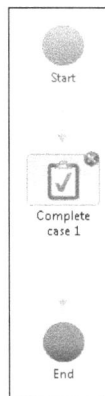

5. Notice that there is an alert in the **Complete case 1** step in the workflow showing that you have some configuration information required before this is a valid workflow. Select the workflow element, and in the ribbon bar, a **Modify element** group will appear.

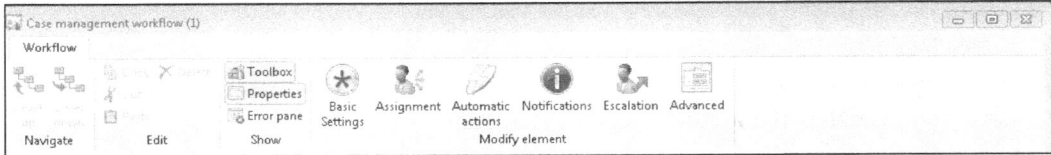

6. Click on the **Basic Settings** button to open up the element properties.

7. In the **Basic Settings** panel, give your step a better name, subject, and work instructions. When notifications are delivered to the users, this is the information that will show up in the message or alert.

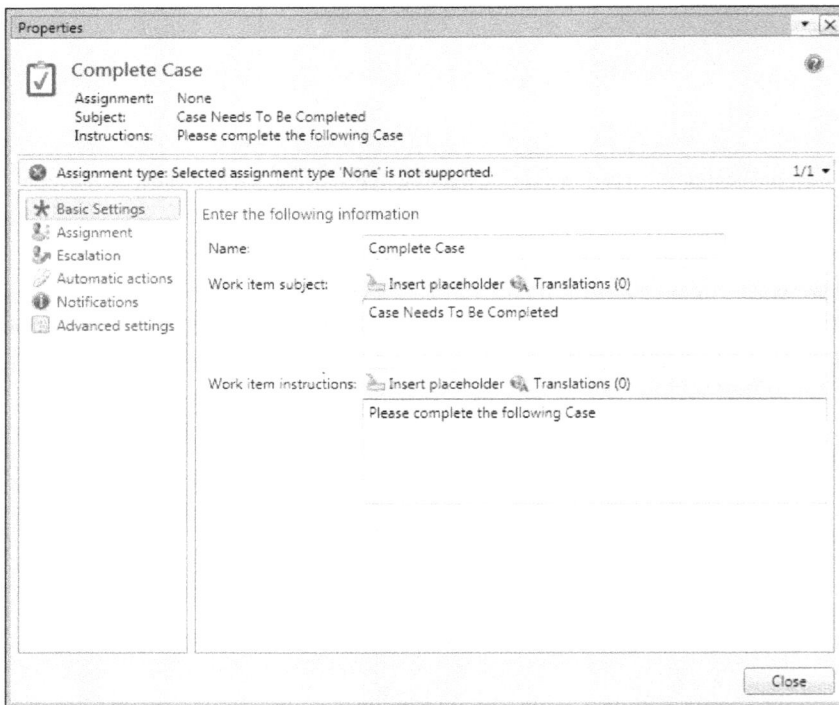

8. Now, we need to assign the task to someone within the organization. To do this, click on the **Assignment** item. From the **Assignment type** tab, select the **User** option so that we can assign this task by the username.

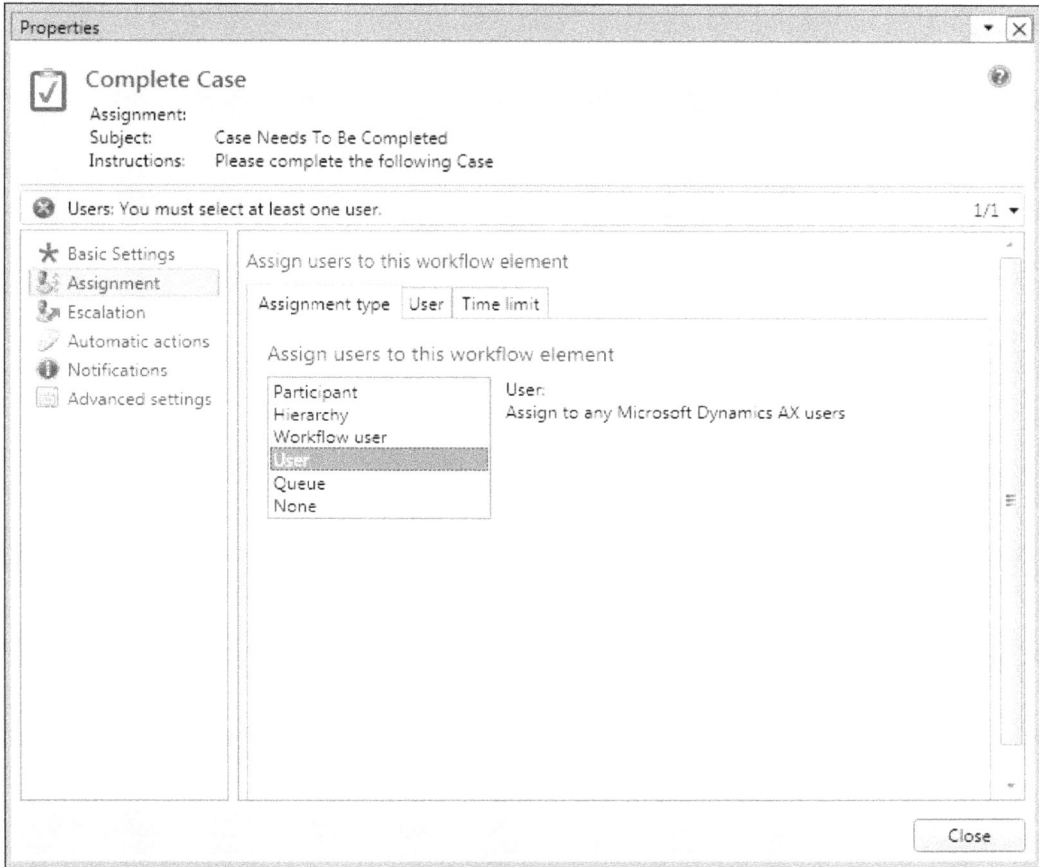

Properties

Complete Case
Assignment:
Subject: Case Needs To Be Completed
Instructions: Please complete the following Case

Users: You must select at least one user.   1/1

- Basic Settings
- Assignment
- Escalation
- Automatic actions
- Notifications
- Advanced settings

Assign users to this workflow element

Assignment type | User | Time limit

Assign users to this workflow element

Participant
Hierarchy
Workflow user
User
Queue
None

User:
Assign to any Microsoft Dynamics AX users

Close

9. Then from the **User** tab, select the user to whom you would like to assign this task and click on the **>** button to move them to the task.

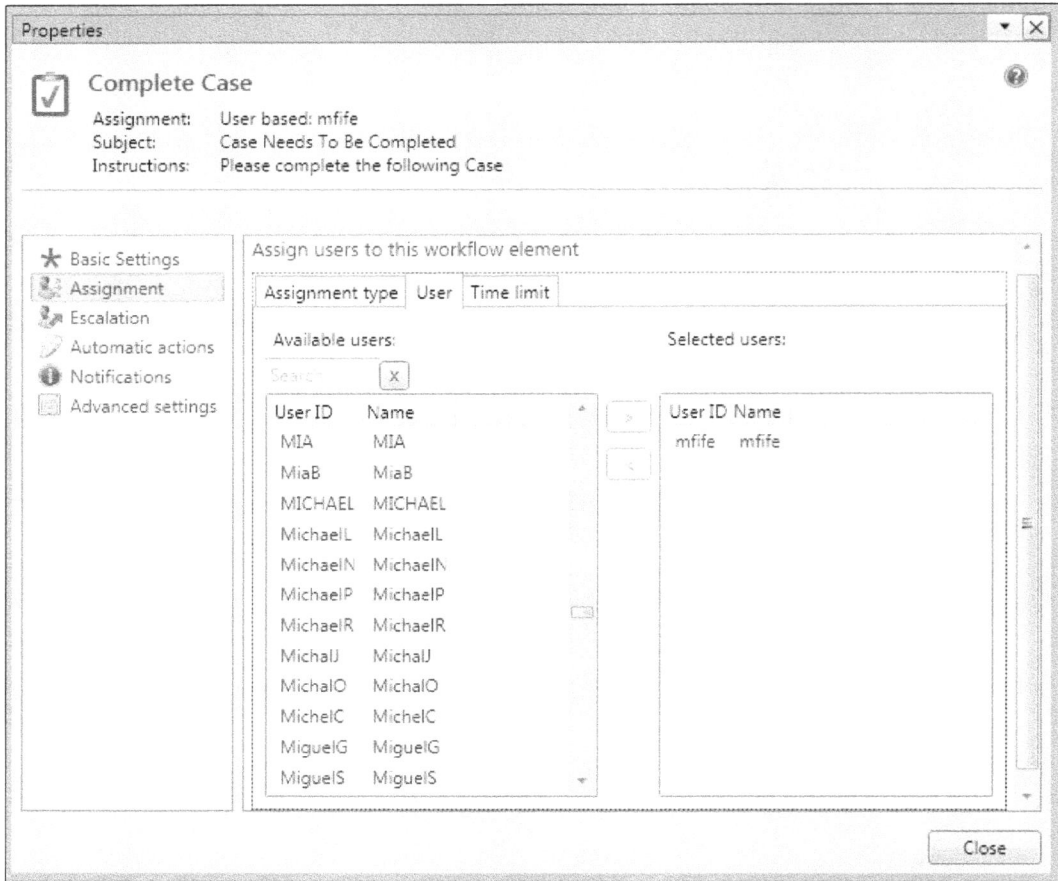

10. Close the element settings form and you should have a workflow with no errors.

Saving and activating workflows

Once you have finished designing your workflow, you can save it and activate it for use within Dynamics AX.

How to do it...

To save and activate a workflow, follow these steps:

1. Click on the **Save and close** button on the workflow designer. Each time you make a change to the workflow and save it, you will create a new version that you will be asked to add notes to, so that you can track what changes have been made.

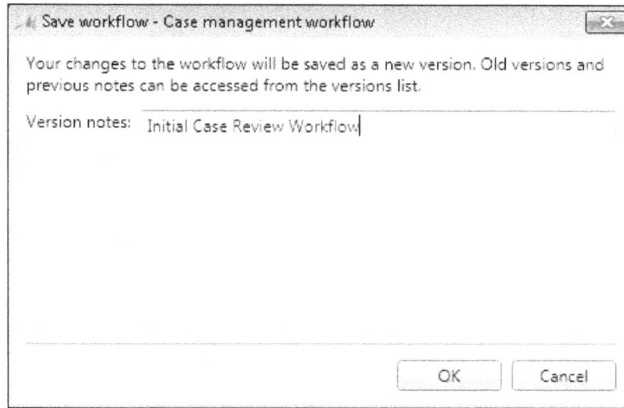

2. If your workflow is valid and has no errors, you will also be asked if you want to activate the workflow on the forms that it is associated with. In this example, we will activate it.

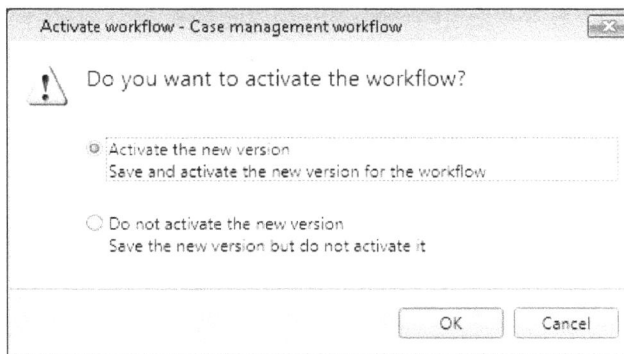

Setting the default workflows

You can create any number of workflow designs based on a workflow template, but Dynamics AX needs to know which one to use. To do this, you need to select a default workflow design.

How to do it...

To mark a workflow as the default workflow, follow these steps:

1. Select the workflow that you want to use as the default workflow. In the **Manage** group of the **Workflow** ribbon bar, click on the **Set as default** button.

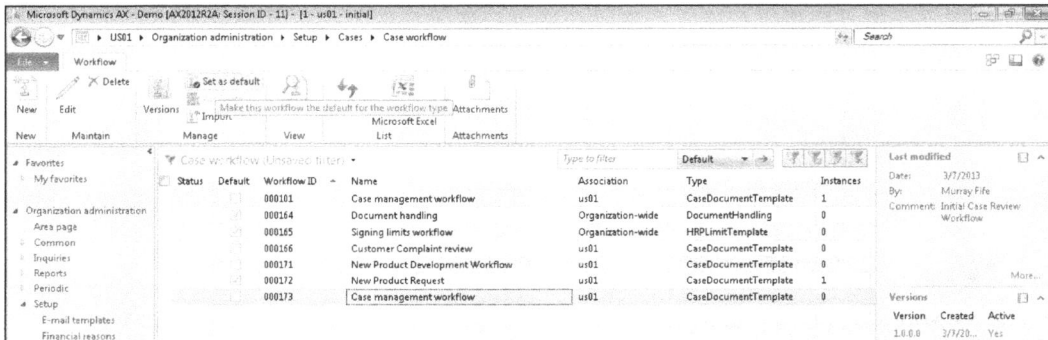

How it works...

When you set a workflow as the default one, it becomes the default workflow for all future workflows that are generated by the system. If you have used another version of a workflow already, those workflows will still continue to run using the other workflow as a template.

Once you have a default valid and activated workflow, a **Submit** button will start showing up on the forms that the workflow is associated with. In this example, our workflow is associated with cases; so when we create a new case, we see it on the **Case** form.

Submitting and using workflows

Once you have your workflows designed and activated, you can start submitting workflows and then using it to perform approvals and send notifications related to your business processes.

Getting ready

In order to have the system process your workflows, you will need to turn on the workflow processor. This is a process that runs in the background that coordinates all the workflow steps, and also creates all the notifications and e-mails related to the workflow steps.

When you are using this within your live system, you will want to configure the workflow processor as a batch process through the **Workflow Infrastructure Configuration** wizard, which you can find in the `Workflow` folder of the **Common** group of the **System administration** area page. But while you are just testing, you may just want to use the **Workflow Processor** tool that is hidden within AOT. To enable this option, follow these steps:

1. Open up the **AOT** explorer and expand the **Forms** group.
2. Find the **Tutorial_WorkflowProcessor** form, right-click on it, and select the **Open** option.
3. When the **Workflow Processor** dialog box is displayed, click on the **Start** button.

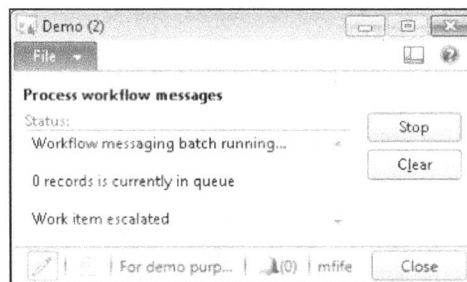

How to do it...

To submit and use a workflow, follow these steps:

1. Clicking on the **Submit** button will allow you to start a workflow that is associated with this record. As part of the workflow submission process, you will be able to add personal instructions that will be associated with the workflow.

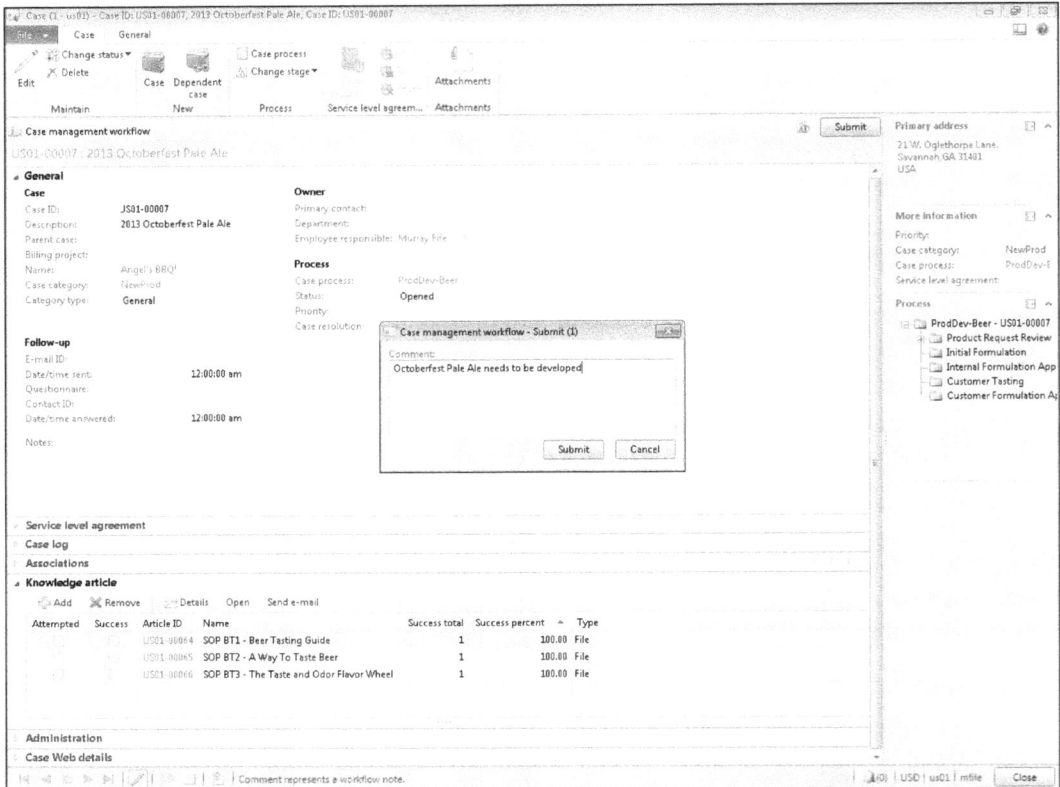

How it works...

As users are assigned tasks, they will be notified in a number of different ways. If they are using the Dynamics AX Windows client, they will receive a pop-up notification in their task tray, and the task will be shown in their **Notifications list** form.

From the **Home** area, all the active workflow tasks that are assigned to the user can be accessed by opening up the **Workflow items assigned to me** form in the `Work Items` folder of the **Common** group.

Additionally, if you are using the Employee self-service portal, the users are able to access all their assigned workflow tasks through a web browser by opening the **My Approvals** page within the **Approvals** group.

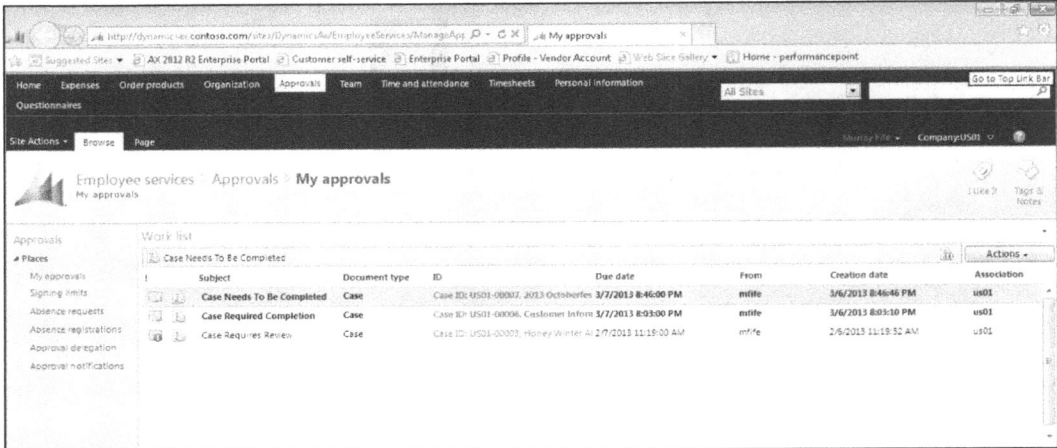

Adding conditional decisions to a workflow

Sometimes you want to have a workflow act one way, sometimes in another way. Usually, this is because of the value of a field in the record. Maybe you want one person to approve a step, unless the dollar value is above a certain amount, in which case it goes to another.

You can do this by using the **Conditional decision** element to create routes through the workflow.

In this recipe, we will show how you can use this element to create multiple workflow processes within one.

How to do it...

To add a conditional decision to a workflow, follow these steps:

1. Open your workflow in design mode, and from the **Workflow elements** palette, select the **Conditional decision** element and drop it onto your workflow.

2. Re-link the workflow process so that the **Conditional decision 1** element is a step in the workflow process.

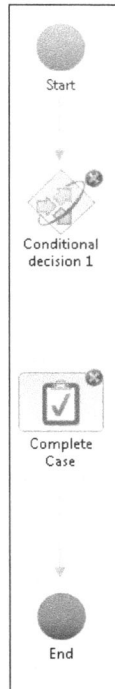

3. Select the **Conditional decision 1** node so that the **Basic Settings** button shows up in the **Workflow** ribbon bar within the **Modify elements** group. Then, click on the **Properties** button to open up the settings form.

4. The **Conditions** tab that is displayed allows you to build a condition that you want to check. Beside the **Where** statement, you can select the field that you want to use in the condition from the dropdown. You can select any field that is linked to the table record that created the workflow. In this case, we want a route based on the case category, so that we don't have to change anything.

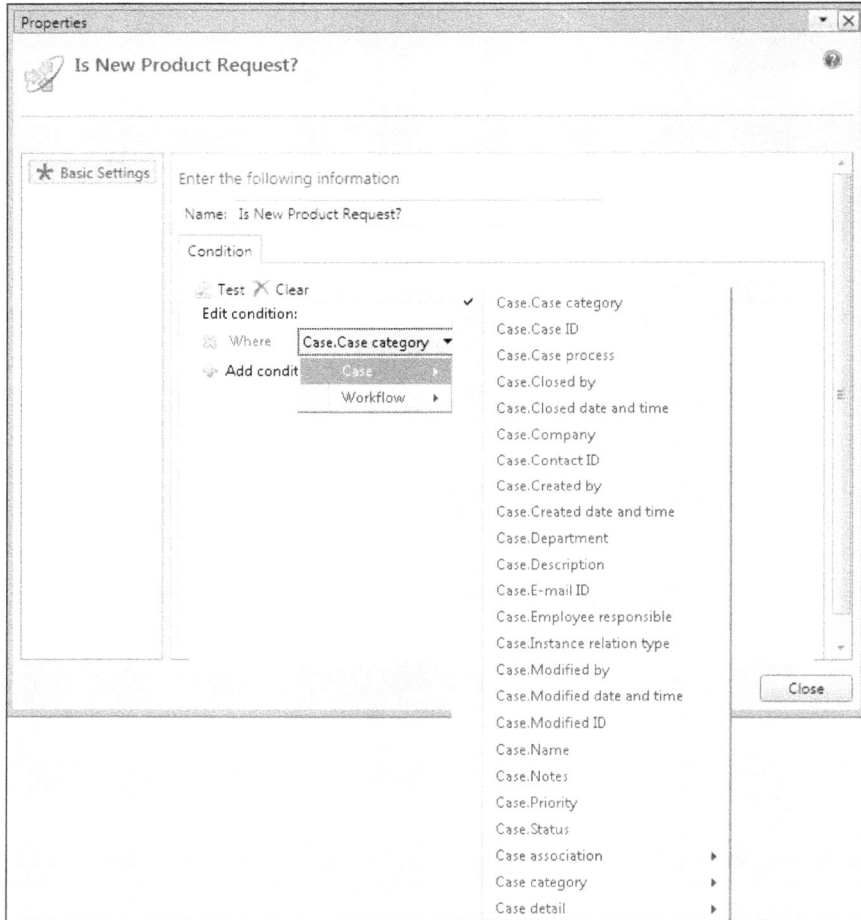

5. The next field that you can choose within your condition is the comparison type that you want to use. Examples of the types of comparisons that you can use include **is**, **is not**, **is greater than**, and **is between**.

6. The next field in the condition is the value that we want to check. Click on the **...** button, and you will be able to get a list of possible field values to compare against.

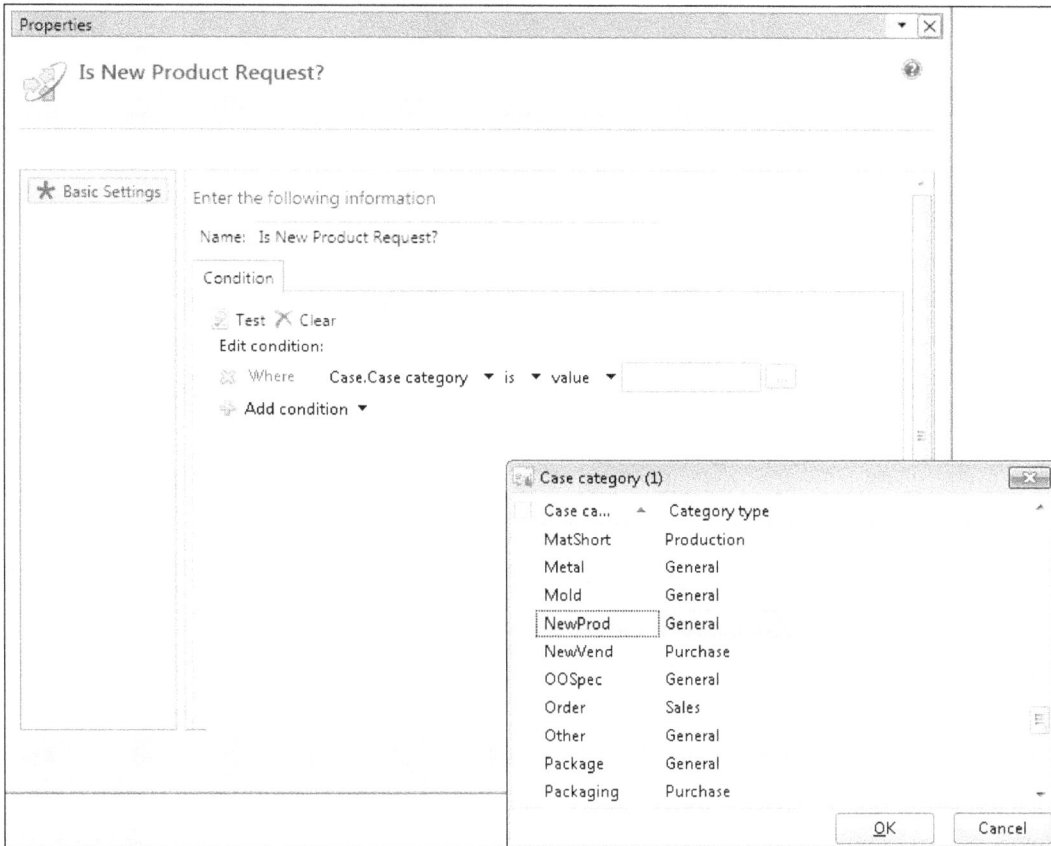

7. After creating the condition, you can close the **Properties** window and return to the workflow designer canvas. The condition has **True** and **False** branches based on the condition, so we just have to create two possible routes for the workflow.

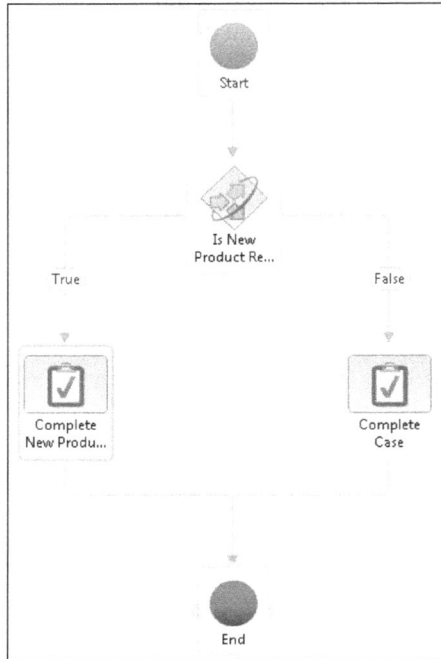

How it works...

Now when the workflow is submitted, it will check to see if the case is a new product case category and run two separate approval processes.

Adding manual decisions to a workflow

Many times in a workflow process people need to make decisions that will affect the path that the process will take. Most of the time these are approvals that need to be obtained, reviews that need to be performed, or tests that need to be taken.

You can build this into your workflow by adding **Manual decision** workflow elements, which can be assigned to a single person, or multiple people. If you assign a decision to multiple people, the approval step could require one, a majority, or all the people in order to complete successfully.

In this recipe, we will show how you can add a Manual decision workflow element to allow users to control the workflow process.

How to do it...

To add a Manual decision workflow element to a workflow, follow these steps:

1. Open your workflow in design mode, and from the **Workflow elements** palette select the **Manual decision** element and drop it onto your workflow.

2. Re-link the workflow process so that the **Manual decision** element is a step in the workflow process.

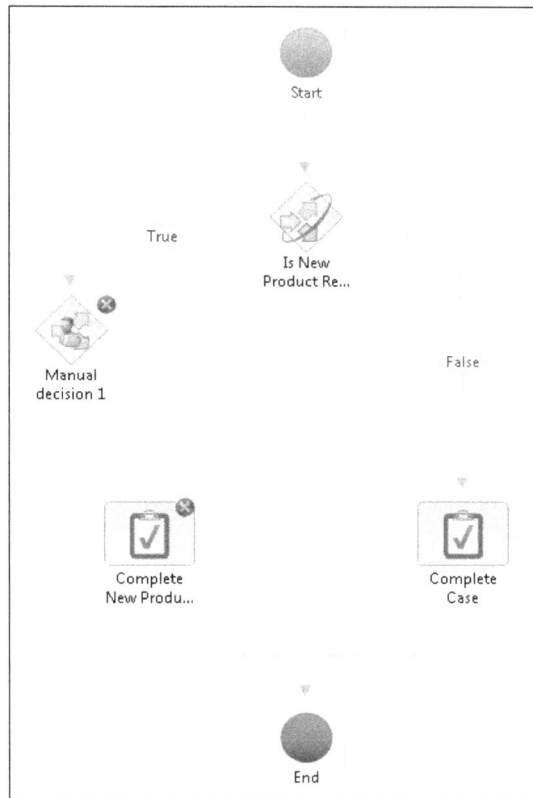

3. Select the **Manual decision** node so that the buttons show up in the **Workflow** ribbon bar within the **Modify elements** group, and then click on the **Properties** button to open up the settings form.

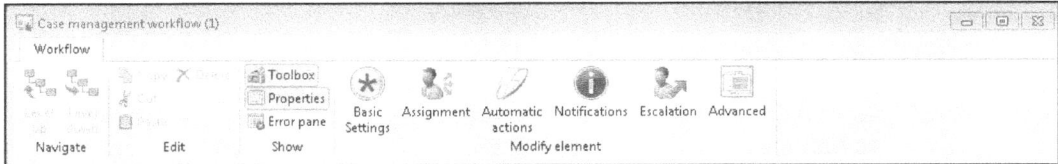

4. In the **Basic Settings** group, you can change the **Name:** field of the step to something a little less generic, and also update the **Work item subject:** and **Work item instructions:** fields. The last two fields will be the descriptions used when sending messages to the users who have been assigned the tasks, so it's important to make these as useful as possible.

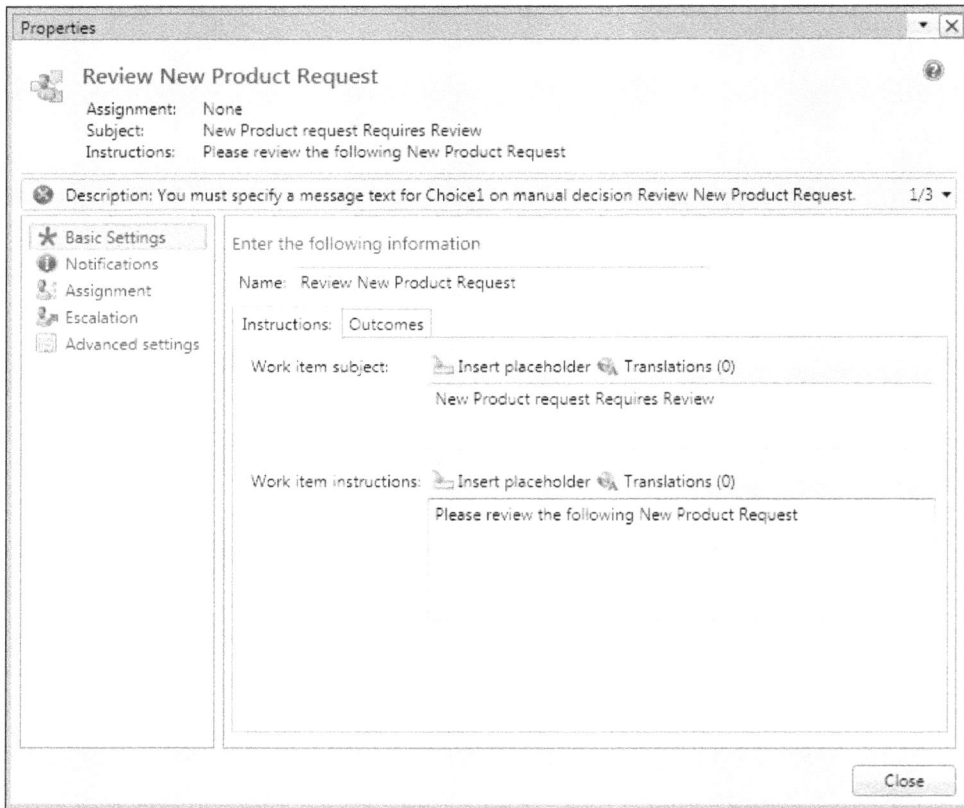

5. Now click on the **Outcomes** tab. Here, you will see two fields **Outcome 1:** and **Outcome 2:**, which you can give descriptions for. When the user is asked to make a decision, these are the options that they will be presented with.

Properties   ▼ ✕

Review New Product Request   ⓘ

Assignment: None
Subject: New Product request Requires Review
Instructions: Please review the following New Product Request

⊗ Assignment type: Selected assignment type 'None' is not supported.   1/1 ▼

- ★ Basic Settings
- ⓘ Notifications
- Assignment
- Escalation
- Advanced settings

Enter the following information

Name: Review New Product Request

Instructions: Outcomes

Type in a meaningful name for each outcome, as these will be displayed to users. Create translations of these names if required.

Outcome 1:   Translations (0)

    Approved

Outcome 2:   Translations (0)

    Rejected

Close

6. Now, you need to assign the workflow task to a user or a group of users. Click on the **Assignment** group on the left of the form, and then select the user(s) whom you want to perform this decision.

7. After creating the decision, you can close down the **Properties** window and return to the workflow designer canvas. The decision has **True** and **False** branches based on the condition, so we just have to create two possible routes for the workflow.

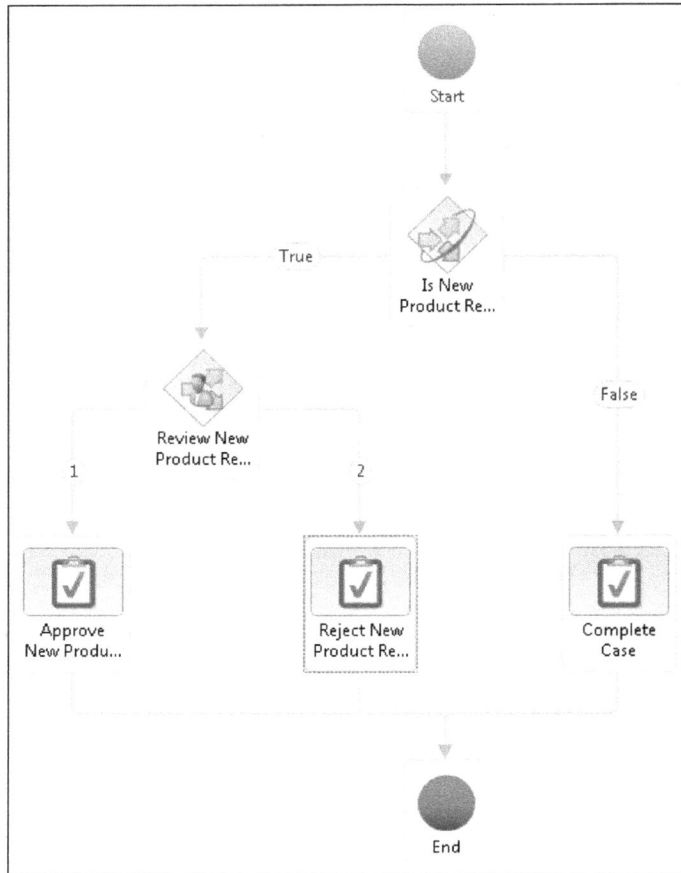

How it works...

You can nest as many of these decisions as you like within the workflow to create more elaborate decision trees to model your business process. In our workflow example, if it is a new product request, it will be routed to an approver. If the request is approved, the administrator will be able to complete the case, otherwise they will reject it.

Adding workflow status notifications

There is nothing more frustrating than having to follow a process, but never being notified when the process has been completed, or even worse, rejected. In our example of the new product request, the person who initiated the request will probably want to know when the approvals have been processed, so that they can contact the customer to tell them if they are able to develop the product.

You can build this into your workflows through the notifications option on any of the workflow steps or on the whole workflow; so when a step is completed, you will automatically receive a status update, and when the process is finished, you will be alerted immediately.

In this recipe, we will show how you can add a notification to a step in the workflow, and also how to send it to the person who started off the workflow rather than to a specific person, making the notification a little more dynamic.

How to do it...

To add a user notification to a workflow, follow these steps:

1. Open your workflow in design mode and select the workflow element that you want to associate the notification with. When the **Modify element** group shows up in the **Workflow** ribbon bar, click on the **Notifications** button.

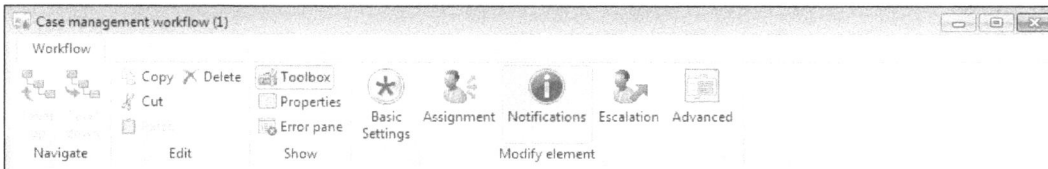

2. This will open up the notification options with a list of notification events that are available, which will vary by workflow element. To add a notification when the step has been completed, check the **Complete** event, and in the **Notification text** memo field, add a subject that you want to use when the user is notified.

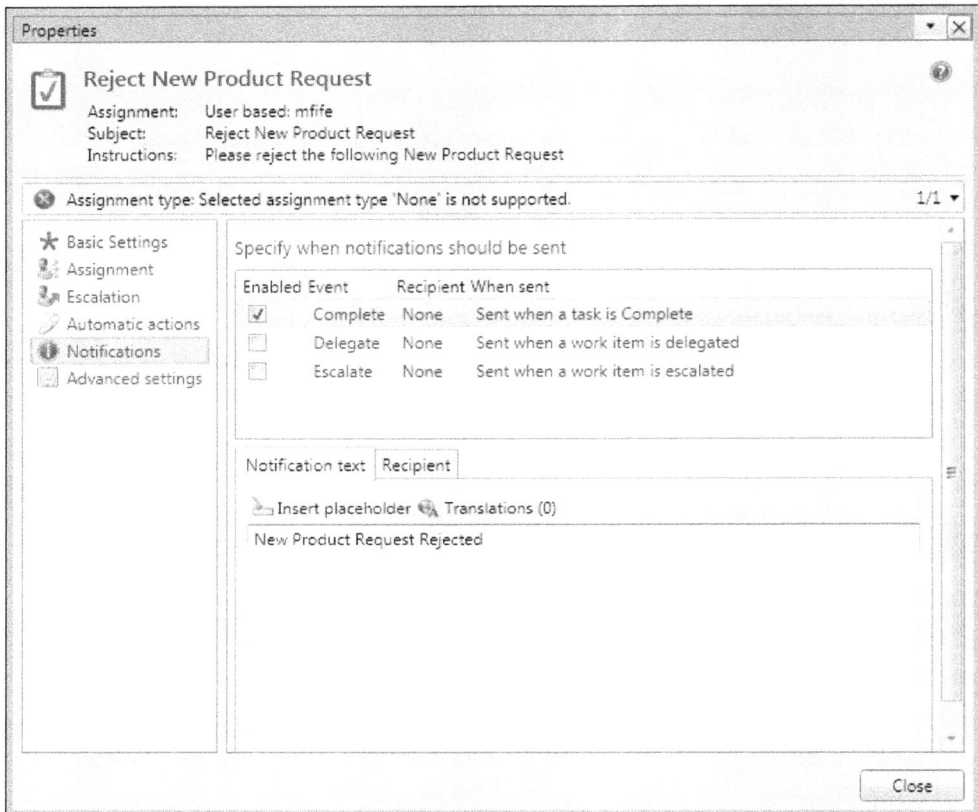

Properties

Reject New Product Request

Assignment: User based: mfife
Subject: Reject New Product Request
Instructions: Please reject the following New Product Request

Assignment type: Selected assignment type 'None' is not supported.   1/1 ▾

★ Basic Settings
Assignment
Escalation
Automatic actions
Notifications
Advanced settings

Specify when notifications should be sent

Enabled	Event	Recipient	When sent
☑	Complete	None	Sent when a task is Complete
☐	Delegate	None	Sent when a work item is delegated
☐	Escalate	None	Sent when a work item is escalated

Notification text | Recipient

Insert placeholder Translations (0)

New Product Request Rejected

Close

3. To select the person to be notified, click on the **Recipient** tab. If you want a certain user to be notified, you can select the **User** option from the assignment list box, but in this example we want to notify the person who submitted the workflow; so select the **Workflow user** option.

Properties

Reject New Product Request

Assignment: User based: mfife
Subject: Reject New Product Request
Instructions: Please reject the following New Product Request

* Basic Settings
* Assignment
* Escalation
* Automatic actions
* Notifications
* Advanced settings

Specify when notifications should be sent

Enabled	Event	Recipient	When sent
✓	Complete	Role ba:	Sent when a task is Complete
☐	Delegate	None	Sent when a work item is delegated
☐	Escalate	None	Sent when a work item is escalated

Notification text | Recipient | Workflow user

Assign users to this notification

Participant
Workflow user
User
None

Workflow user:
Send notifications to users of this workflow

Close

4. This will enable a tab for the **Workflow user** selection. To send the notification to the user who initiated the workflow, select the **Workflow originator** option from the **Workflow user** combobox.

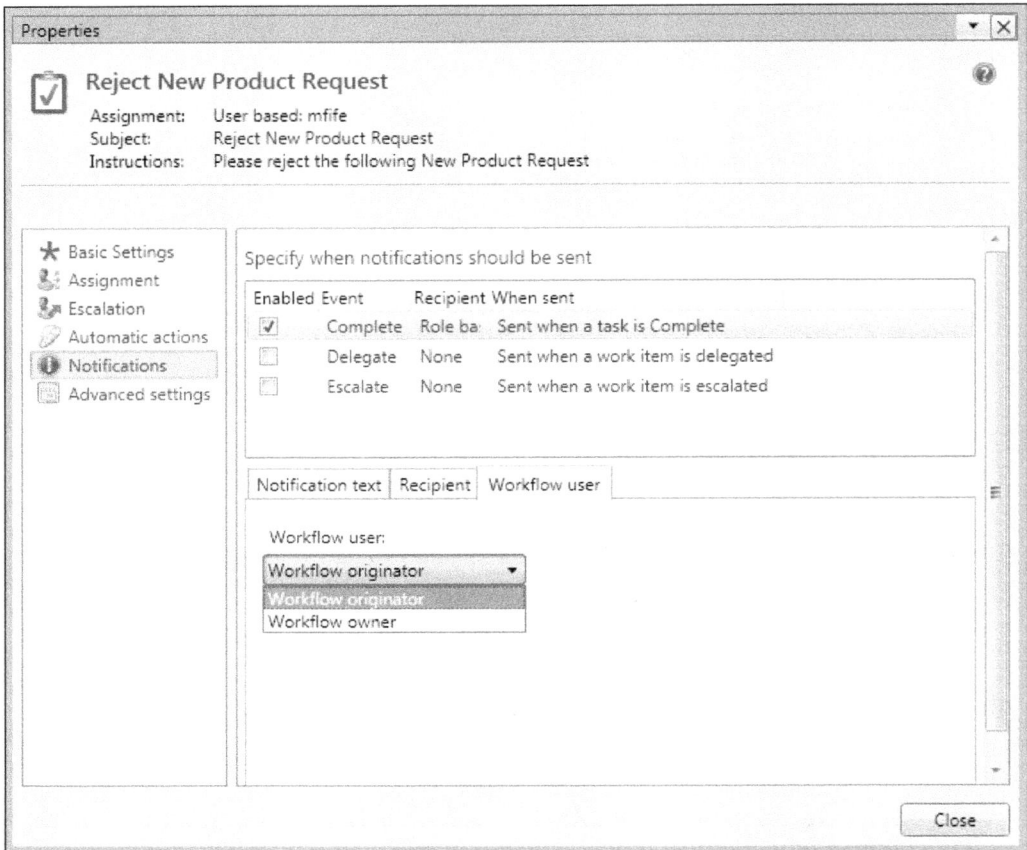

Properties	▾ ☒

☑ **Reject New Product Request** ⊙

Assignment: User based: mfife
Subject: Reject New Product Request
Instructions: Please reject the following New Product Request

★ Basic Settings
🎯 Assignment
🏃 Escalation
✏ Automatic actions
ⓘ Notifications
🖼 Advanced settings

Specify when notifications should be sent

Enabled	Event	Recipient	When sent
☑	Complete	Role ba:	Sent when a task is Complete
☐	Delegate	None	Sent when a work item is delegated
☐	Escalate	None	Sent when a work item is escalated

Notification text | Recipient | Workflow user

Workflow user:

Workflow originator ▾
Workflow originator
Workflow owner

Close

5. Now click on **Close** to finish updating the workflow element and to save the workflow.

How it works...

You can configure these notifications at any stage in the workflow process and also against the workflow itself, so that users are notified of status changes and also when the workflows are completed.

Adding text placeholders to workflow messages

When users receive notifications or are assigned tasks through the workflow process, the more information that they are given, the quicker they should be able to act. A subject line that says *Approve NPD – 72632: New Summer Pale Ale for Angel's BBQ* is much more useful than something that says *Approval Required*.

In this recipe, we will show you how you can embed text from your workflow record into the messages that you send to the users, so that you can help your users help themselves.

How to do it...

To embed text placeholders into notification messages, follow these steps:

1. Open your workflow in design mode and select the workflow element that you want to include record-specific text within the notification messages. On all the message fields where you can add text from the workflow record, you will be able to see an **Insert placeholder** button.

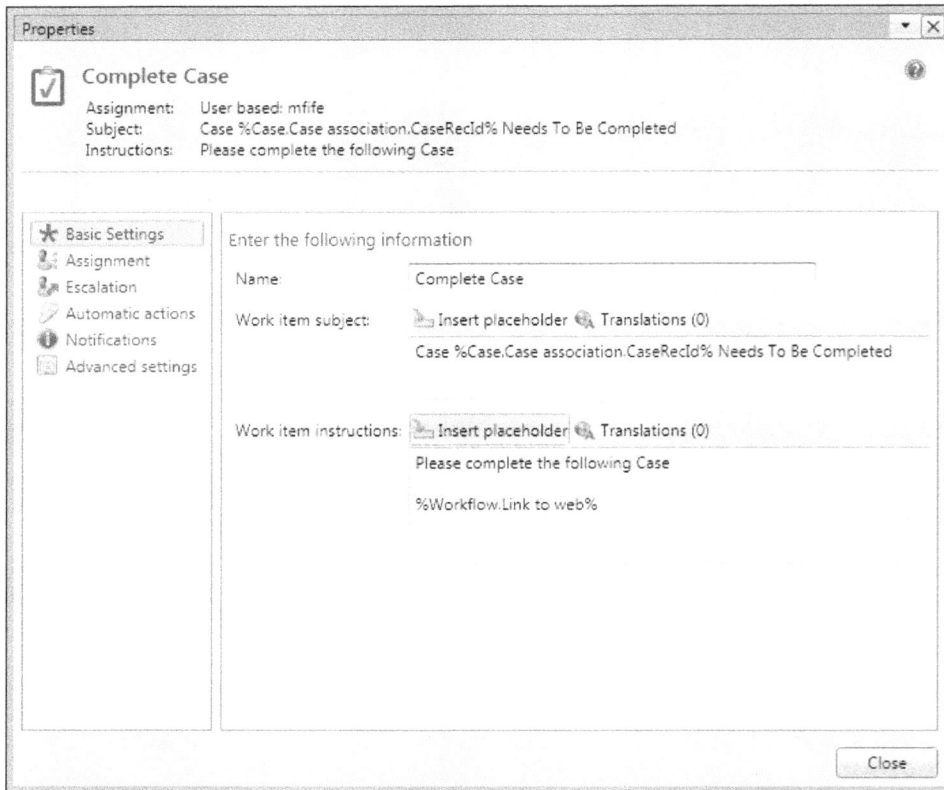

```
Properties                                                                 ▾ ⌧

    ✓   Complete Case                                                        ⊙
    ☑
        Assignment:     User based: mfife
        Subject:        Case %Case.Case association.CaseRecId% Needs To Be Completed
        Instructions:   Please complete the following Case


    ★ Basic Settings          Enter the following information
    ♟ Assignment
    ♟ Escalation              Name:                  Complete Case
    ✎ Automatic actions
    ❶ Notifications           Work item subject:      ▤ Insert placeholder  ✇ Translations (0)
    ▦ Advanced settings                               Case %Case.Case association.CaseRecId% Needs To Be Completed


                              Work item instructions: ▤ Insert placeholder  ✇ Translations (0)

                                                      Please complete the following Case

                                                      %Workflow.Link to web%














                                                                            Close
```

2. When you click on **Insert placeholder**, a list of valid text placeholders will be shown. Some of these will be from the source table of the workflow and some will be related to the workflow. In this example, we want to add a hyperlink from the notification to the workflow, so that the user is able to click on the link from the e-mail notification and open up the workflow. To do this, scroll to the bottom of the list, select the **%Workflow.Link to web%** element and click on **Insert** to add it to your workflow message.

Text placeholder	Label	Description
%Case.Priority%	Priority	View or select the priority of the selected case
%Case.Process%	Case process	The defined process that the case will follow
%Case.Status%	Status	View or update the status of a case
%Workflow.Last note%	Last note	The last note entered in the workflow.
%Workflow.Link to web%	Link to web	The web link to the workflow document.
%Workflow.Workflow originator%	Workflow originator	The user that initiated the workflow.
%Workflow.Work item owner%	Work item owner	The user that has work item assigned.
%Workflow.Workflow owner%	Workflow owner	The user configured as the workflow owner.

Insert

How it works...

You can add as many of these text placeholders to the subject and also the body of the workflow messages and notifications to make them as descriptive as you like.

Properties

Complete Case

Assignment: User based: mfife
Subject: Case %Case.Case association.CaseRecId% Needs To Be Completed
Instructions: Please complete the following Case

* Basic Settings
* Assignment
* Escalation
* Automatic actions
* Notifications
* Advanced settings

Enter the following information

Name: Complete Case

Work item subject: Insert placeholder Translations (0)

Case %Case.Case association.CaseRecId% Needs To Be Completed

Work item instructions: Insert placeholder Translations (0)

Please complete the following Case

%Workflow.Link to web%

Close

When these messages are sent out by the workflow engine, it simply replaces the placeholder with proper values.

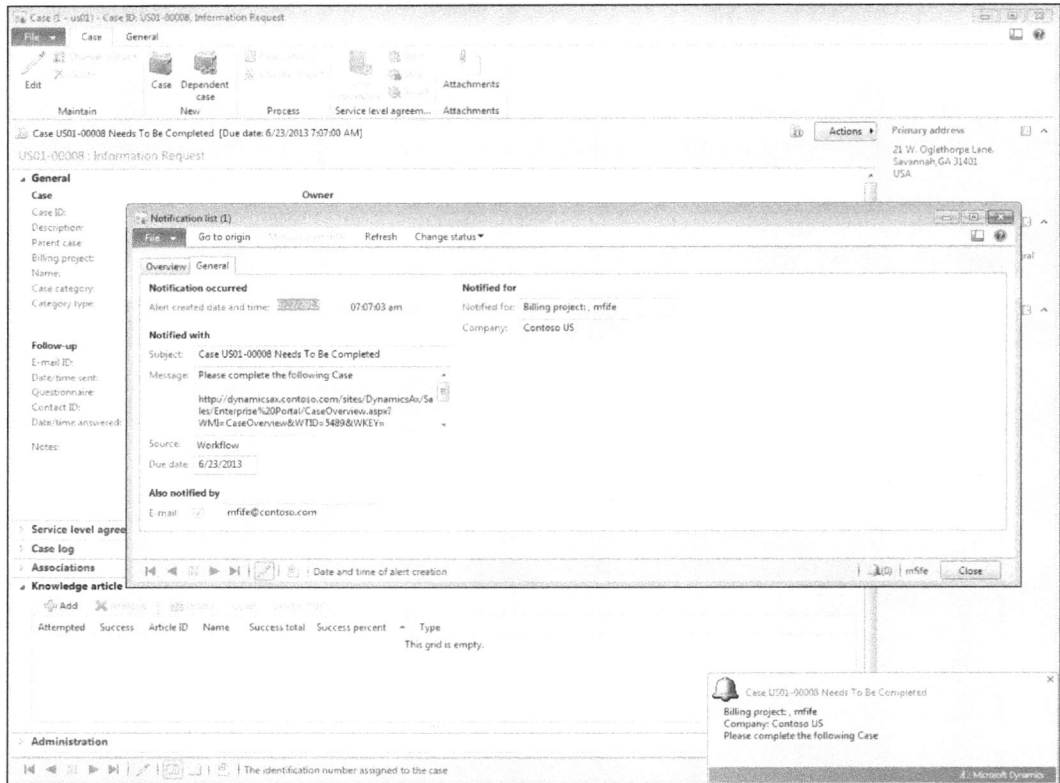

Summary

In this chapter, we showed a simple example of how to design and enable a simple workflow with conditional branches, and also approval steps that are delivered out to the appropriate users. For many business cases, this is all that you need to use.

As you work with the workflow designer more though, you will notice other features that you may want to take advantage of, including:

- Assigning decisions and steps to multiple users, and then requiring one, some, or all of them to complete the step before allowing the workflow to continue
- Creating parallel processes allowing multiple decisions and tasks to be performed at once within the workflow
- Implementing escalation rules to make sure that tasks are performed within a certain amount of time, otherwise they get assigned to a superior within the company

Additionally, if you feel like writing some code, you can try developing additional workflow templates and even new workflow steps for the existing workflow templates.

7
Reporting in Office

In this chapter, we will focus on how you can use the Microsoft Dynamics AX Office Add-Ins to create report and form templates in Word that are then accessed through Dynamics AX. You will also learn the following:

- ► Creating a document data source
- ► Creating a Dynamics AX document template within Word
- ► Creating document template libraries
- ► Registering documents to template libraries

Introduction

Microsoft Dynamics AX is delivered with integration to many of the Office applications, including Word, which allows users to create their own reports in an application that they are familiar with and have probably used for years. From an IT point of view, this is a great way to allow the users to create their own reports because the data is secure and ties back to the user's profile and security rights. From the user's point of view, this is great because they can format their reports themselves without having to be technically oriented.

As an added benefit, these Word templates can be saved to a template library in SharePoint that Dynamics AX will be able to access, which will link to the **Attachments** functionality, allowing the users to create filtered Word documents on the fly.

In this chapter, we will show you how to set up document data sources that you can then build reports off from within Word, and then save them to a template library so that everyone is able to take advantage of them.

Creating a document data source

Before you are able to use data from Dynamics AX in a Word report template, you need to register it as a document data source.

In this recipe, we will show how you register a query as a document data source so that you will be able to use it in Word.

How to do it...

To create a new document data source, follow these steps:

1. Open up the **Document data sources** form from the `Document Management` folder of the **Setup** group on the **Organization administration** area page.

2. This will show you a list of available document data sources that have already been registered with your version of Dynamics AX. Click on the **New** button on the menu bar to create a new document data source.

3. Select the module that you want the service to be related to.

4. Word will only read the **Query reference** data source types; so from the **Data source type** dropdown, select **Query reference**.

5.   You can now select any of the queries that have been registered within Dynamics AX from the **Data source name** drop-down box. In this case, we will select the **InventOnHand** query.

6.   Finally, check the **Activated** checkbox and you are done.

Creating a Dynamics AX document template within Word

Once you have a document data source registered with Dynamics AX, you can start using it as a data source within Word documents and templates. This process is similar to creating a mail merge document using Outlook, and only then you can use all of the data in Dynamics AX.

In this recipe, we will show how you can use a document data source within Word to create a custom template report.

Getting ready

Before you start, make sure that you have installed the Office Add-Ins that are part of the standard Dynamics AX 2012 setup. If you don't have this already installed, you will need to run the Microsoft Dynamics AX Setup and install the Office Add-ins feature from within the Microsoft Dynamics AX components group. You may need to get help from your system administrator for this.

How to do it...

To create a new document template in Word, follow these steps:

1.   When you open up Word, you will notice that you have a Dynamics AX ribbon bar, in addition to the standard ones. To add data from Dynamics AX to your Word document, all you need to do is click on the **Add Data** button in the **Design** group of the **Dynamics AX** ribbon bar.

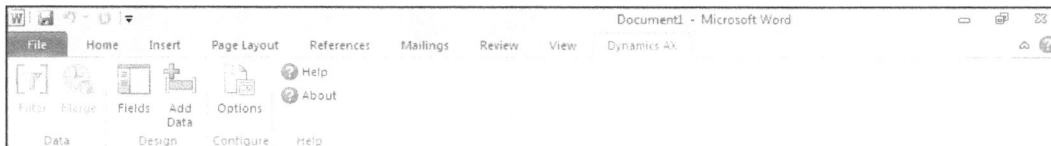

2. This will open up a list of all of the queries that you have defined in your document data sources. You can select as many of these as you like to be data source references within your Word document.

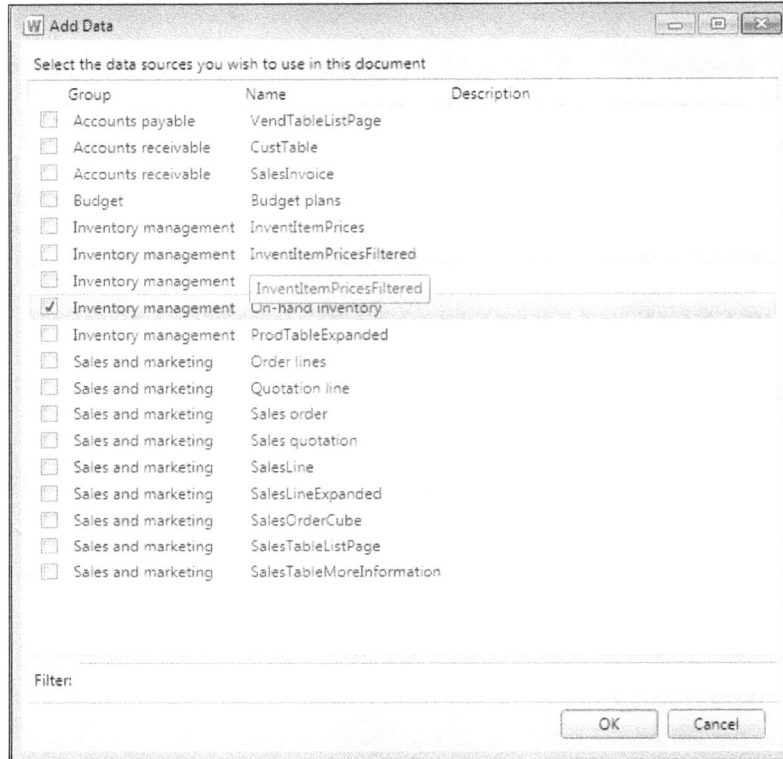

3. After selecting your data source, a new **Microsoft Dynamics AX** field explorer panel will show up within your document. You will be able to see all the related tables and fields used in the query that you can use in your document template.

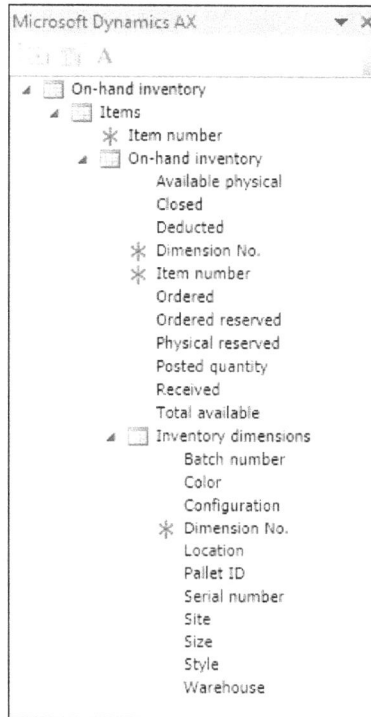

4. To add a field, all you need to do is drag it from the field explorer panel over to your document.

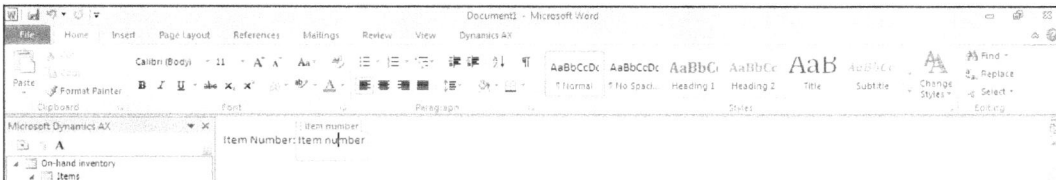

5. If you have repeating data, you can add that to the report as well by creating a table in your report.

6. If you drag a field onto the second row of the table, it will automatically add the title of the field for you in the first row of the table. You can add as many fields as you like to the table.

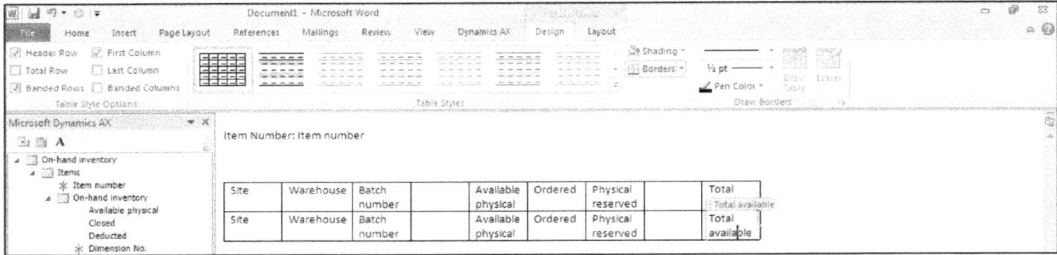

7. Now select **Save As** from the **File** menu, give your document a name, and then save it so that you can re-use this template.

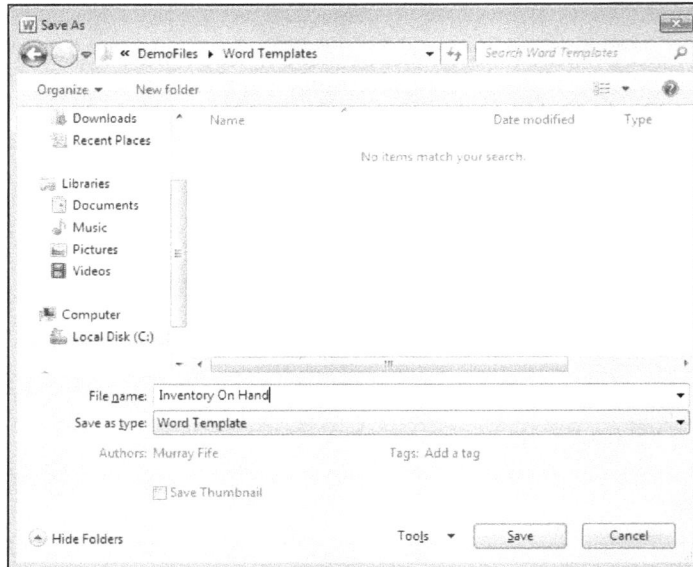

How it works...

To view the report with data in it, all you need to do is click on the **Merge** button from the **Data** group of the **Dynamics AX** ribbon bar.

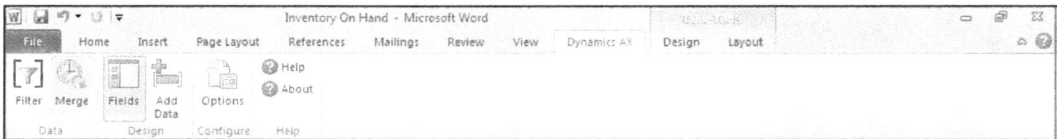

This will create a new Word document for you with all the data coming from Dynamics AX.

If you want to change the company that you are running the report against, you can click on the **Options** button within the **Configure** group of the **Dynamics AX** ribbon bar. This will open up a form allowing you to change the legal entity, and even the AOS server that you are connecting to.

If you click on the **Filter** button within the **Data** group of the **Dynamics AX** ribbon bar, you will be able to add user filters to the report as well.

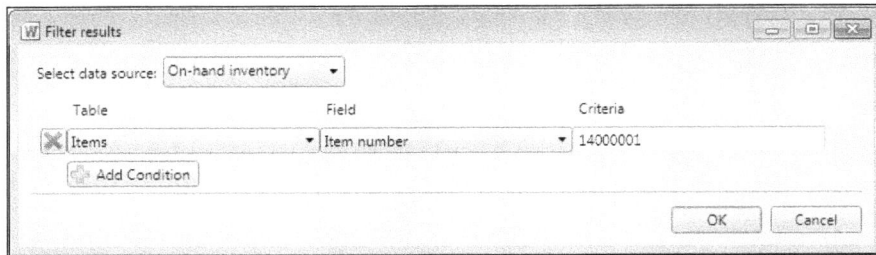

Rerunning the merge function will now just return the records that match your filter.

Since this is Word, you can take advantage of all the formatting features that you are used to, and turn your bland report into something that is a little bit more appealing.

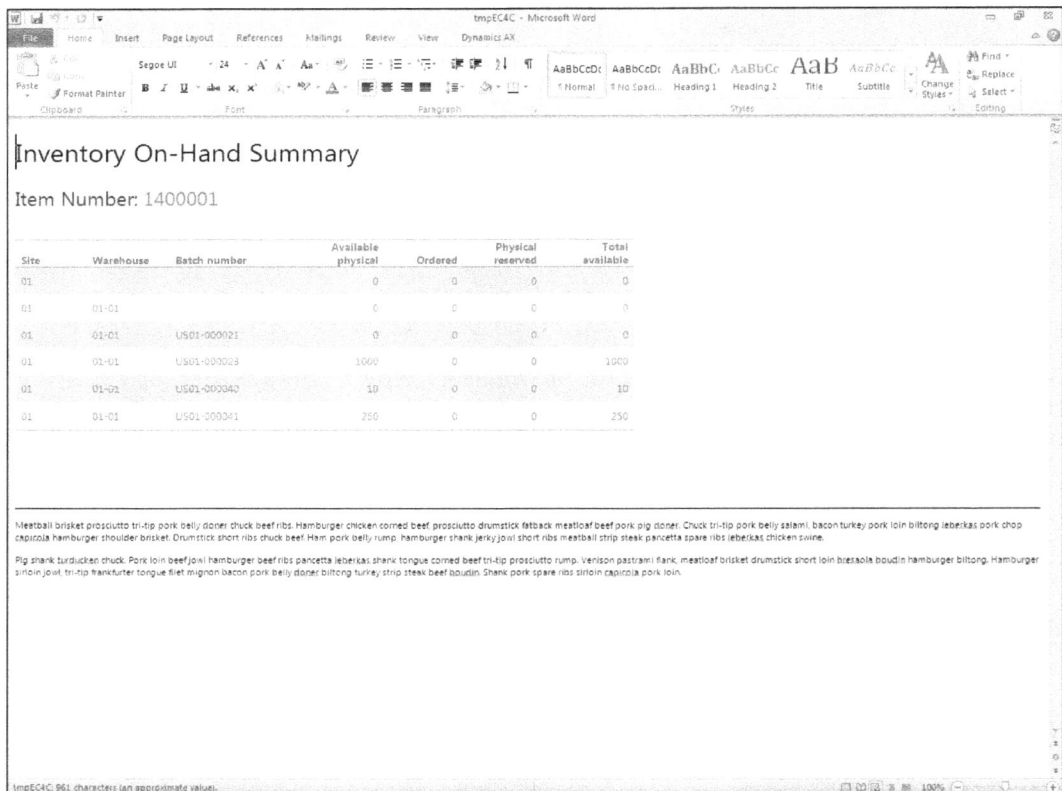

Creating document template libraries

Once you have created a Word template that is connected to a document data source, you can save it to a template library within SharePoint and register it with Dynamics AX. This enables Dynamics AX to see your Word template, and use it within the Attachments feature to create merged documents on the fly.

In this recipe, we will show you how to create a new template library within SharePoint and then link it to Dynamics AX as a template document type.

How to do it...

To create a new document template library in SharePoint, follow these steps:

1. To create a template library, start by opening up SharePoint in a browser.
2. To show all the document libraries that you have on your site, click on the **View: All Site Content** from the **Site Actions** menu.

3. From the **Site Actions** menu, select the **New Document Library** menu item.

4. Give your template library a name and description, select **Microsoft Word document** from the **Document Templates** drop-down box, and then click on the **Create** button.

5. This will create a new document library for you. To register this template library in Dynamics AX, you need to create a new template document type.

6. From within Dynamics AX, click on the **Document types** menu item within the `Document management` folder of the **Setup** group on the **Organization administration** area page.

7. To create a new template document type, click on the **New** button on the menu bar.

8. Give your document type a type and name.

9. In the **Class:** field select **Template library**.

10. Specify a path in the **Archive directory:** field and add a path for where you want the real-generated Word documents to be stored.

11. In the **SharePoint site:** field, paste in the base site URL where you created your document template library within SharePoint.

12. After specifying the correct SharePoint URL, you will now be able to find your library in the **Document library:** dropdown.

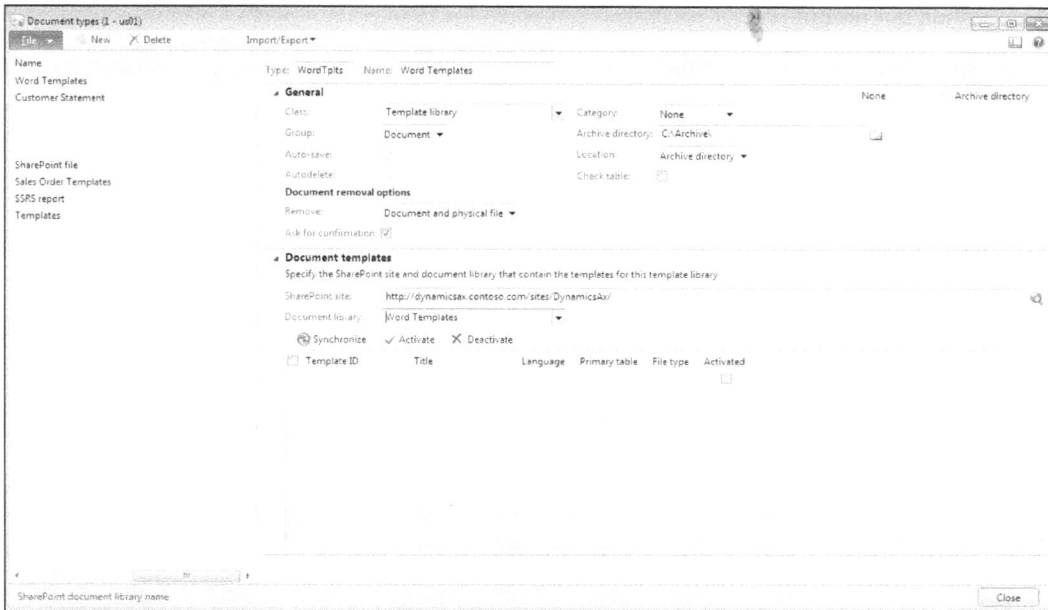

13. Click on the **Close** button and you are now done with the creation of a document template library.

Registering documents to template libraries

Once you have a SharePoint document template library registered within Dynamics AX, you can start adding your Word templates to it and enabling them to be used by the Attachments functions.

In this recipe, we will show you how to add your templates and then synchronize SharePoint with Dynamics AX.

How to do it...

To register a document with the document template library, follow these steps:

1. Open up your document template library within SharePoint and click on the **Add document** link.

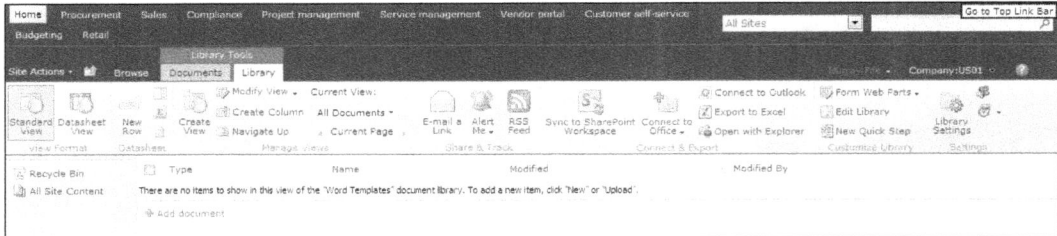

2. Click on the **Browse** button to find your Word template.

3. Within the file explorer, navigate to your Word template file and click on **Open**.

4. To upload your document to SharePoint, click on **OK**.

5. There is one final step required, and that is to synchronize Dynamics AX with the SharePoint template libraries so that it discovers the new template that you added. To do this, click on the **Document types** menu item within the Document management folder of the **Setup** group on the **Organization administration** area page, and select your template document type. In the **Document Templates** section of the form, click on the **Synchronize** button.

Document templates

Specify the SharePoint site and document library that contain the templates for this template library

SharePoint site:	http://dynamicsax.contoso.com/sites/DynamicsAx/	
Document library:	Word Templates	▼

🔄 Synchronize   ✓ Activate   ✕ Deactivate

Template ID	Title	Language	Primary table	File type	Activated
					☐

6. This will search through the SharePoint library for any documents that it is able to use and add them to the templates list.

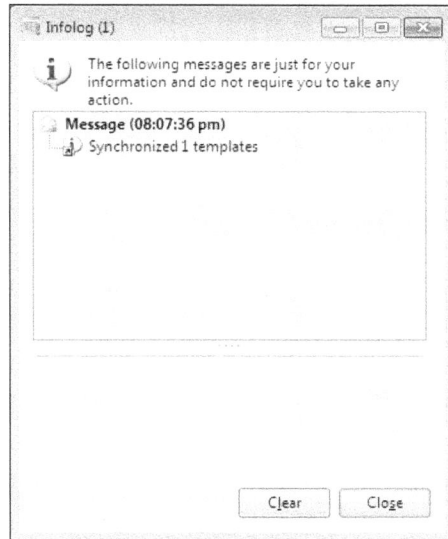

Infolog (1)

ℹ The following messages are just for your information and do not require you to take any action.

Message (08:07:36 pm)
    Synchronized 1 templates

Clear   Close

7. To enable the document for use, make sure you select the **Activated** checkbox.

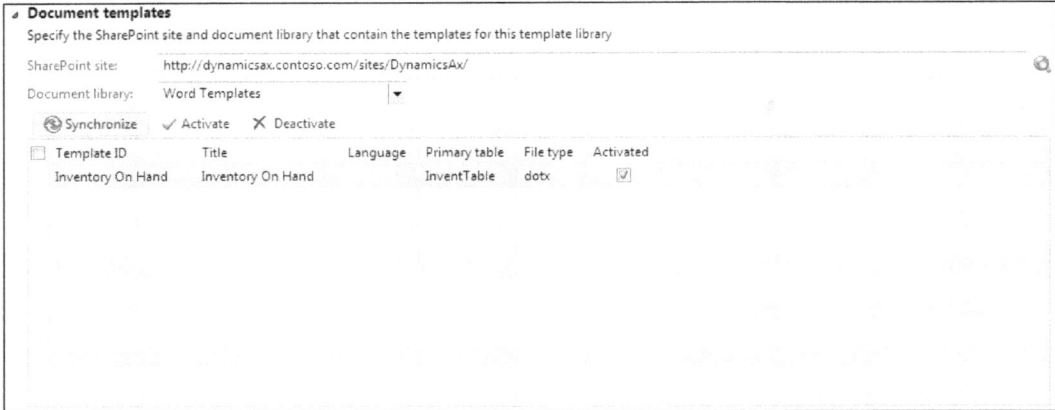

Template ID	Title	Language	Primary table	File type	Activated
Inventory On Hand	Inventory On Hand		InventTable	dotx	☑

Document templates
Specify the SharePoint site and document library that contain the templates for this template library
SharePoint site: http://dynamicsax.contoso.com/sites/DynamicsAx/
Document library: Word Templates
Synchronize ✓ Activate ✗ Deactivate

How it works...

Once your templates are registered with Dynamics AX, something happens that is pretty cool. The Attachments function will look to see if there are any document templates that have the same primary table Id as the current record. If it finds any, they will show up as a document attachment type. When you create the document attachment, it will merge the template into a Word document that will be automatically filtered to the current record that you are looking at.

As a quick note, if you look at your template document type record, each of the templates that you have registered will have a primary table. In this case, it is the **InventTable** table. So anywhere that we are looking at products, the template will show up in the Attachments as a document type.

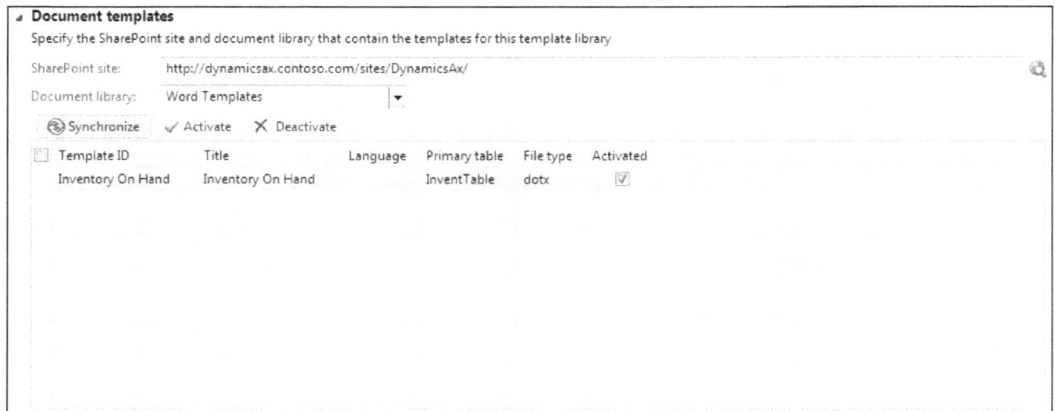

Document templates
Specify the SharePoint site and document library that contain the templates for this template library
SharePoint site: http://dynamicsax.contoso.com/sites/DynamicsAx/
Document library: Word Templates
Synchronize ✓ Activate ✗ Deactivate

Template ID	Title	Language	Primary table	File type	Activated
Inventory On Hand	Inventory On Hand		InventTable	dotx	☑

To create a Word document from a registered template, open up a form where the primary table is the same as your template and click on the **Attachments** button. Usually, this is in the first ribbon bar of the form.

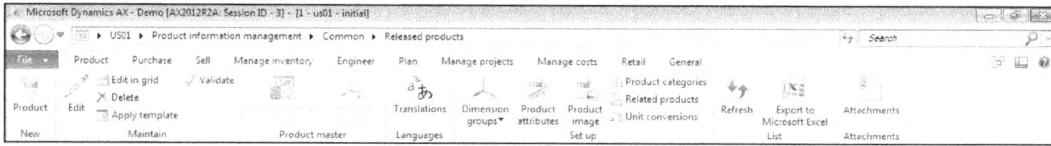

Click on the **New** drop-down button on the menu bar to see all of the available document types that you can attach.

If the current record's primary table is the same as that of any of the templates, they will show up as a document type.

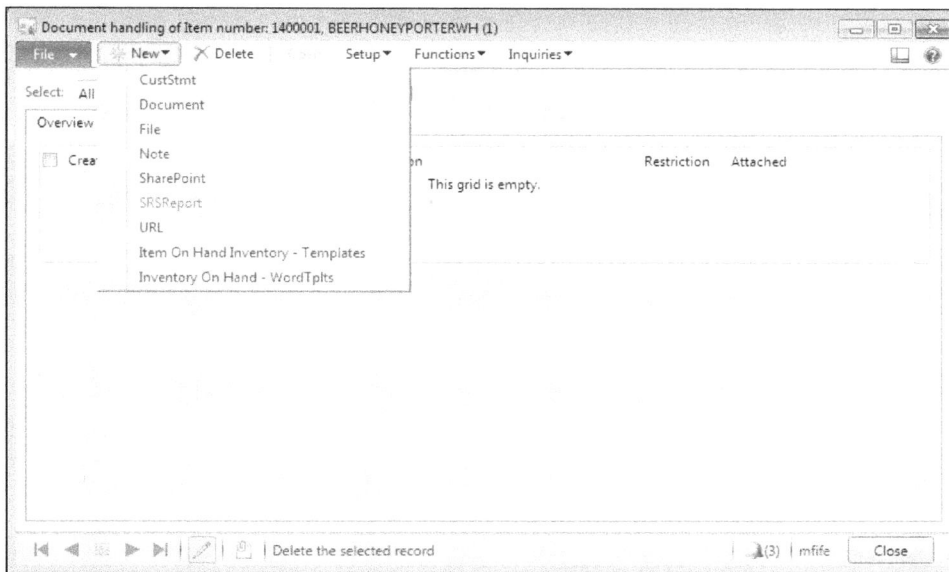

Selecting the document type will automatically create a merged version of the Word template, and also save the file right away and associate it with your document record to reference later on.

Summary

This feature of Dynamics AX is so useful because you don't need to be a reporting expert in order to take advantage of it. Almost everyone within the organization should be able to work with Microsoft Word and Excel, so they are not learning a new tool. Chances are that you are already scavenging information from the database and creating your own reports; this just makes the task a lot easier, and also up-to-date.

You can use this feature to create simple ad hoc reports, and also for creating standard forms and documents that you may use over and over again. For example, you could create:

- Customer and vendor summary sheets
- Sales price lists
- Standard form letters such as collection notices

In this chapter, we only covered using Word to create templates. You can do exactly the same within Excel, so you may want to try that as well.

8
Talking to the Outside World

In this chapter, we will show how you can use the Customer and Vendor portals that are delivered with Dynamics AX to share information with people outside the organization. You will also learn the following:

- ▶ Adding login accounts for customers in Active Directory
- ▶ Configuring customer accounts in Dynamics AX
- ▶ Associating customer logins with customer accounts
- ▶ Configuring a product catalog
- ▶ Adding images and presentation information to product catalogs

Introduction

The Enterprise portal templates that are delivered with Dynamics AX 2012 include three self-service portals, which allow you to reach out to users who would not normally have access to the system. You can allow:

- ▶ Employees to make requests and update their information through the Employee self-service portal
- ▶ Customers to access their sales orders, receipts and invoices, update their contact information, and also use the shopping cart to place new orders through the Customer self-service portal
- ▶ Vendors to update contact information, and respond to bids through the Vendor self-service portal

All the hard work has been done for you. All that you need to do is set them up and start using them.

In this chapter, we will show how you can configure one of these portals: the Customer self-service portal.

Adding login accounts for customers in Active Directory

In order for an external user to log in and access the Dynamics AX self-service portals, they need to have a username and password. This Active Directory account is used to authenticate the user in SharePoint and can be linked to a Dynamics AX user account, so that we are able to configure them as a valid external user.

In this recipe, we will walk you through the steps required to create the Active Directory user account.

Getting ready

Before you start this recipe, you will want to make sure that you have access to the server that manages your Active Directory configuration. If you don't have access, you may want to contact your system administrator to get access, or have them help you with this step.

How to do it...

To add a new login account for a customer in Active Directory, follow these steps:

1. From within the server that manages your Active Directory accounts, open up the **Active Directory Users and Computers** administration console from the **Administrative Tools** menu group within the Start menu.

2. Rather than mingle all the customer and vendor logins with all your user logins, you may want to create a new organizational unit for each of them. To do this, just right-click on your domain and select **Organizational Unit** from the **New** menu item.

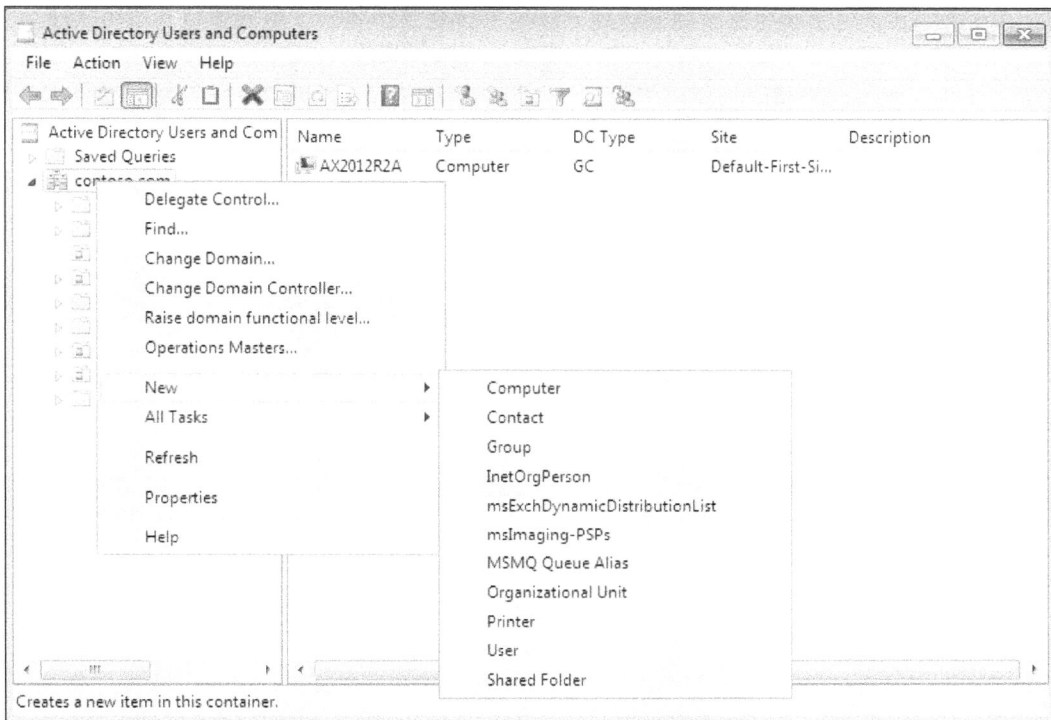

3. Give your organizational unit a name in the **Name:** field and then click **OK**.

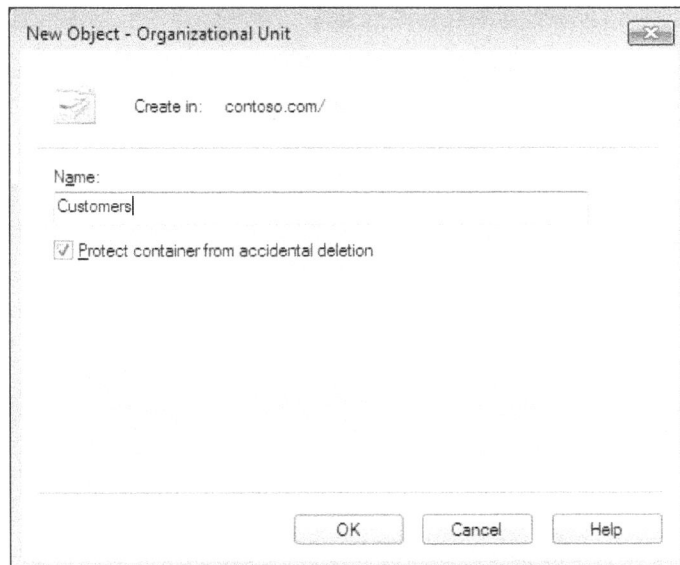

4. Next, create a user account for your customer by right-clicking on the **Customers** organizational unit and selecting **User** from the **New** menu item.

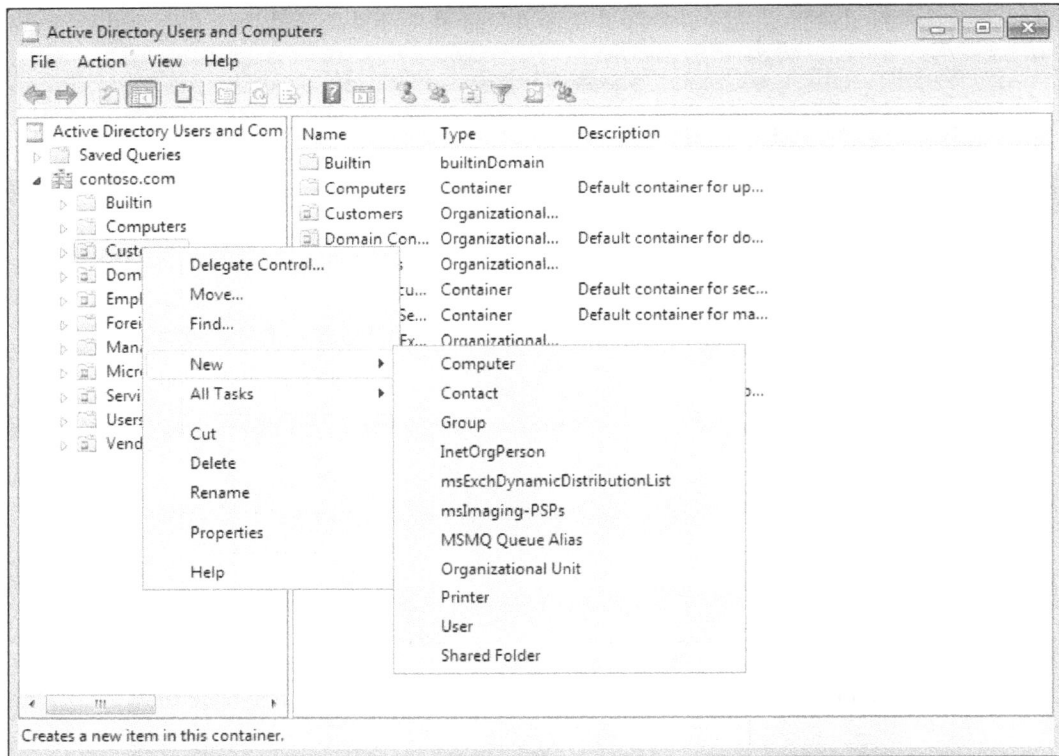

5. In the **Full name:** field, type in the customer's name and give your user a unique username to log in with, and click on **Next**.

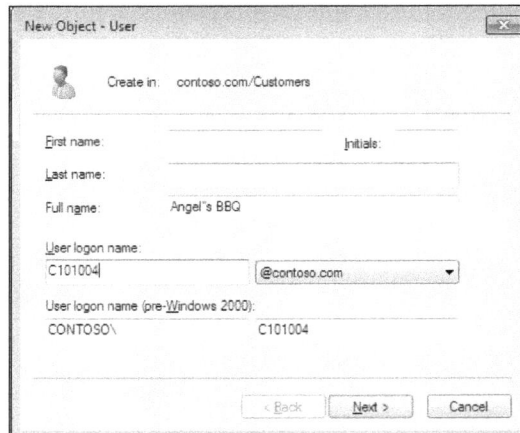

> In this example, we just use the customer number prefixed with "C". Using just the customer number by itself may create conflicts with vendors having the same ID.

6. Assign your customer a new password and then click on **Next**.

7. On the confirmation screen, just click on **Finish** to end the process.

You can repeat this process for each of your customers.

Configuring customer accounts in Dynamics AX

In order for the user to be able to access the self-service portals within the Enterprise portal, they need to be registered in Dynamics AX as a valid user with the correct roles and profiles.

In this recipe, we will show you how to create an external user account within Dynamics AX.

How to do it...

To configure a new customer account in Dynamics AX, follow these steps:

1. Select the **Users** menu item from the Users folder of the **Common** group within the **System administration** area page.

2. You can create the user the hard way or the easy way. The easy way is to create the user account from Active Directory by clicking on the **Import** button within the **New** group of the **Users** ribbon bar.

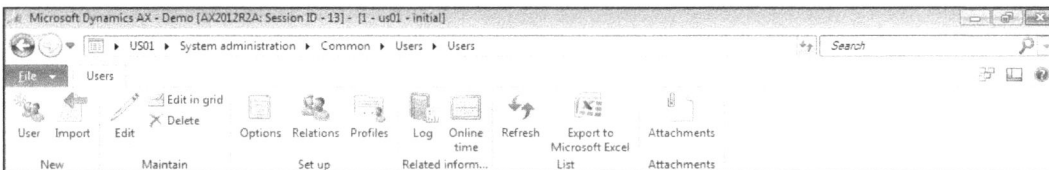

3. When the **Active Directory Import Wizard** starts up, click on the **Next** button.

4. Select your domain from the **Domain name:** drop-down box, and then select a search filter for the criteria fields. Click on **Next**.

5. This should show you a list of all the user accounts within Active Directory that match your search criteria, and you can select the user(s) who you want to import into Dynamics AX. Once you have selected the users, click on **Next**.

6. On the confirmation screen, click on **Next** again.

7. When the **Select roles** dialog box is shown, find the **Customer (external)** role and then click on the **<** button to move it to the **Selected Roles** list. Then click on **Next**.

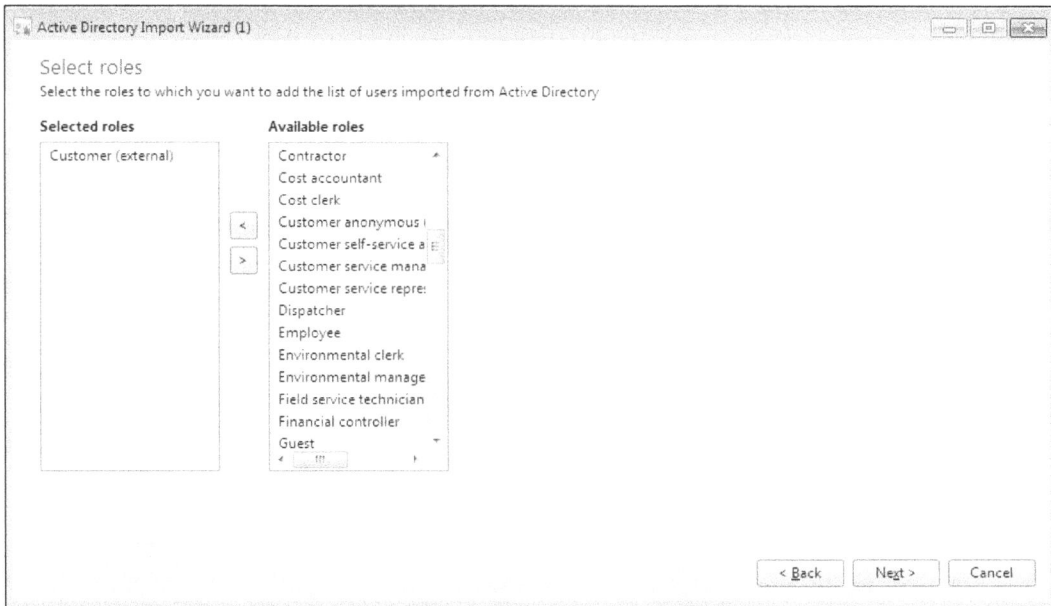

8. On the **Select profile** dialog box, assign your customer a profile and then click on the **Next** button. Without a profile, they may not be able to see any of their data within Dynamics AX.

9. To complete the process, just click on **Finish**.

Associating customer logins with customer accounts

In order for an external user to see their account information and just their account information, you need to create a relationship between the user account within Dynamics AX and the customer account. This is done through the user relationships.

In this recipe, we will show how to create a relationship between a user account and a customer account.

Getting ready

In order to create a user-to-customer relationship, you need to have a contact for the customer account. If you don't have a contact, you may want to quickly create one.

How to do it...

To associate a customer login with a customer in Dynamics AX, follow these steps:

1. Select the **Users** menu item from the `Users` folder of the **Common** group within the **System administration** area page.

2. Select the user account that you want to link to a customer account, and then click on the **Relations** button within the **Setup** group of the **Users** ribbon bar.

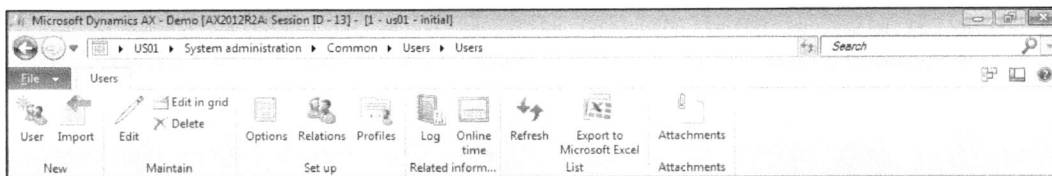

3. In the **User relations** form, click on the **New** button in the menu bar.

4. From within the **Person:** drop-down field, select the contact for the customer account that you want to link to the customer.

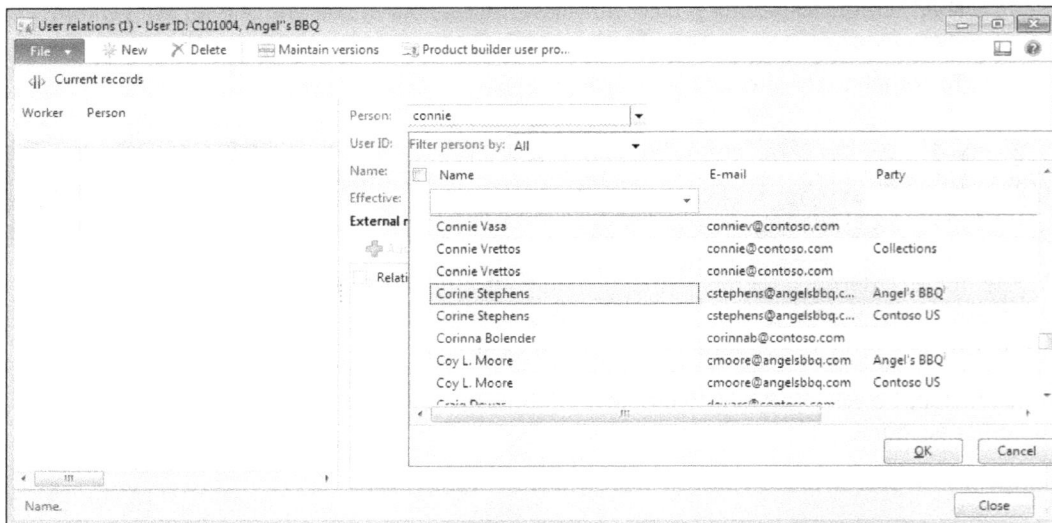

5. This should automatically populate the user IDs. Now, click on the **Add** button from the menu bar of the **External relations** group.

6. From the **Name:** dropdown, select the customer account that you want to associate with the customer, and then click on the **Close** button.

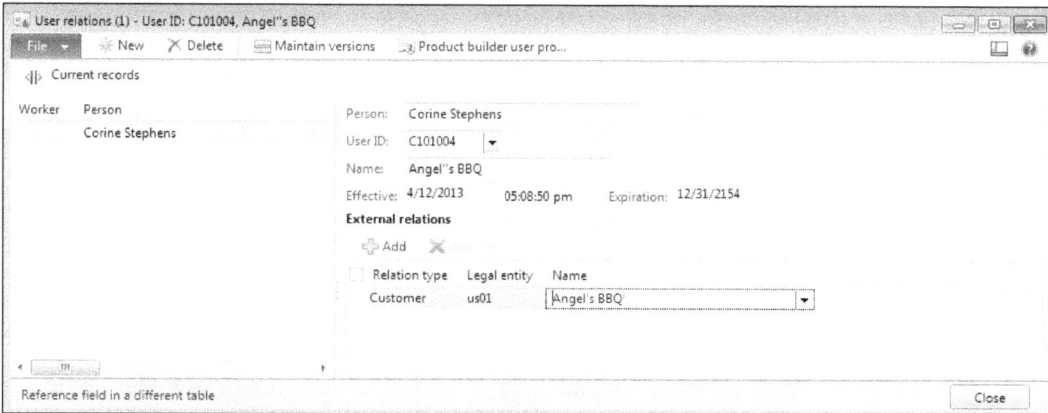

How it works...

This will now allow the user to log in to the Customer self-service portal, and the information that will be displayed will be only for the related customer account.

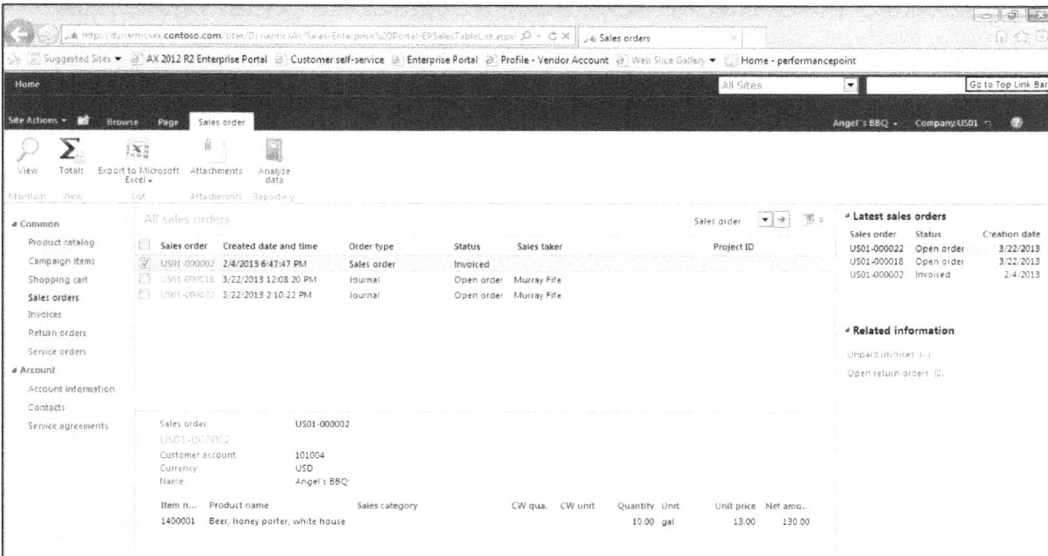

The user will be able to access all their information such as address and contact information. If the user creates new contacts or addresses, this information will be immediately changed within Dynamics AX.

Configuring a product catalog

The Customer self-service portal has a simple e-commerce feature that allows customers to enter orders. To do this, though, you need to publish the products that you want to allow customers to order, and this is done by defining a product catalog for the Customer self-service portal.

In this example we will show how you can create a product catalog and link it with the self-service portal.

How to do it...

To configure a new product catalog, follow these steps:

1. Select the **Product groups** menu item from the `Product catalogs` folder of the **Setup** group on the **Product Information Management** area page.
2. To create a parent group for our product catalog, click on the **New** button.
3. Give your product group a name and make sure that the **Type** field is set to **Group node**.

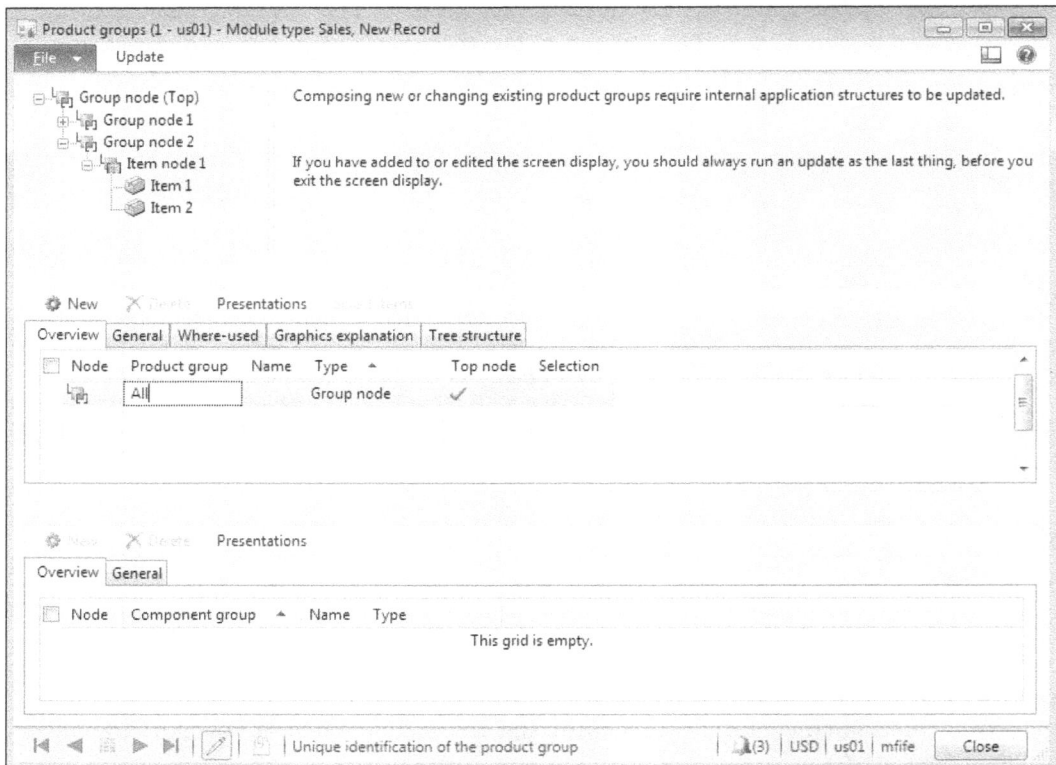

4. Continue and create subgroups in exactly the same way.

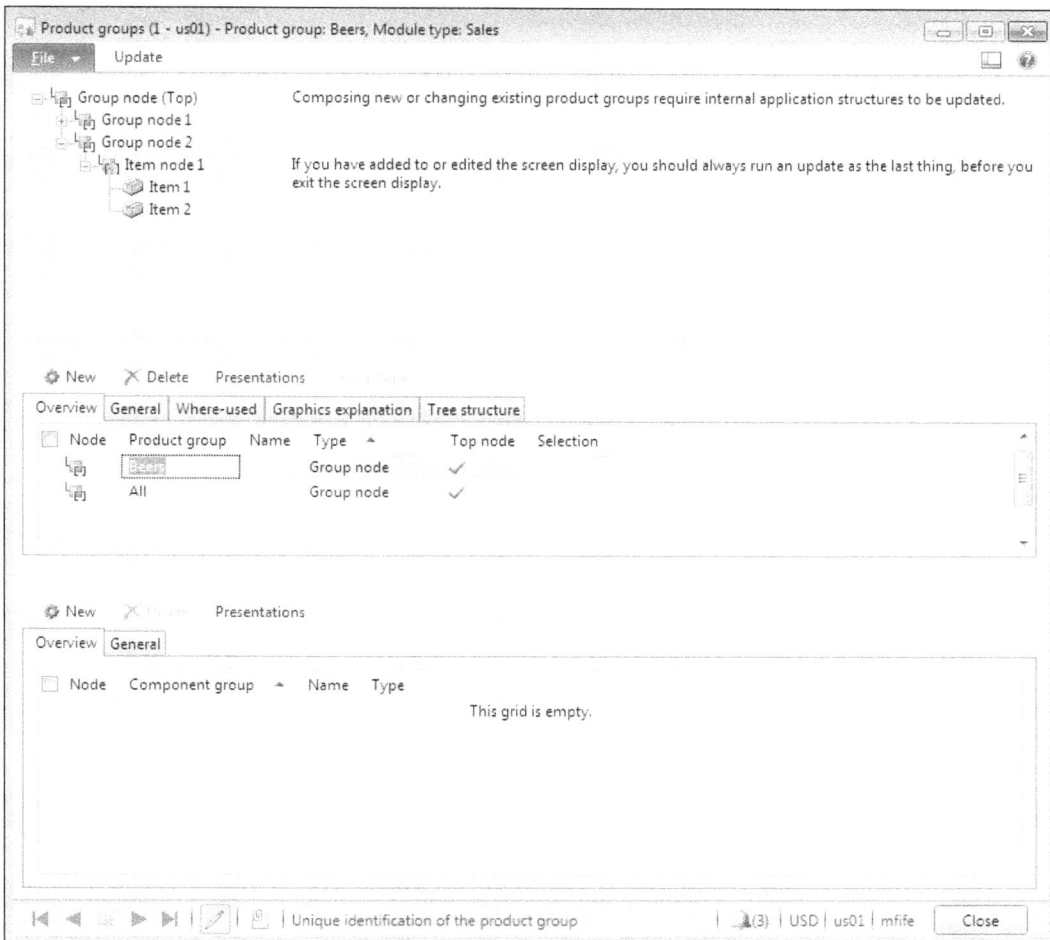

Product groups (1 - us01) - Product group: Beers, Module type: Sales

File | Update

- Group node (Top)
  - Group node 1
  - Group node 2
    - Item node 1
      - Item 1
      - Item 2

Composing new or changing existing product groups require internal application structures to be updated.

If you have added to or edited the screen display, you should always run an update as the last thing, before you exit the screen display.

New | Delete | Presentations

Overview | General | Where-used | Graphics explanation | Tree structure

Node	Product group	Name	Type ▲	Top node	Selection
			Group node	✓	
	All		Group node	✓	

New | Delete | Presentations

Overview | General

Node	Component group ▲	Name	Type
		This grid is empty.	

Unique identification of the product group   (3) | USD | us01 | mfife   Close

5. Link your parent group to the subgroup by selecting the parent group and then clicking on the **New** menu button in the subitems group. From the **Component group** dropdown, select the subgroup.

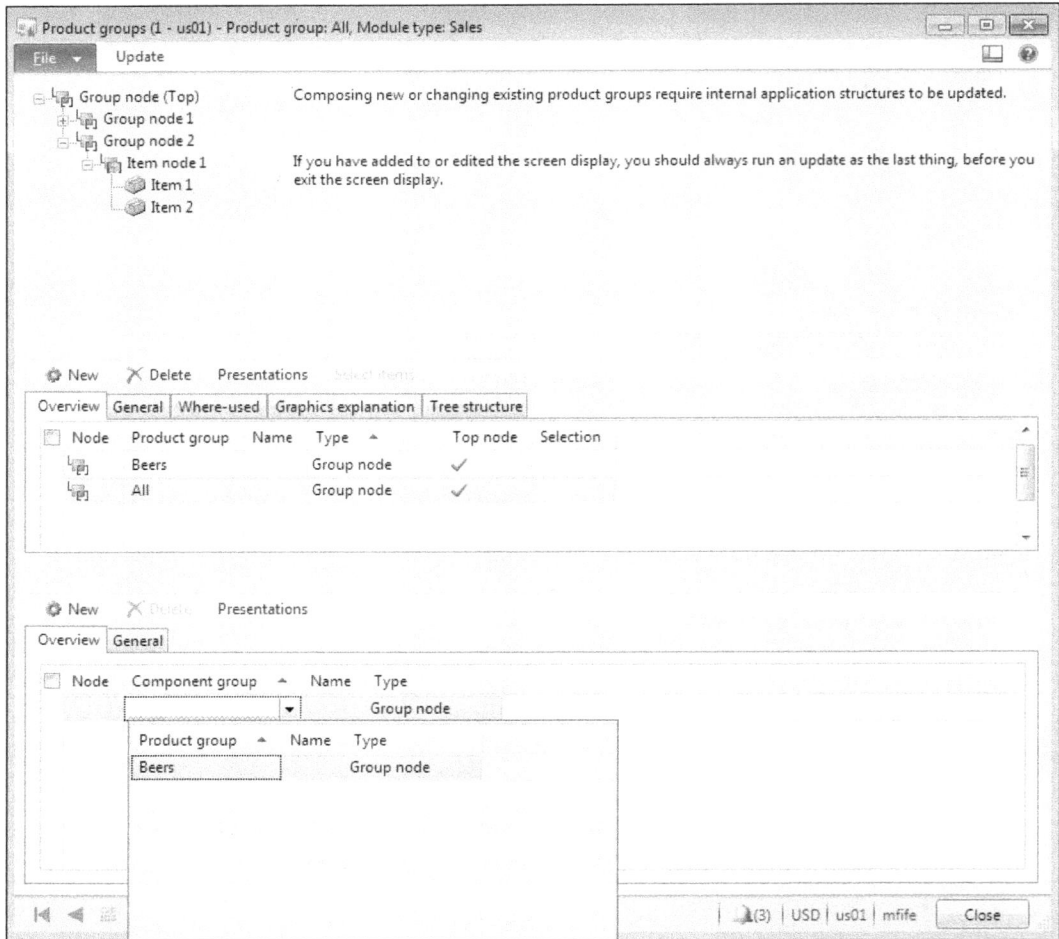

6. You can create subgroups that are linked to items rather than other groups. To do this, click on the **New** menu button and create a new group node, but set the type to **Item node**. Link the **Item node** group to a parent group. Then in the child nodes list, click on the **New** button and within the **Item number** drop-down box, select the products that you want to include in the group.

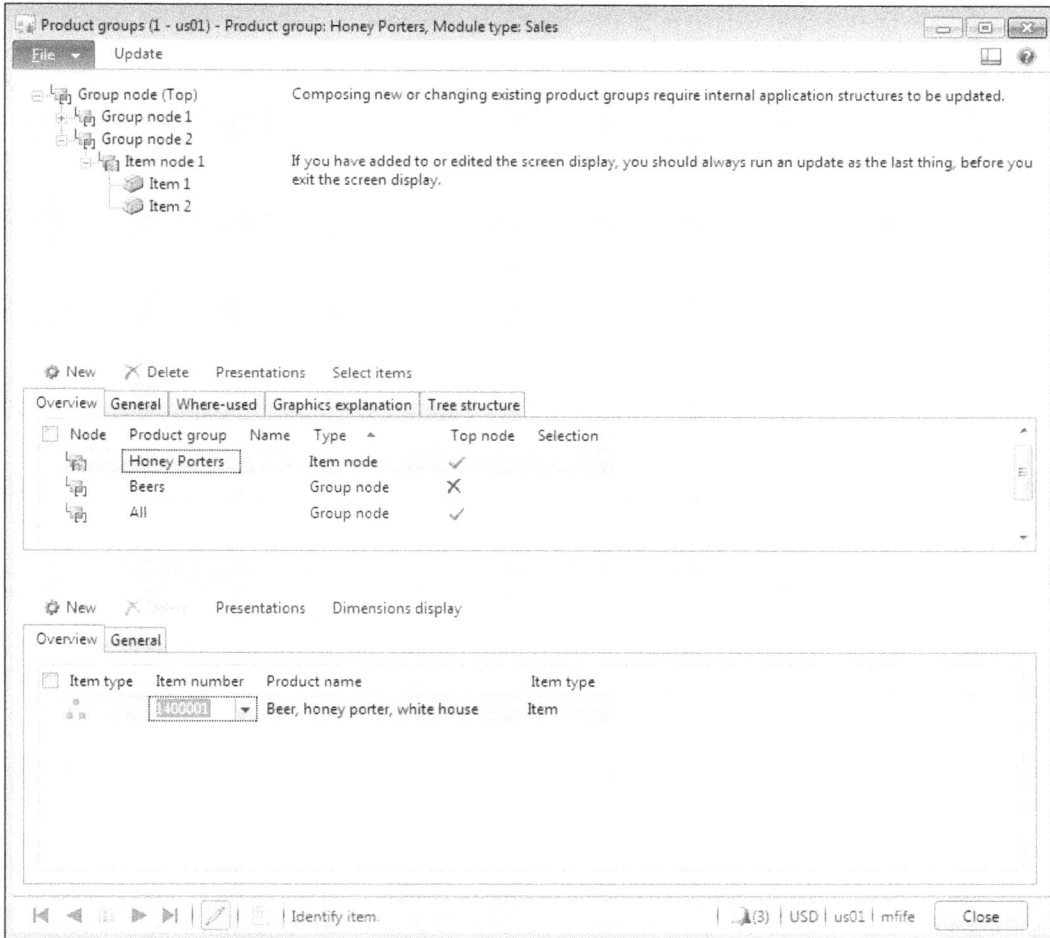

7. After you have created the product hierarchy that you want publish to the Customer self-service portal, click on the **Update** button in the menu bar of the **Product group structure** form. Then, check the **Update product group structure** field and click on the **OK** button.

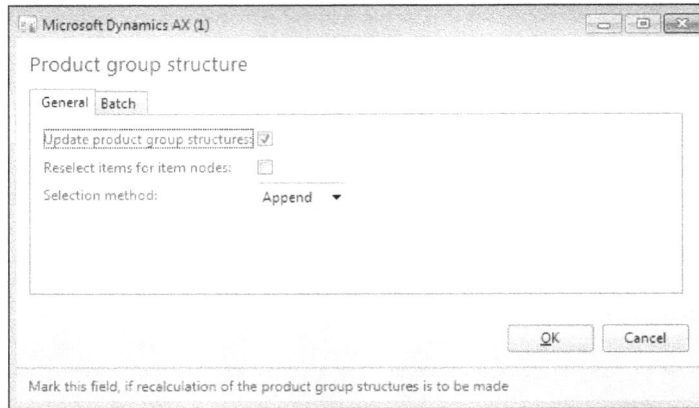

8. Now, we need to link the product catalog to the Enterprise portal. To do this, select the **Customer self-service parameters** menu item from the `Customer self-service` folder of the **Setup** group within the **Sales and Marketing** area page.

9. Finally, choose the **Product structures** tab, select the parent product group that you defined from the **Product group** field, and then click on the **Close** button.

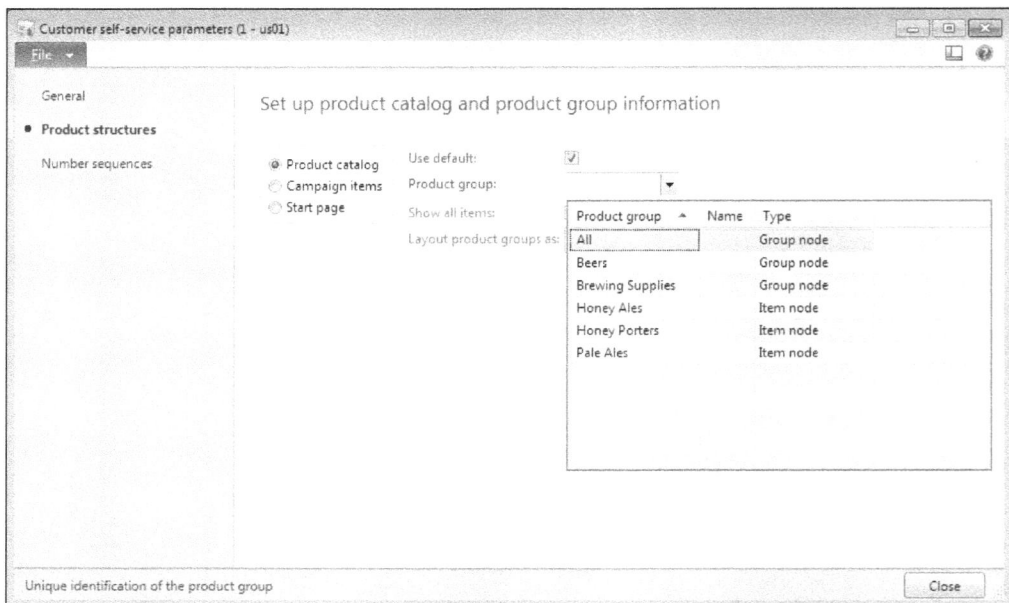

How it works...

Now when the customer logs in to the Customer self-service portal and selects the **Product catalog** option, they will see the product catalog that you have defined.

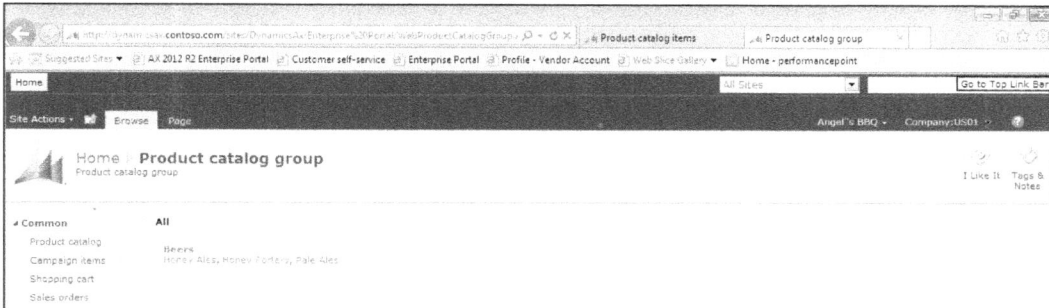

They will be able to drill down to the base product, see the product details and price information directly from Dynamics AX, and add it to their cart.

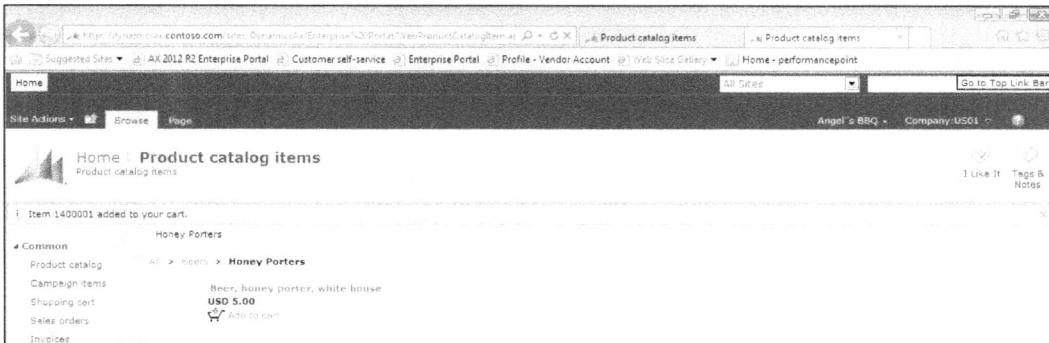

From this point on, the user can add products to their shopping cart, update the quantities, and place their orders just as you would expect within a web product catalog. The default information from their customer account will be populated at checkout, and they will be able to confirm their orders.

Checkout						□ x

Complete general information > **Confirm order**

Confirm your order

Customer reference:	ANGELS-2893266		Total:	5.00
Requisition:			Total discount:	0.00
Ship date:	4/12/2013		Charges amount:	0.00
Contact:	Corine Stephens		Sales tax amount:	0.00
Delivery name:	Angel's BBQ		Total amount:	5.00
Address:	21 W. Oglethorpe Lane. Savannah, GA 31401 USA		Currency:	USD

Item number	Product name	Product number	Quantity	Price unit	Unit price	Discount percent	Cash discount amount	Net amount
1400001	Beer, honey porter, white house		1.00	1.00	5.00	0.00	0.00	5.00

Previous   Finish   Cancel

Once orders are placed through the Customer self-service portal, they are immediately created within Dynamics AX.

Adding images and presentation information to product catalogs

You can make your product catalog look a lot better by adding pictures and detailed information to your products through the presentation options available within the product groups.

In this recipe, we will show you how to add product images and details.

How to do it...

To add presentation details to your product catalog, follow these steps:

1. Select the **Product groups** menu item from the `Product catalogs` folder of the **Setup** group on the **Product Information Management** area page.

2. Select the item node from your item groups that you want to add more detailed information to, and click on the **Presentations** menu button.

3. From the **Presentations** dialog box, select the **Description** tab and click on the **Edit** button to add a more detailed customer facing description.

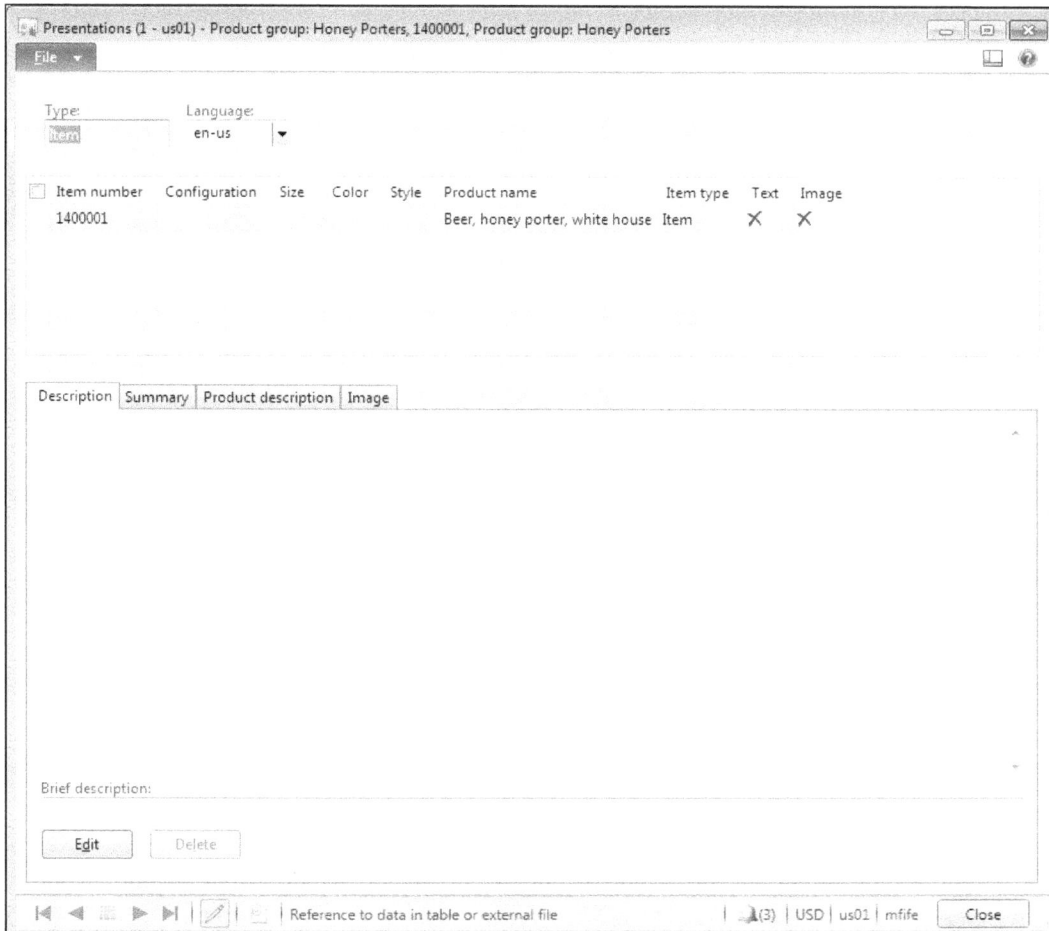

4. Type in the detailed description that you want to show on the self-service portal and then click on the **Save** button.

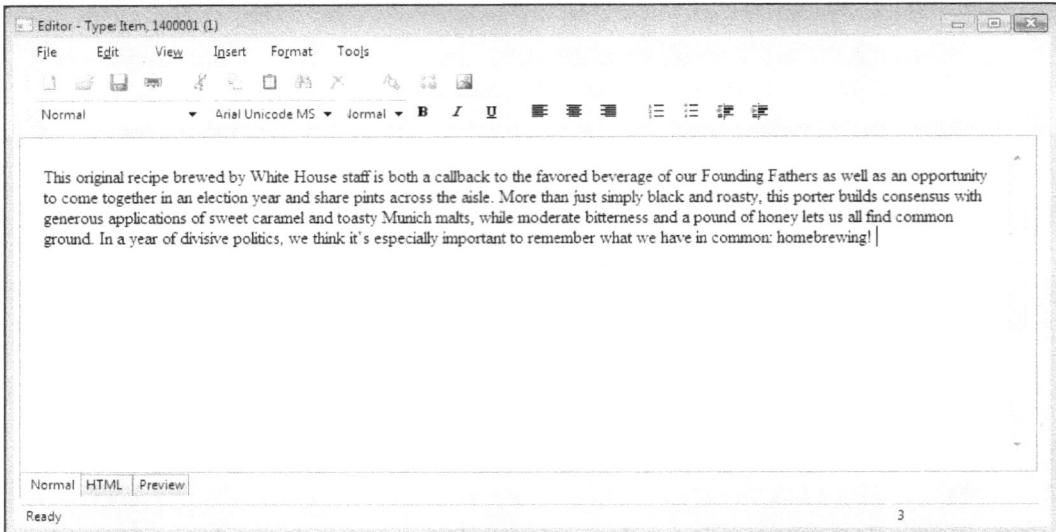

5. To add a thumbnail image to the product, click on the **Image** tab and then click on the **Add image** button.

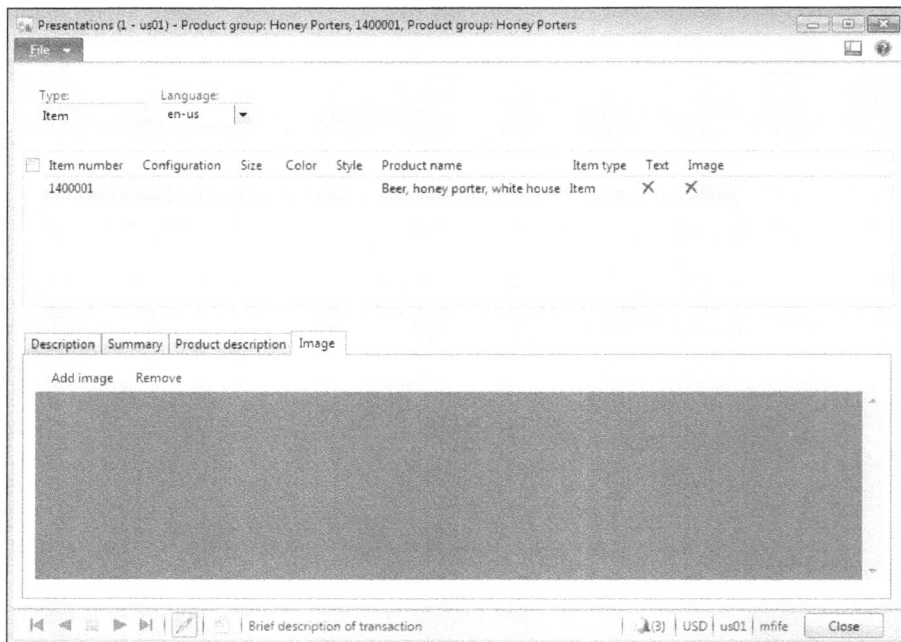

6. A dialog box will show up asking if you want to update all of the languages. If you have a system with multiple languages in use, you may want to check this option. Then, click on the **OK** button.

7. Now select the image file that you want to use as the product thumbnail and click on **Open**.

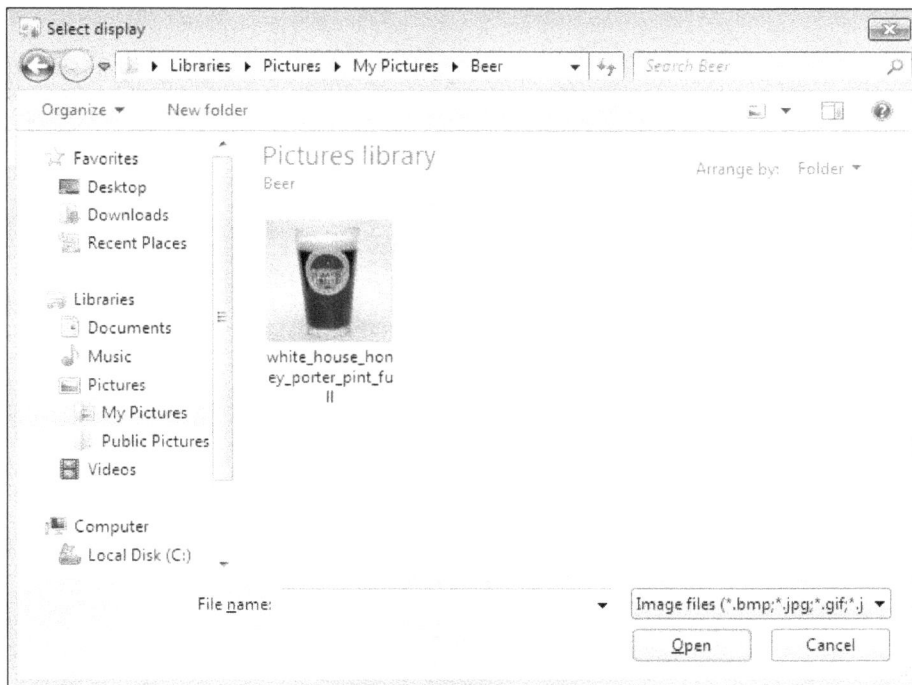

8. The final step in this process is to synchronize all the images that you have associated with the product catalog with your Enterprise portal. To do this, click on the **Publish images** menu item in the `Enterprise Portal` folder of the **Setup** group within the **System administration** area page.

9. To sync the images, click on the **OK** button in the publishing dialog box:

How it works...

Now when the user browses the catalog, they will see an image associated with the product.

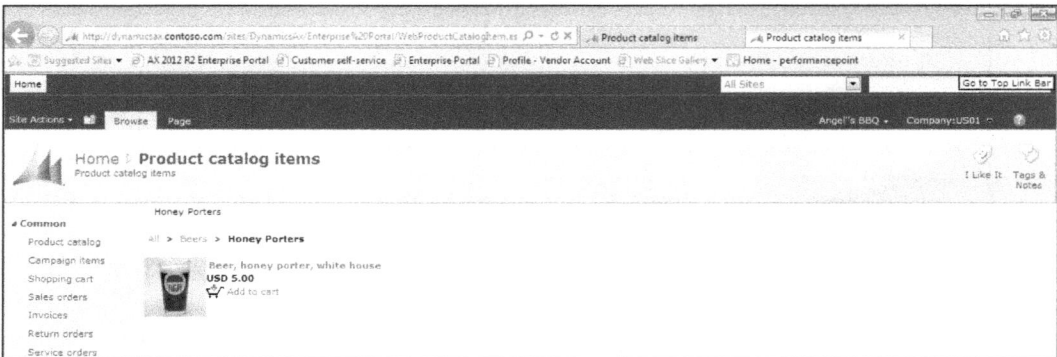

And when they drill into the detail for the product, they will see more information coming from the detailed description that was created for the product.

View product details: 1400001, Beer, honey porter, white house

Page | View

Add to cart | Close

Commit

⊿ **Select item**   1400001

	Item number:	1400001
	Product name:	Beer, honey porter, white house
	Unit:	gal
	List price:	5.00
	Currency:	USD
	On hand quantity:	0.00
Summary:	Quantity:	1.00

⊿ **Details**

Description

This original recipe brewed by White House staff is both a callback to the favored beverage of our Founding Fathers as well as an opportunity to come together in an election year and share pints across the aisle. More than just simply black and roasty, this porter builds consensus with generous applications of sweet caramel and toasty Munich malts, while moderate bitterness and a pound of honey lets us all find common ground. In a year of divisive politics, we think it's especially important to remember what we have in common: homebrewing!

Add to cart | Close

Summary

You may have thought that to allow others to access information within the ERP system is a lot of work to build and set up. Through this chapter, you have seen that the Customer self-service portal that you get with Dynamics AX is not that hard to configure, and you can quickly set it up and let customers use it.

In addition to what we showed in this chapter, there are other features within the Customer self-service portal that you may want to try taking advantage of. If you want to dig in deeper, try:

- Formatting your descriptions through the HTML designer within the product groups presentation editor
- Adding images and descriptions to the group nodes as well as the item nodes in the product catalog
- Creating other root product catalogs for the highlighted campaigns and start pages of the self-service portal

Also, you may want to look at the other self-service portals that are delivered with Dynamics AX. You can:

▶ Create logins for vendors much the same way as you do for customers, allowing them to log in to the Vendor self-service portal. From there, they will be able to access all of their POs, invoices, and so on, and also respond to quotation requests that you send them.

▶ Allow more casual users to access the Employee self-service portal to update their HR contact information, request training, submit requisitions, and also enter timesheets and expense reports online.

All the portals are built and delivered out of the box with Dynamics AX. Why not take advantage of them?

9
Creating Help

In this chapter, we will introduce the help authoring system that is built into the Dynamics AX framework, and show you how you can take advantage of it to build your own integrated help system and knowledgebase. You will also learn the following:

- ▶ Creating a new help publisher ID
- ▶ Creating a new help publisher content folder
- ▶ Creating your help content
- ▶ Creating a Task Recorder walkthrough
- ▶ Turning a task recording document into a help topic

Introduction

Dynamics AX has a help engine that is installed along with the base installation that is used for searching and displaying all of the standard help files, and the help files are also indexed and searchable through the **Enterprise Search** feature. If you want to, you can have full access to all the default help source files, and you can easily add your own twists to the standard documentation.

This becomes even more useful to you because it not only provides a way for you to edit the default help to add your own nuances to the documentation, but it also allows you to create your very own help topics that the users are able to search for alongside the standard help.

In this chapter, we will show you how you can create your own help documents for reference information, and also how to use the Task Recorder that is built into Dynamics AX to document and publish business procedures for the users to reference directly from the Dynamics AX help service.

Creating a new help publisher ID

Help files are separated within the help service by publisher, allowing the user to further refine their help searches if they want, and also allowing publishers to update their help independently. In the following examples we will be creating new help content, so it's probably a good idea to register a new publisher within the help service before continuing.

In this recipe, we will show you how to create a new publisher within the help service.

Getting ready

All the help service files should be located in the following directory on the Dynamics AX server: `c:\inetpub\wwwroot\DynamicsHelpServer\DynamicsAXHelpServer`.

How to do it...

To create a new help publisher ID, follow these steps:

1. Find the `web.config` file and open it up in an editor such as Notepad or Visual Studio.

2. Within the `dynamicsHelpConfig` section of the `web.config` file will be a `publishers` section. There may be multiple entries here if there are add-ons installed for Dynamics AX, but in the base image, there should just be one `publisherId` for Microsoft.

3. Make a copy of the Microsoft `publisherId` entry and paste it below. Then change `publisherId` and `name` to be a unique publisher.

4. Then, save your `web.config` file.

How it works...

Now when you open up the Dynamics AX help, if you click on the **Options** button, you will see your new publisher as a filter option.

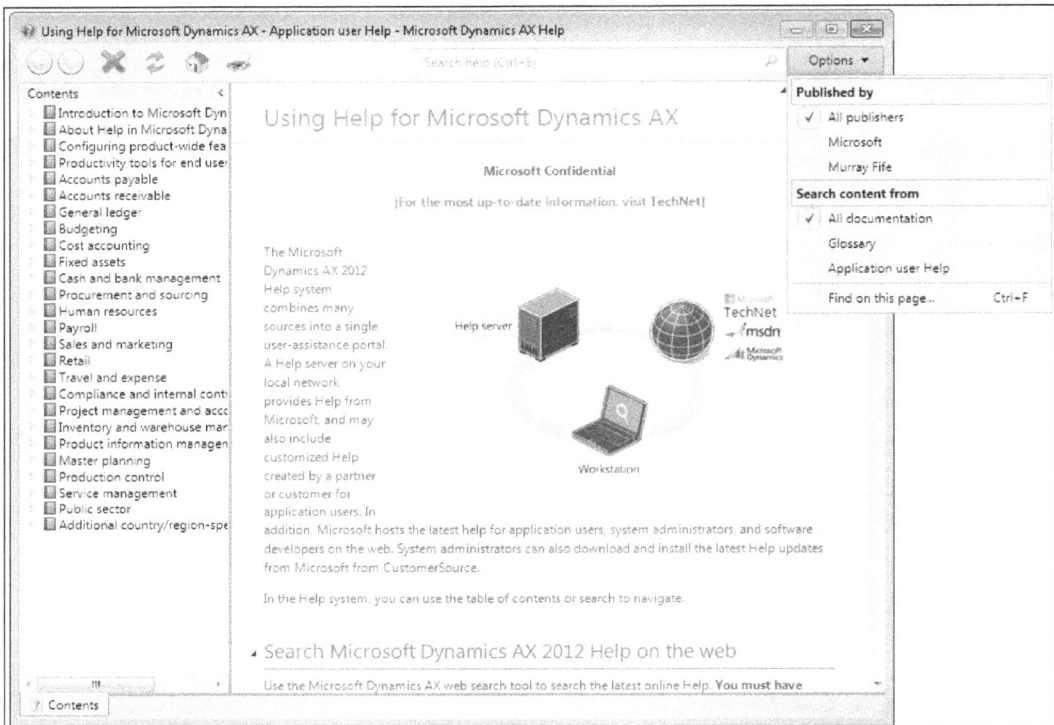

Creating a new help publisher content folder

Once you have a publisher ID defined, you need to create a folder structure to store all your help content.

In this recipe, we will show you how to create the publisher folder structure.

Getting ready

Each publisher should have their own `Content` folder located in the following directory on the Dynamics AX server: `c:\inetpub\wwwroot\DynamicsHelpServer\DynamicsAXHelpServer\Content\`.

How to do it...

To create a new help publisher `Content` folder, follow these steps:

1. Create a new folder in the `Content` folder with the same name as your `publisherID`.

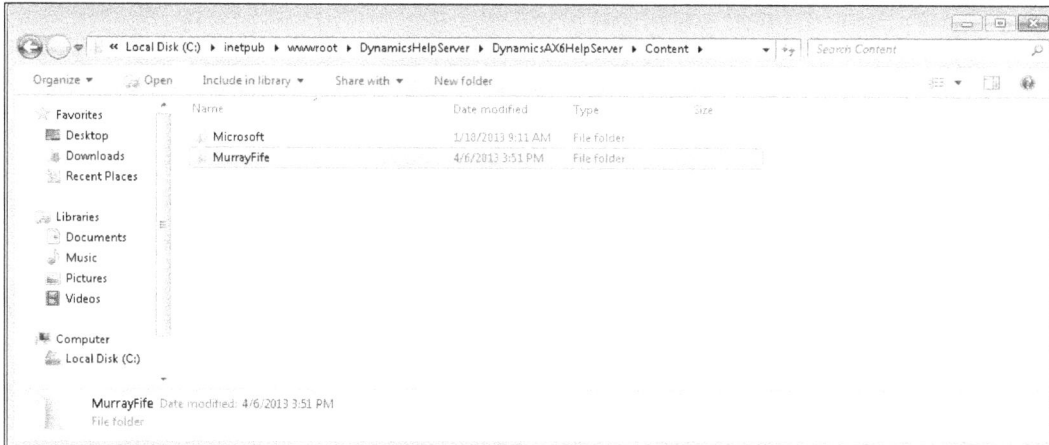

2. Within the new publisher directory, create a subdirectory for each language that you want your documentation published in using the language code naming convention. In this case, we will just publish in US English (EN-US).

3. Then, create a subfolder within the `Language` folder called `UserDocResources`.

4. Within the `UserDocResources` folder, create a new XML file called `TableOfContents.xml`. This will store your table of contents' definition for your help files.

> If you want, you can also look in the same folder for the Microsoft help publisher and just copy that file over to your publisher's folder.

5. Open the `TableOfContents.xml` file in a text editor (Notepad or Visual Studio) and add the following XML using your own publisher ID.

```
<?xml version="1.0" encoding="utf-8"?>
<tableOfContents xmlns="http://schemas.microsoft.com/
dynamicsHelp/2008/11" xmlns:xsi="http://www.w3.org/2001/XMLSchema-
instance">
  <publisher>MurrayFife</publisher>
  <documentSet>UserDocumentation</documentSet>
```

```
  <ms.locale>EN-US</ms.locale>
  <entries>
  </entries>
</tableOfContents>
  <entries>
    <entry>
      <text>Brewerpedia</text>
      <Microsoft.Help.F1></Microsoft.Help.F1>
    </entry>
  </entries>
</tableOfContents>
```

6. Add a new base folder to your help TOC by adding an `entry` node to the `entries` group.

    ```
    <entries>
      <entry>
        <text>Brewerpedia</text>
        <Microsoft.Help.F1></Microsoft.Help.F1>
      </entry>
    </entries>
    ```

7. To add child topics to that folder, just add more entries with the `children` nodes under your base `entry` node. You can embed as many levels of child nodes this way within your TOC.

    ```
    <entries>
        <entry>
          <text>Brewerpedia</text>
          <Microsoft.Help.F1></Microsoft.Help.F1>
          <children>
            <entry>
              <text>About Beer</text>
              <Microsoft.Help.F1></Microsoft.Help.F1>
            </entry>
          </children>
        </entry>
    </entries>
    ```

8. Each help topic that you create needs to have a `Microsoft.Help.F1` GUID value. A quick and simple way to create a unique GUID is to go to `http://createguid. com`. Every time you refresh this page it will show you a new GUID.

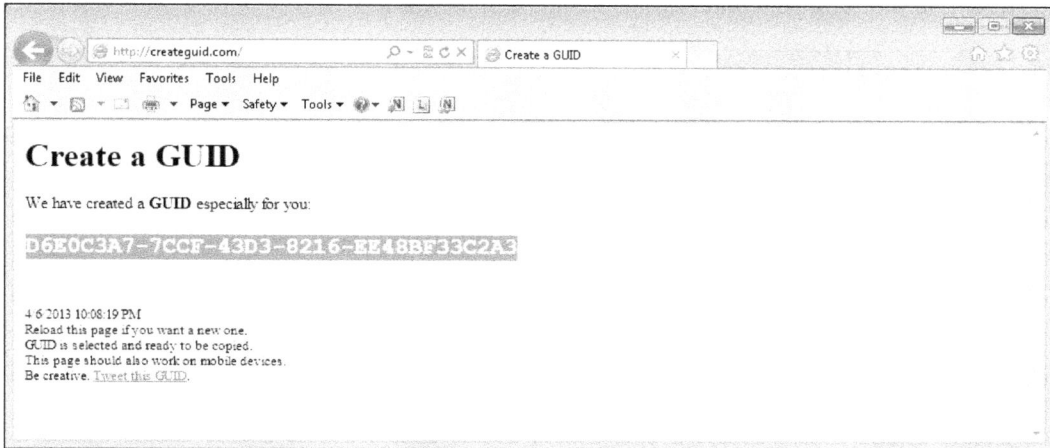

9. Create a new GUID for each entry that you have in your TOC.

```xml
<?xml version="1.0" encoding="utf-8"?>
<tableOfContents xmlns="http://schemas.microsoft.com/dynamicsHelp/2008/11" xmlns:xsi="http://www.w3.org/2001/XMLSchema-instance">
    <publisher>MurrayFife</publisher>
    <documentSet>UserDocumentation</documentSet>
    <ms.locale>EN-US</ms.locale>
    <entries>
      <entry>
        <text>Brewerpedia</text>
        <Microsoft.Help.F1>5C2FC46F-76F3-4647-9084-CDDE6E509D0B</Microsoft.Help.F1>
        <children>
          <entry>
            <text>About Beer</text>
            <Microsoft.Help.F1>D6E0C3A7-7CCF-43D3-8216-EE48BF33C2A3</Microsoft.Help.F1>
          </entry>
        </children>
      </entry>
    </entries>
</tableOfContents>
```

10. Finally, save your table of contents.

How it works...

Now when you open up the Dynamics AX help, you should see a new entry for the help that you added to your table of contents, including the subfolders.

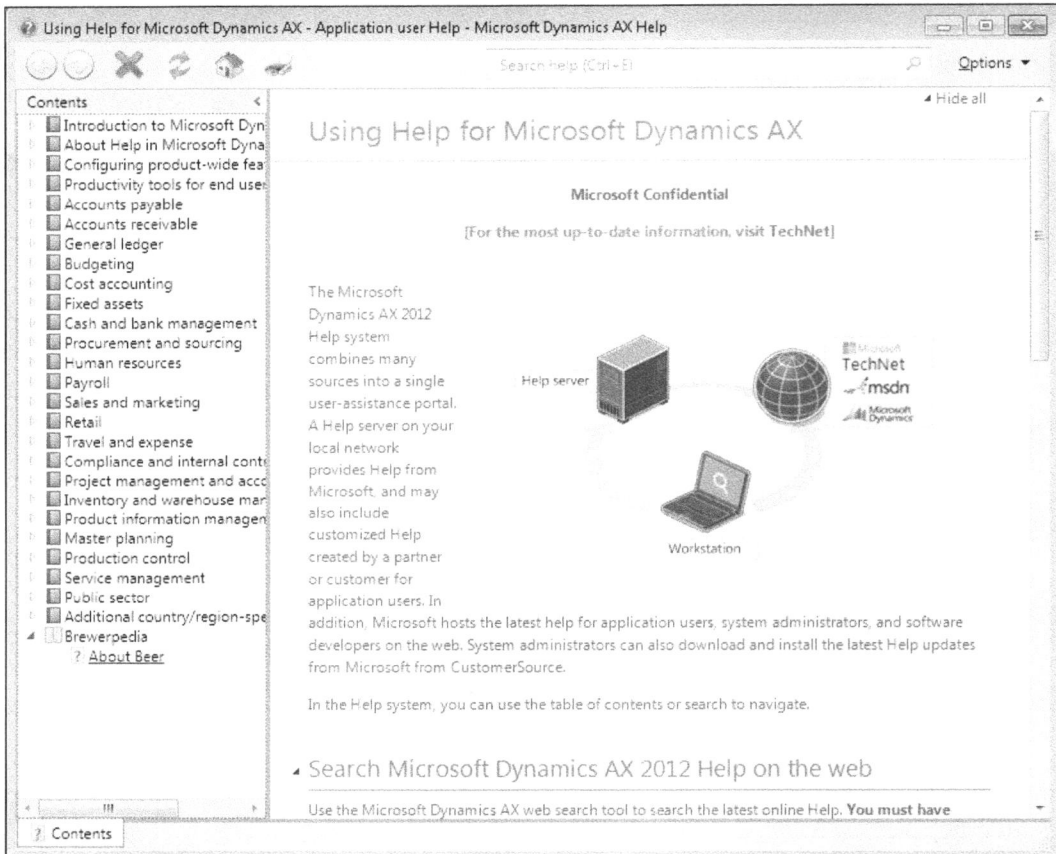

Creating your help content

Creating your own help is a pretty simple exercise and doesn't require any special applications or tools. All you need is a copy of Microsoft Word and directions on where to find the help template that is embedded in the Dynamics AX help system.

In this recipe, we will show you how to create and publish your own help topics.

How to do it...

To create new help content, follow these steps:

1. To find the help template that you can use to publish your own help, just open up the Dynamics AX help and type in `template for help documentation`.

2. When the search results are returned, select the **Templates for Help Documentation** help topic.

3. Scroll down through the help topic and there will be a link to a `Dynamics Help Content Template.docm`. Click on this link to download the help content template.

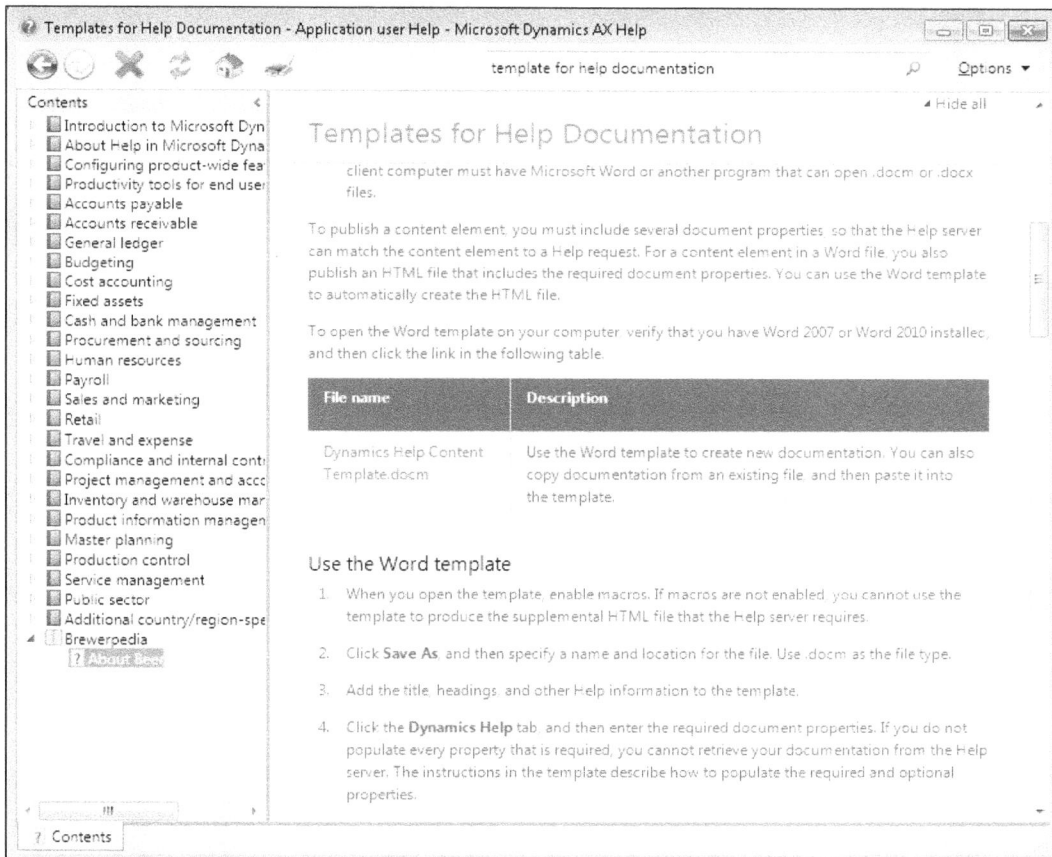

4. This will open up the help template. Since this is just a Word document, you can create your help content by hand or just cut and paste from any existing documentation that you may have.

5. On the Word ribbon bar, you will see an additional tab for the **Microsoft Dynamics Help** metadata. In that ribbon bar, update the **Title** and **Publisher ID**, and set the **Topic ID** to match the GUID for the topic in the publisher table of content's XML file.

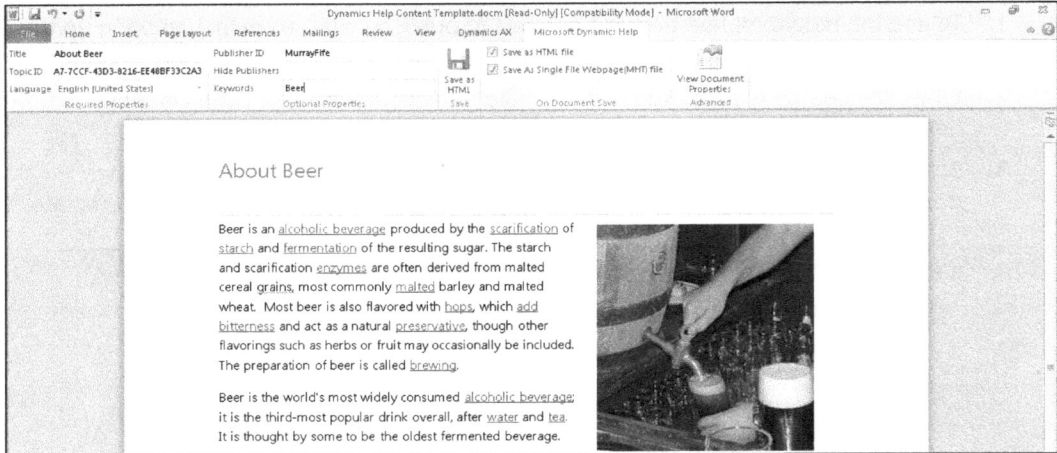

6. From the **File** menu, select the **Save As** option and navigate to the `Content` folder for your publisher and save the file. The name of the file does not matter, but for this example, we will use the GUID to identify the document. Also, to separate out each chapter in the help documentation, we created a subdirectory for the chapter.

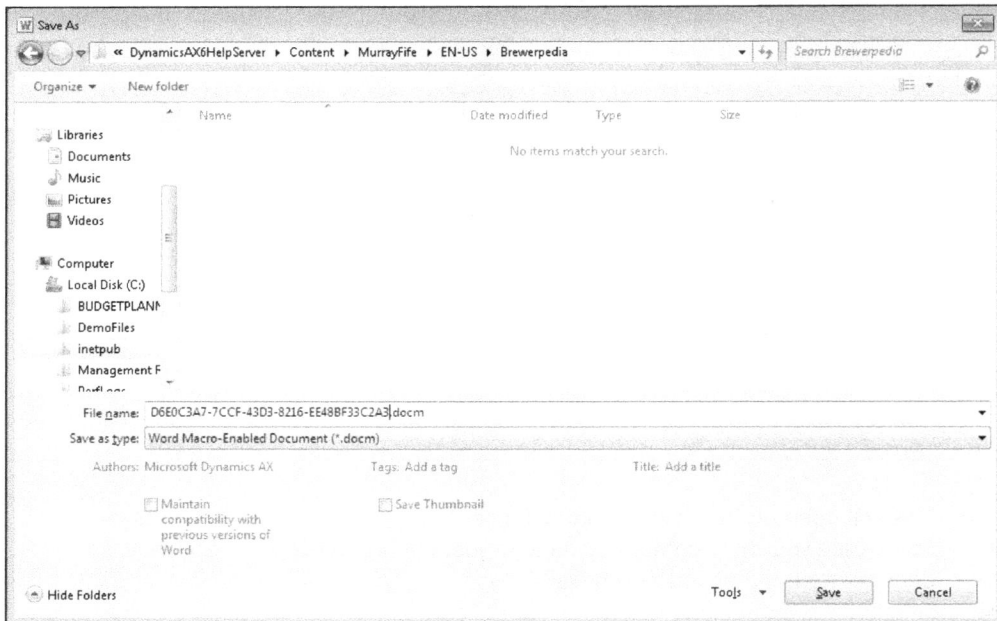

7. To finish the publication process, click on the **Save as HTML** button within the **Save** group of the **Microsoft Dynamics Help** ribbon bar.

How it works...

If we look into our Content folder, there will now be three files for the help topic: `.docm`, `.htm`, and `.mhtml`.

When you open up help and select your new topic, you will be able to see the content that you just created.

Additionally, since the help server is watched by the Enterprise Search service, searching for any keyword that is embedded in the help documentation will return your help content.

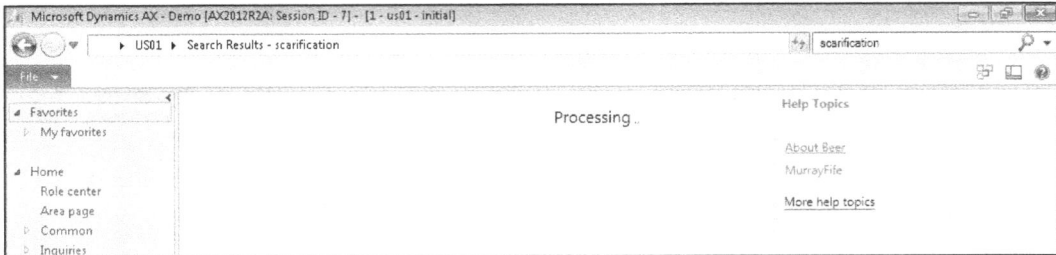

Creating a Task Recorder walkthrough

Dynamics AX has an in-built tool called the **Task Recorder**. This is a tool that allows you to record exactly what you are doing within Dynamics AX. The recordings can then be turned into Word, Visio, and/or PowerPoint documents that play back your recorded steps. This makes it a great way to create user guides and process documentation, which could then be embedded within the Dynamics AX help.

In this recipe, we will show you how to use the Task Recorder to create process documentation.

How to do it...

To create a new Task Recorder recording, follow these steps:

1. Access the Task Recorder from the **Tools** submenu of the **File** menu in the Dynamics AX Rich Client.

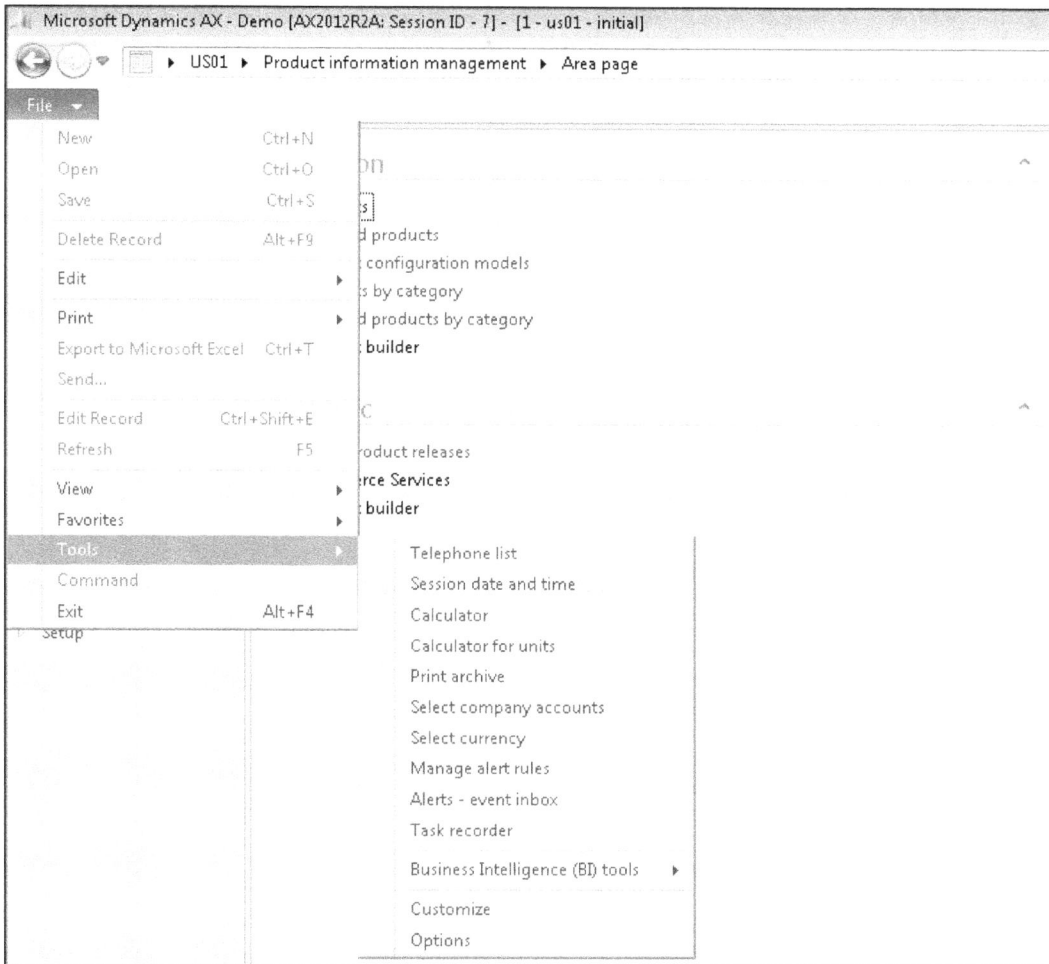

2. This will open up the **Task recorder** dialog box. To start recording, just click on the Record button (in red).

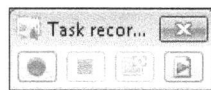

3. After performing the task that you want to record, click on the Stop button (in blue) in the Task Recorder and save the task. Give your task recording a name, a brief description for reference, and then click on the **Save** button.

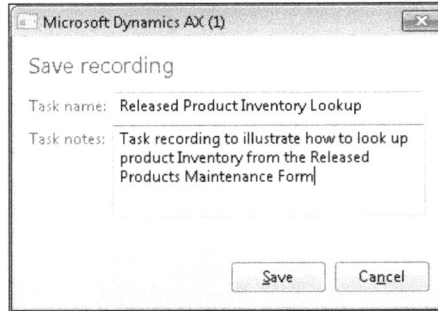

Microsoft Dynamics AX (1)	
Save recording	
Task name:	Released Product Inventory Lookup
Task notes:	Task recording to illustrate how to look up product Inventory from the Released Products Maintenance Form
	Save Cancel

4. You will then be taken to a list of all your recordings. Select your new recording and click on the **Generate document...** button.

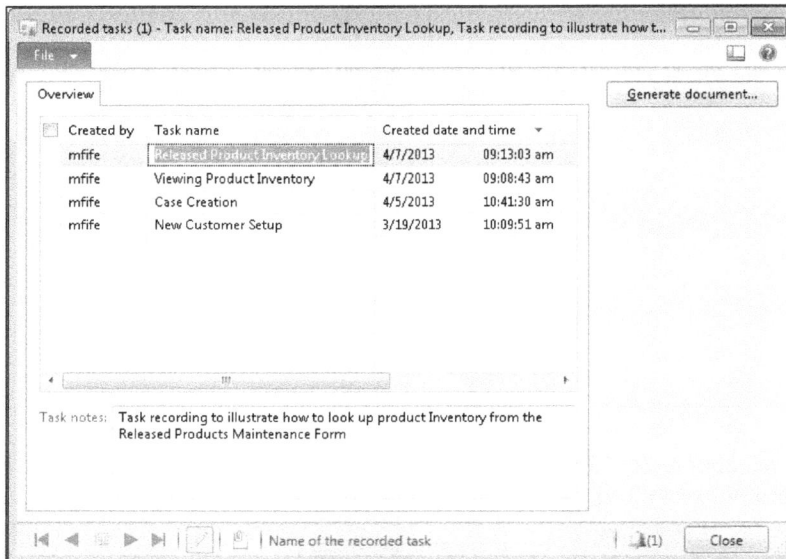

Recorded tasks (1) - Task name: Released Product Inventory Lookup, Task recording to illustrate how t...				
File ▾				
Overview				Generate document...
Created by	Task name	Created date and time		
mfife	Released Product Inventory Lookup	4/7/2013	09:13:03 am	
mfife	Viewing Product Inventory	4/7/2013	09:08:43 am	
mfife	Case Creation	4/5/2013	10:41:30 am	
mfife	New Customer Setup	3/19/2013	10:09:51 am	

Task notes: Task recording to illustrate how to look up product Inventory from the Released Products Maintenance Form

◄◄ ◄ ▶ ▶▶		Name of the recorded task	(1)	Close

5. When the **Generate document** dialog box is displayed, you can select the format of the document. Choose the **Microsoft Word** document type and click on the **OK** button.

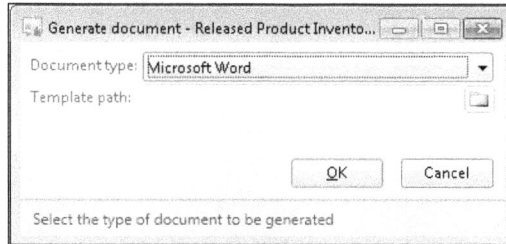

How it works...

This will then open up Word, along with the narrative and screenshots, replaying the steps that were recorded.

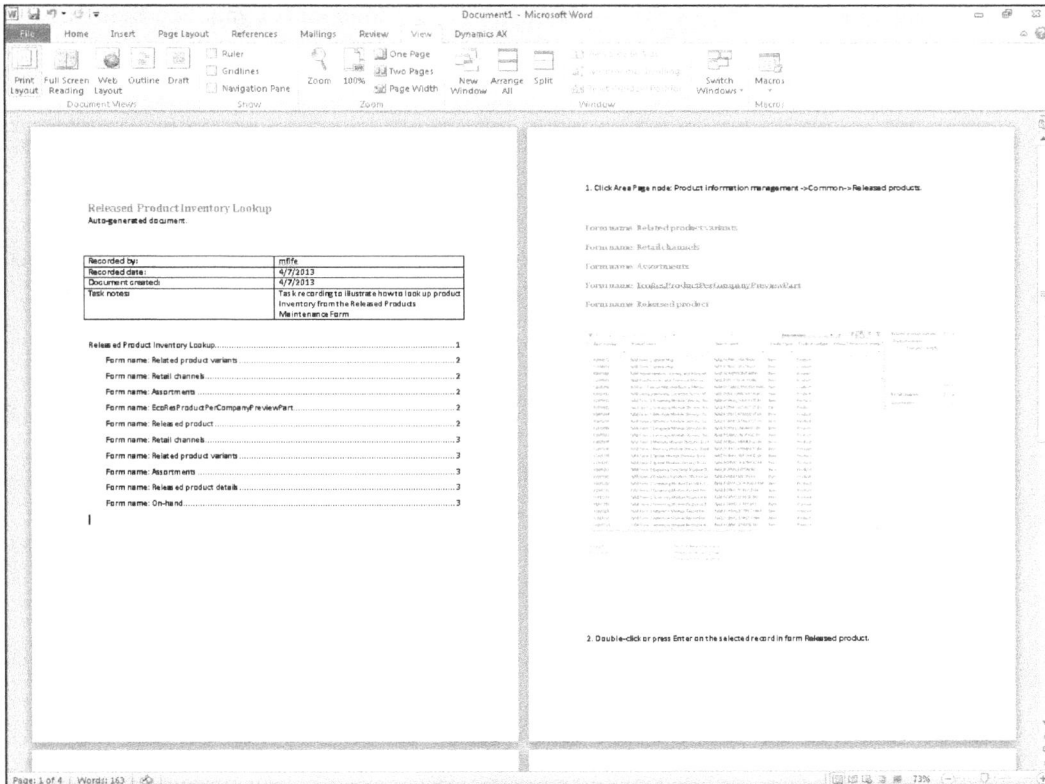

Turning a task recording document into a help topic

Once you have a task recording document, you can turn this into a help entry very quickly; you just need to cut and paste the task recording details into the help template.

In this recipe, we will show how to create procedural help documentation.

How to do it...

To convert a task recording into a help topic, follow these steps:

1. Find the Dynamics Help template through the help system.

2. When the template opens, click on the **Save As** option.

3. Save the help template document to your publisher content folder, with a unique GUID as the document name.

4. Change the title in the Word document, and on the **Microsoft Dynamics Help** ribbon bar, update the **Title** and **Publisher ID**, and set the **Topic ID** to match the GUID for the topic in the publisher table of contents' XML file.

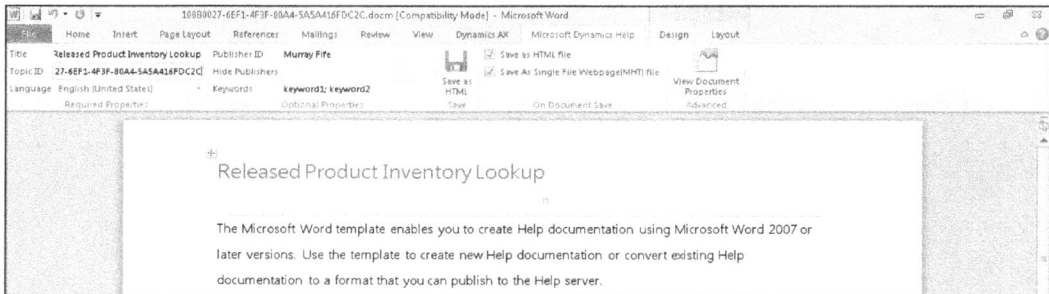

5. Copy the content from the document generated by Task Recorder into the help template file.

6. Tidy up the detailed task description by removing sections that you are not interested in showing.

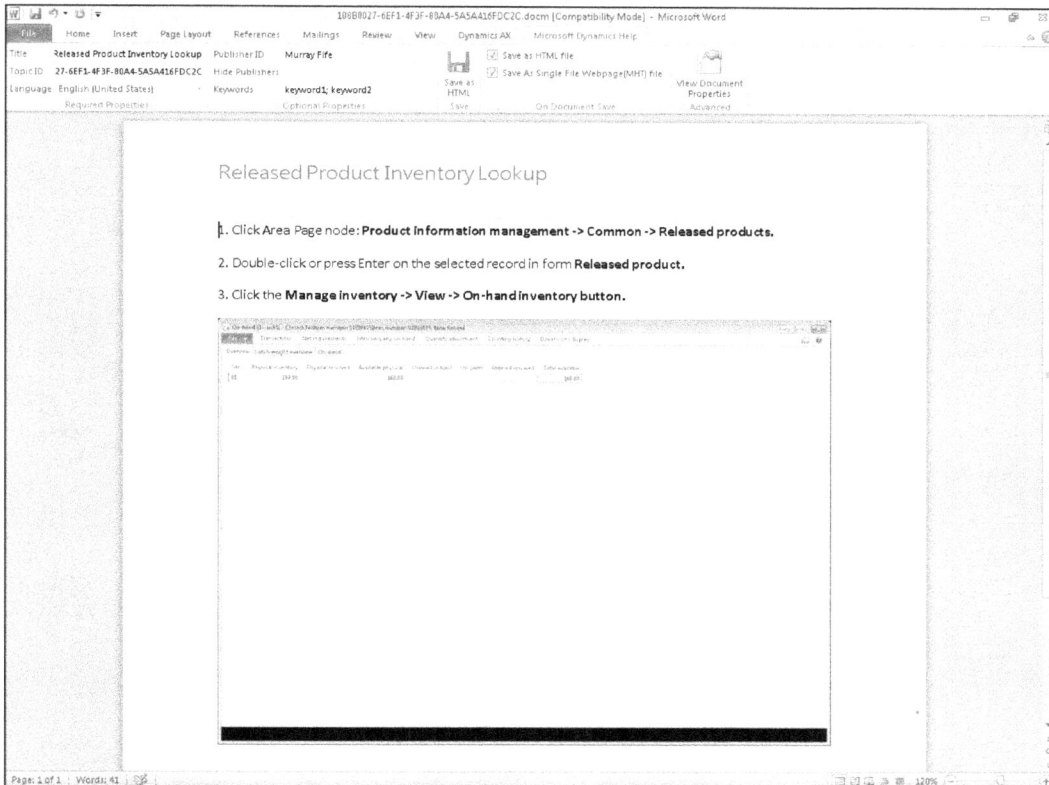

7. Then click on the **Save as HTML** button within the **Save** group of the **Microsoft Dynamics Help** tab to publish the HTML files.

8. Now open up your publisher table of contents' XML file, and add an entry for your user documentation using the GUID that matches the GUID defined in the Word document.

```
<entry>
  <text>Walkthroughs</text>
  <Microsoft.Help.F1></Microsoft.Help.F1>
  <children>
    <entry>
      <text>Released Product Inventory Lookup</text>
      <Microsoft.Help.F1>108B0027-6EF1-4F3F-80A4-
5A5A416FDC2C</Microsoft.Help.F1>
    </entry>
  </children>
</entry>
```

9. Finally, save your table of contents file.

How it works...

When you open up Dynamics AX help, the users will now be able to find documentation specific to your business processes.

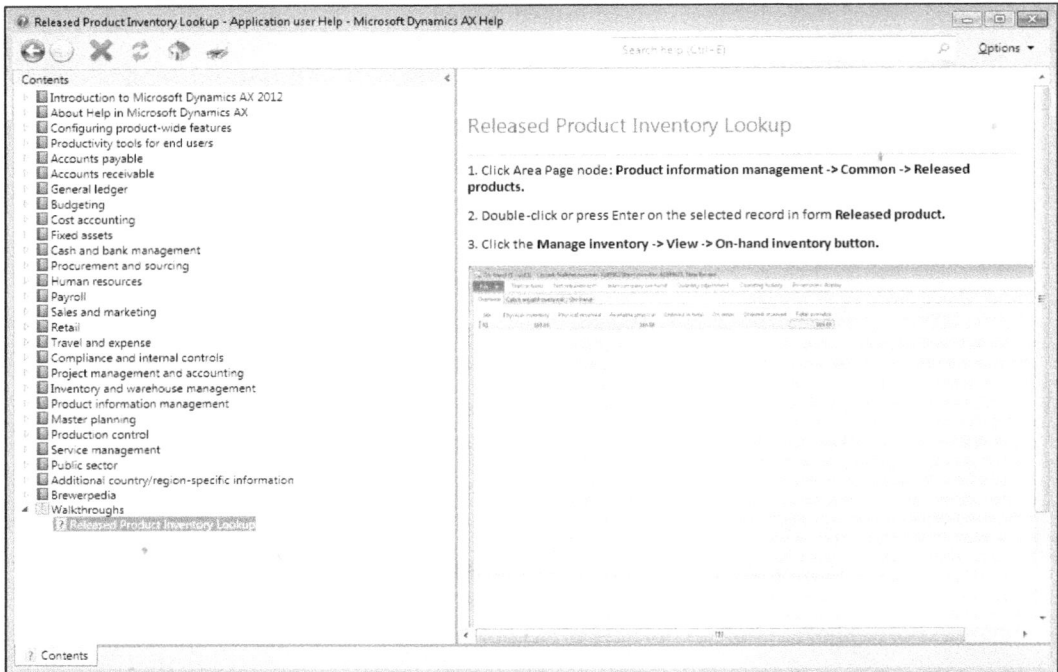

Summary

Although the standard help that is delivered with Dynamics AX is good, your own help files with your own examples is better. Making it almost impossible for users to avoid finding it by integrating it with Dynamics AX is the best of all.

The help service has a number of other more advanced features that you can take advantage of if you want to delve into it further. You can:

▸ Create links from your help documentation to other websites by embedding hyperlinks

▸ Create links to Dynamics AX data through Dynamics AX specific hyperlinks that are enabled when you install Rich Client

▸ Embed other media files such as videos for more dynamic help content

▸ Add keywords for context-sensitive searches

Other types of help content that you might want to publish through the help could include:

▸ Standard operating procedures

▸ Terminology and glossaries

▸ A detailed product documentation

All of this information will then be linked into the Help and Enterprise Search allowing users to find it quickly and directly from the application, without a lot of technical work.

10
Web Services and Forms

In this chapter, we will show you how you can use Microsoft InfoPath in conjunction with web services linked to Dynamics AX to create smarter forms. You will also learn the following:

- ▶ Creating a Dynamics AX web service
- ▶ Creating a web service wrapper
- ▶ Using a Dynamics AX web service in an InfoPath form
- ▶ Creating custom OData queries to retrieve Dynamics AX data
- ▶ Building InfoPath lookups using OData queries

Introduction

Web services are a great way for other applications to connect with Dynamics AX, and are also very easy to create and use through the tools that are delivered with Dynamics AX. You can create new web services that you can use to perform updates in the system, and you can also use the standard query services to get data from the database, all through a secure method.

InfoPath is a great Office application that you may already have installed, but not know what you can use it for. It allows you to create forms and documents that can read and update databases, and also use web services to grab and update data. When you combine these two, you will be able to create simpler forms very quickly that the users can use for Dynamics AX without having to be an expert programmer.

In this chapter, we will show you how you can use web services and InfoPath to create a simple update form for Dynamics AX.

Creating a Dynamics AX web service

There are a number of web services that have already been created and deployed with the standard Dynamics AX install. There are a lot more services that you can publish as web services through the AOT in just a matter of minutes, allowing you to access and update almost any area of Dynamics AX from other applications.

In this recipe, we will show you how you can create new web services from within the Dynamics AX development environment.

How to do it...

To create a new web service within Dynamics AX, follow these steps:

1. From within the **AOT** explorer, create a new project for the web service.

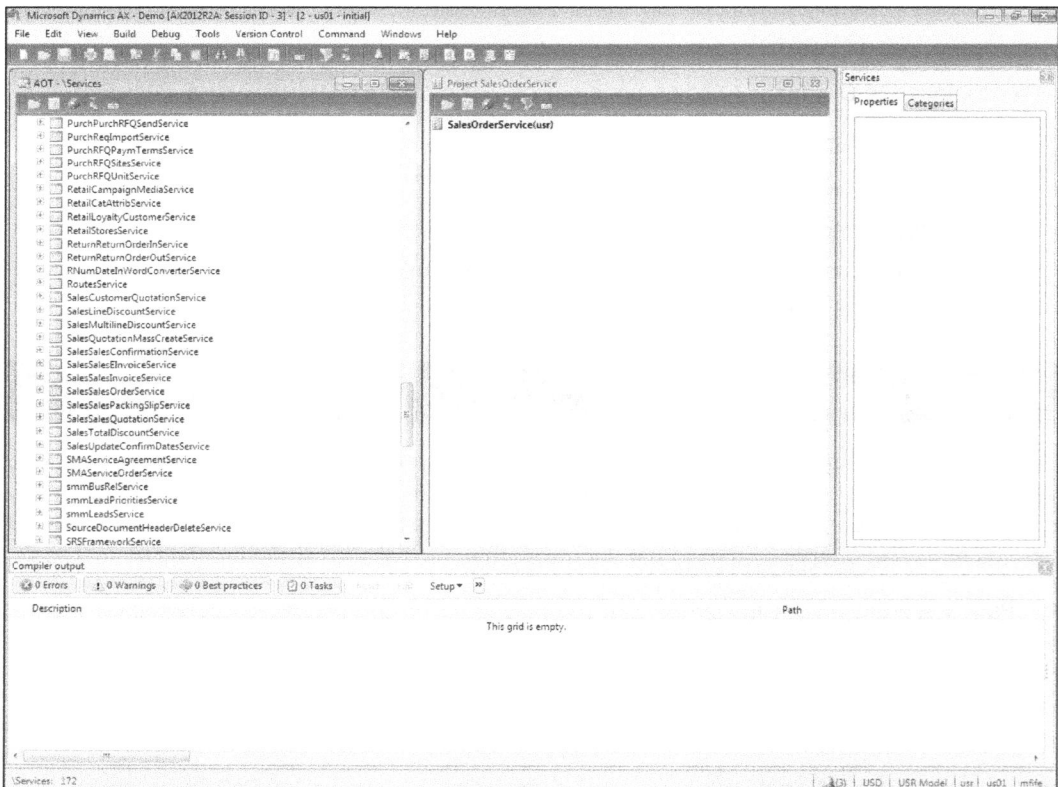

2. From inside the project, right-click on the project name and from the **New** submenu, select **Service Group** to create a new web service group.

3. Rename your service group to be something a little more appropriate. In this case, we are creating a sales order web service; so we will rename it as `SalesOrderService`.

4. From the **AOT** browser, open up the **Services** group, find the service that you want to publish as a web service, and then drag it over onto your new project service group. In this recipe, we selected the **SalesSalesOrderService**, which has all of the logic to create sales orders.

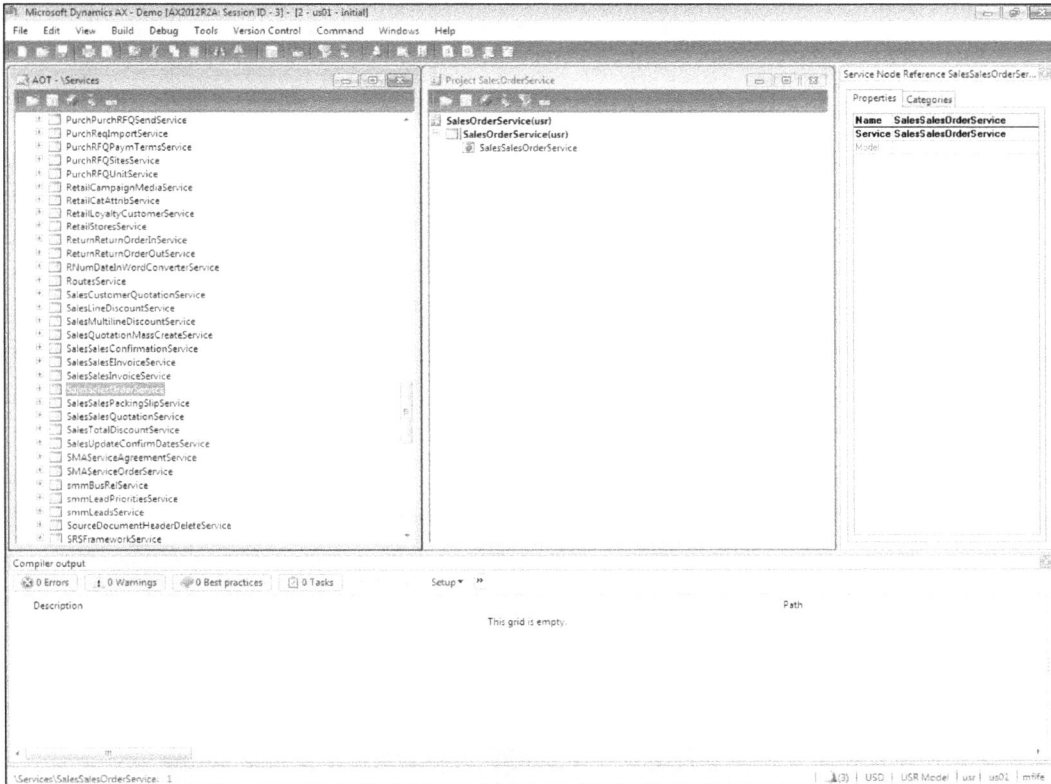

You can continue adding as many services into your service group as you like.

5. When you have finished adding services, right-click on the service group that you created and select the **Deploy Service Group** menu item. This will process the service group and create a web service for you.

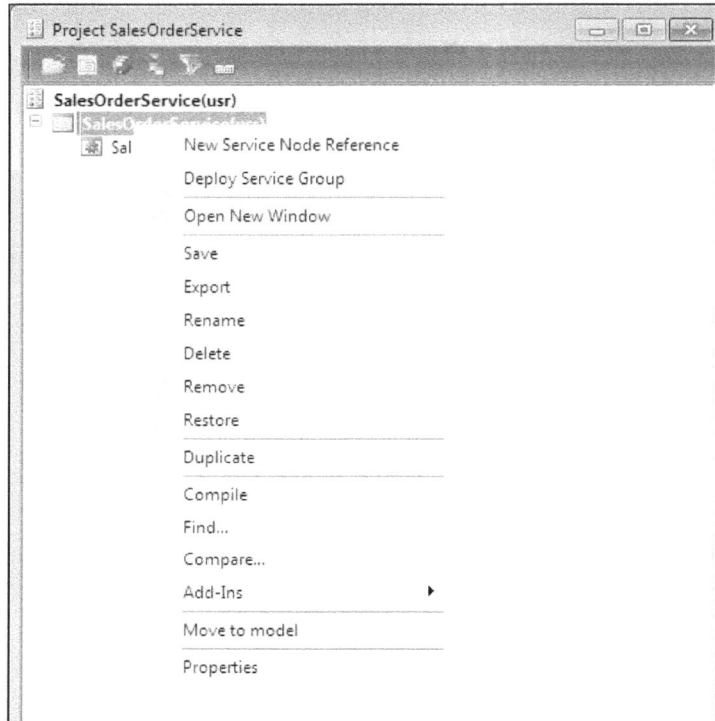

How it works...

To see the web service that was created, open the **Inbound ports** option from the `Services and Application Integration Framework` folder of the **Setup** group in the **System administration** area page.

Your new service should show up there. If you look at the **WSDL URI:** field for the inbound port, you will find the URL for the web service itself.

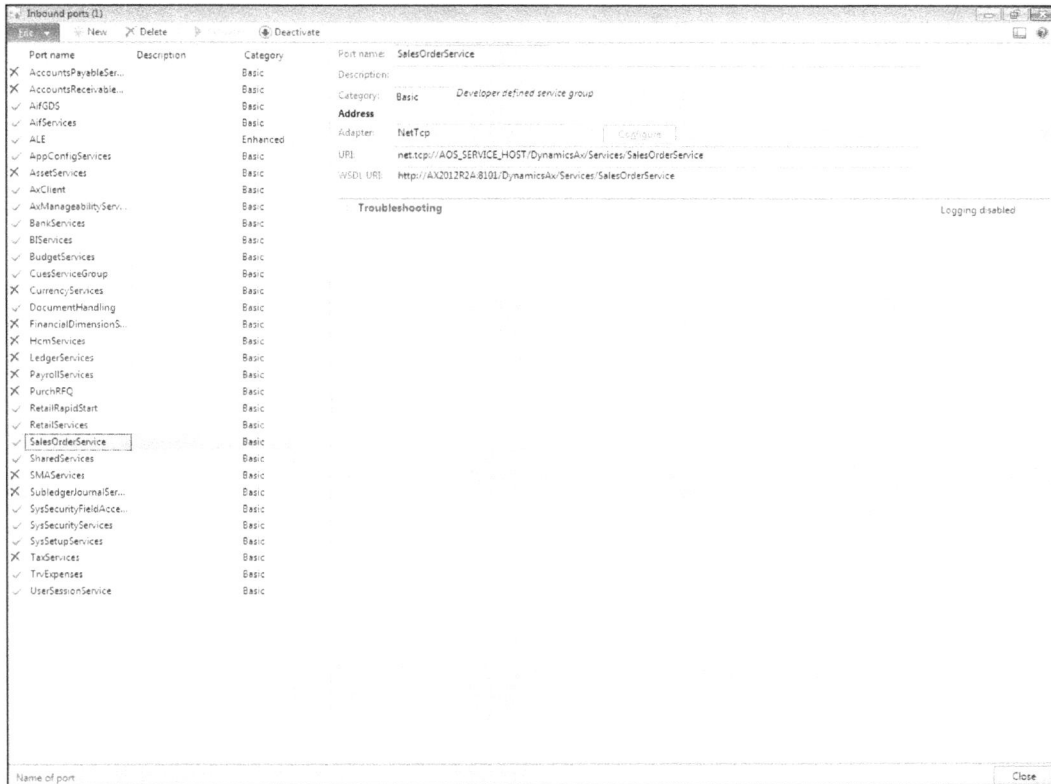

If you browse to that location, you will see the schema for the web service that you will use for other applications to call, in order to update Dynamics AX. For us it's not that user-friendly, but for applications, this is all they need to know.

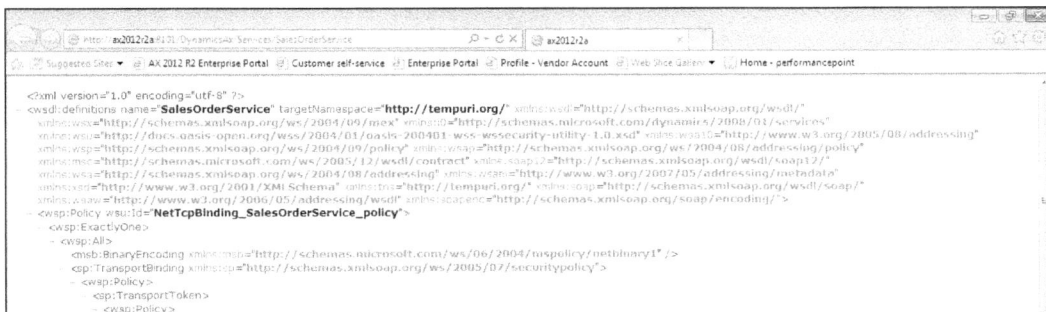

Creating a web service wrapper

The web services that Dynamics AX creates seem to work best for programming interfaces, and sometimes programs have problems with the format of the web service call. InfoPath is one of these programs. So, we need to wrap the Dynamics AX service within a web service wrapper that InfoPath is able to use. This is not as complicated as it sounds though, and you can quickly do this with Visual Studio.

In this recipe, we will show how you can create a web service wrapper through Microsoft Visual Studio that we can use from within InfoPath.

Getting ready

In order to do this you need to have a copy of Visual Studio. We will be using Visual Studio 2010 in our example, but you should be able to create similar web service wrappers using earlier versions as well.

How to do it...

To create a web service wrapper, follow these steps:

1. From within Visual Studio, create a new web project and from the template library, select the **ASP.NET Web Service Application** template.

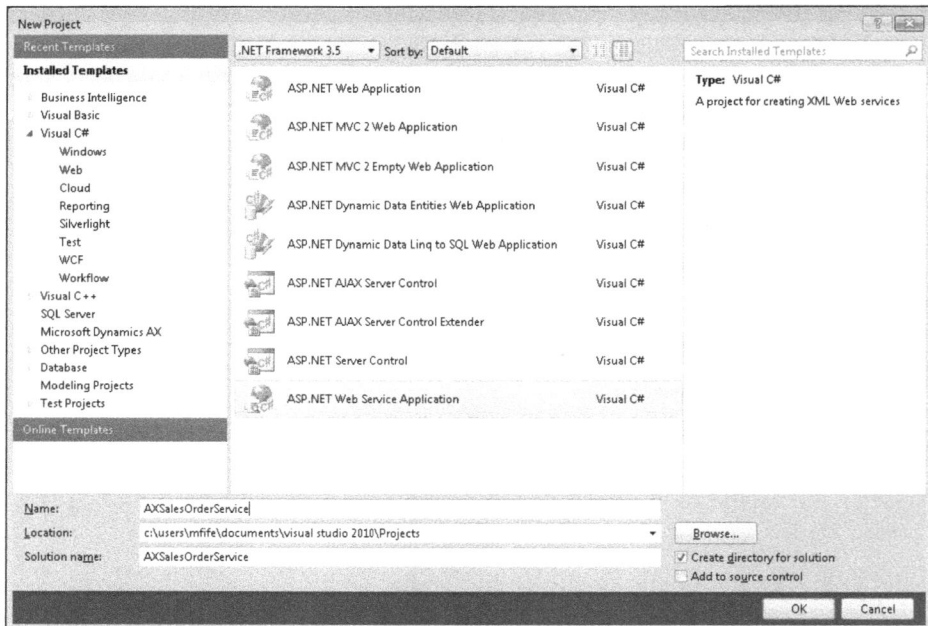

2. This will create your web service shell that will be modified to call the Dynamics AX web service. To link the Dynamics AX web service to our project so that we are able to call it, right-click on the `References` folder in **Solution Explorer** and select the **Add Service Reference...** menu item.

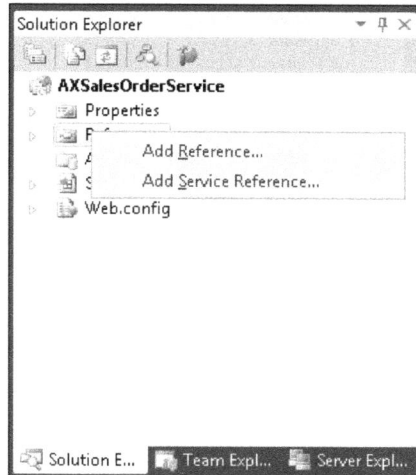

3. From within the **Add Service Reference** dialog box, paste the URL for your Dynamics AX web service and click on the **Go** button. This will allow Visual Studio to discover the web service, and you will be able to see all of the operations that are exposed.

4. Change the name in the **Namespace:** field to match the web service name so that it will be easier to remember in the later steps, and then click on the **OK** button.

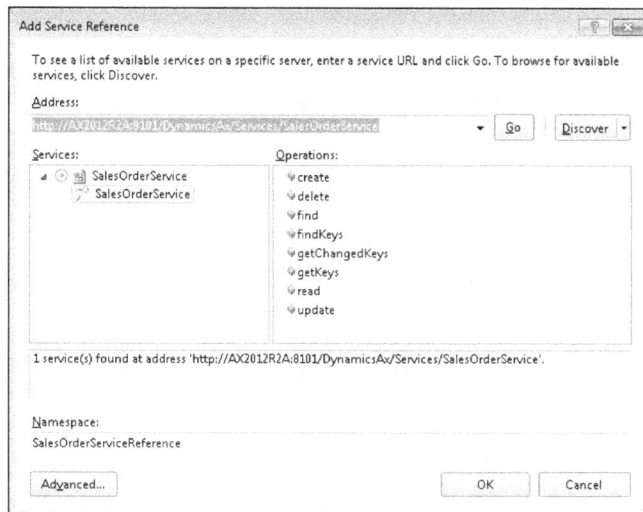

When you return to your web service project, you will be able to see the web service reference in the **Service References** group within **Solution Explorer**.

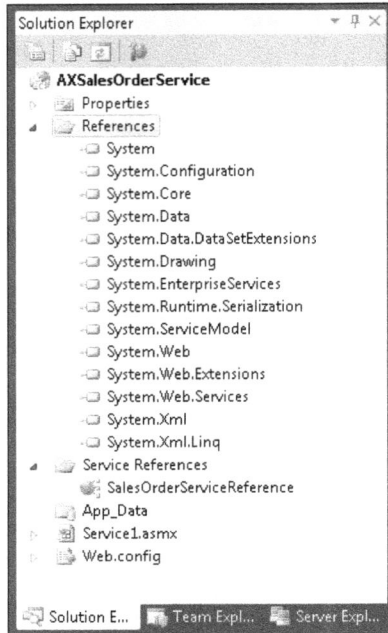

5. Within the header of the web service code, add an entry for your service reference as follows:

```
using AXSalesOrderService.SalesOrderServiceReference;
```

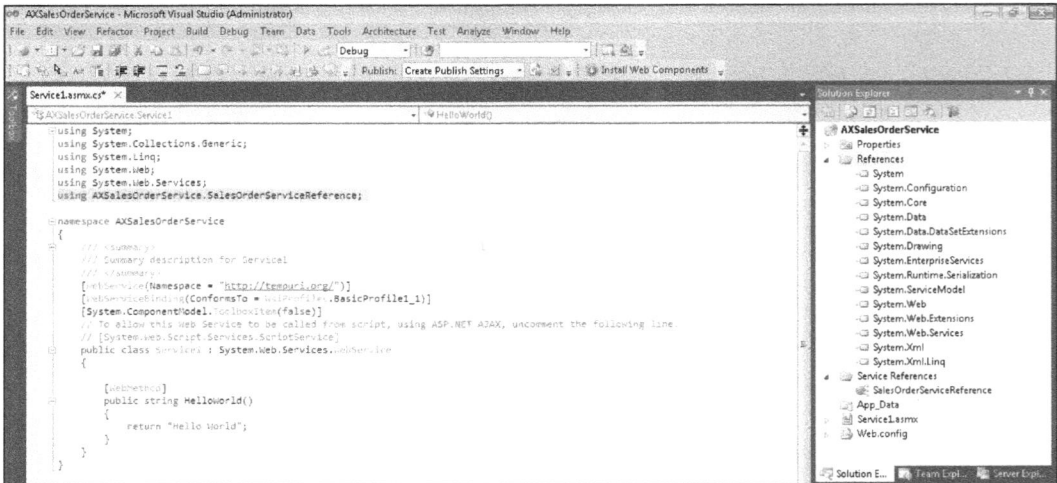

6. Now, replace the `HelloWorld` web method code that is added to the web service by default with the following code that will use the web service to create a new sales order:

```
[WebMethod]
public string NewSalesOrder(
        string company,
        string language,
        string custAccount,
        string PONumber,
        string itemID,
        decimal salesQty,
        string salesUnit
        )
{
      SalesOrderServiceClient client = new
SalesOrderServiceClient();
      AxdSalesOrder salesOrder = new AxdSalesOrder();
      AxdEntity_SalesTable salesTable = new AxdEntity_
SalesTable();
      AxdEntity_SalesLine salesLine = new AxdEntity_
SalesLine();
      CallContext callContext = new CallContext();
      EntityKey[] keys;
      EntityKey key;
      KeyField fld;
      salesTable.CustAccount = custAccount;
      salesTable.ReceiptDateRequested = new DateTime(2013,
03, 20);
      salesLine.ItemId = itemID;
      salesLine.SalesQty = salesQty;
      salesLine.SalesUnit = salesUnit;
      salesTable.SalesLine = new AxdEntity_SalesLine[] {
salesLine };
      salesTable.PurchOrderFormNum = PONumber;
      salesTable.SalesType = AxdEnum_SalesType.Sales;
      salesOrder.SalesTable = new AxdEntity_SalesTable[] {
salesTable };
      callContext.Company = company;
      callContext.Language = language;
      keys = client.create(callContext, salesOrder);
      key = keys[0];
      fld = key.KeyData[0];
      return fld.ToString();
}
```

You can see this in the following screenshot:

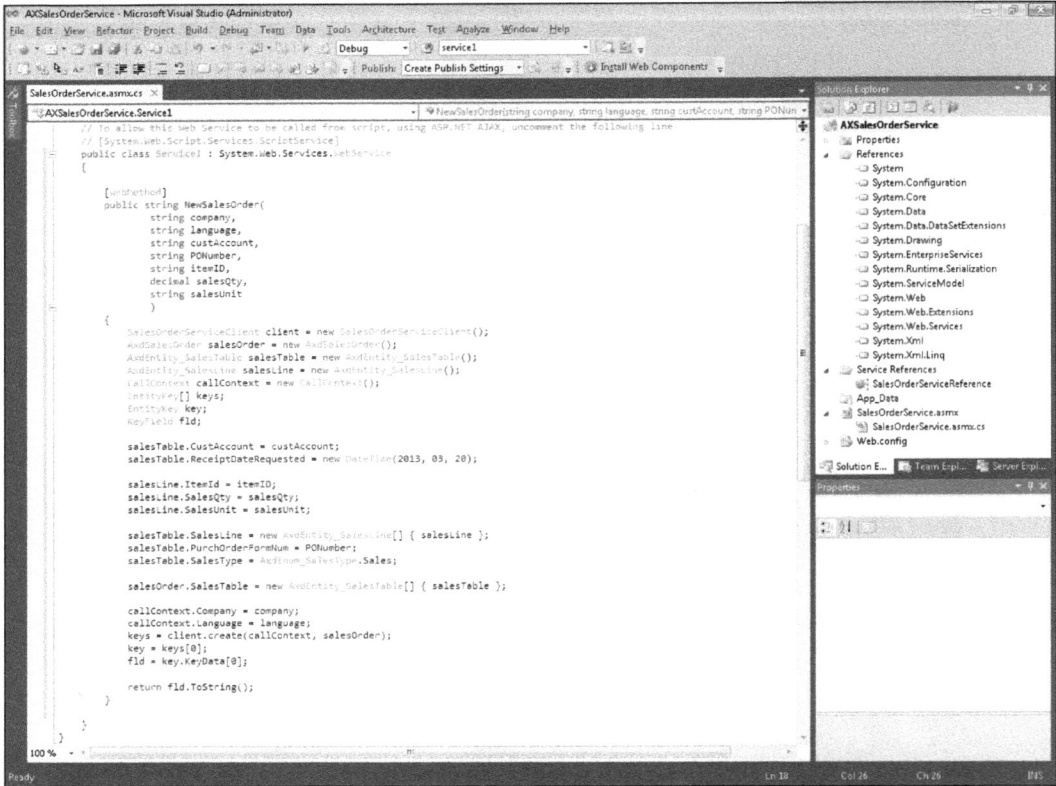

7. Then, compile your web service.

How it works...

When you compile your program and run it, you will be taken to the web interface for the new web service showing all of the methods that you've exposed.

If you click on the **NewSalesOrder** web service call, you will be able to see all the parameters that are required to perform the web service.

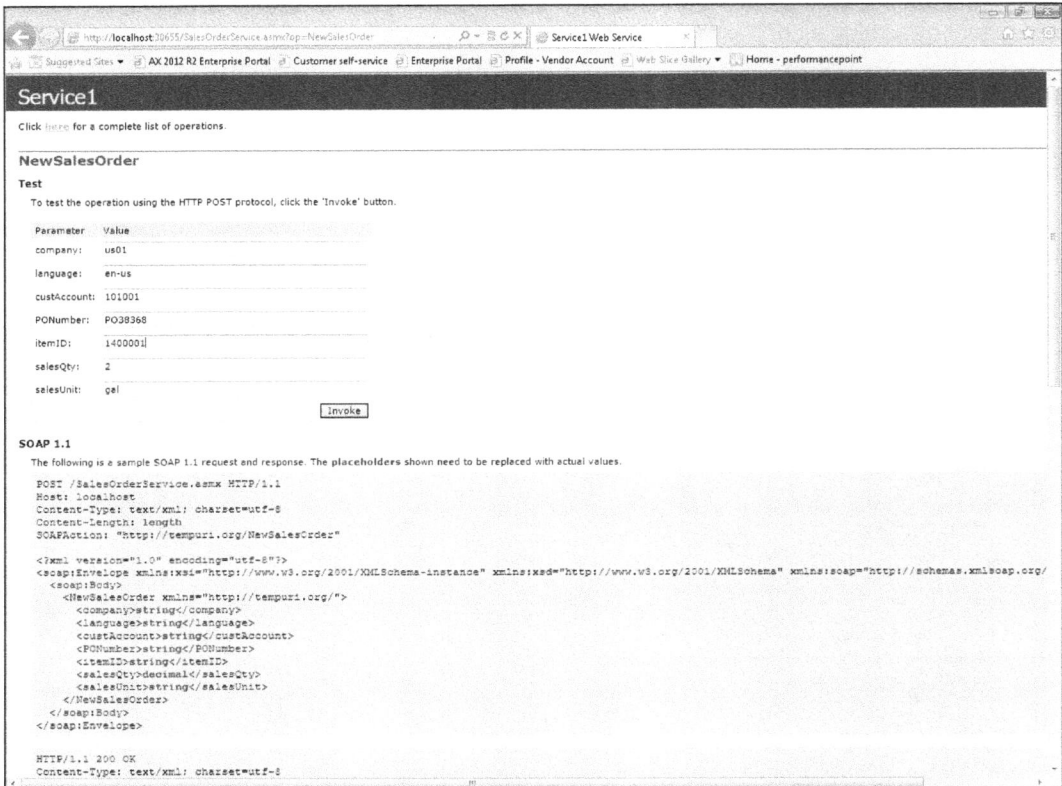

You can test your web service by filling in the parameters and then clicking on **Invoke**. This will perform the web service and return with the results of the call.

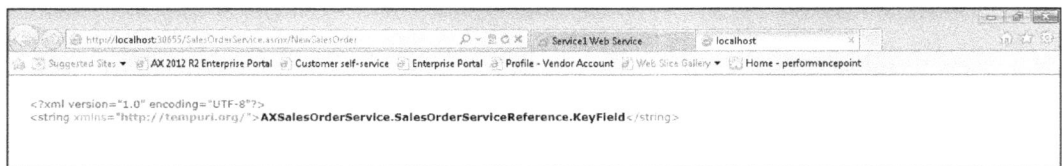

With a little bit of extra code, you can have the web service return back the order number as well.

To double-check if that everything worked, you can open up Dynamics AX and you should be able to see the new sales order.

Using a Dynamics AX web service in an InfoPath form

InfoPath allows you to quickly create data entry forms that can be saved locally, to SharePoint, and also update data in databases. Additionally, it is able to connect to web services and send and receive data through that channel as well. So once we have a web service wrapper built that links to Dynamics AX, we can create a form that will send information to it in order to add and update data.

In this recipe, we will show how you can create an InfoPath form that uses a Dynamics AX web service wrapper to publish information.

Getting ready

For this recipe, you need to make sure that you have InfoPath installed, since it is usually part of Office Professional Plus or Office 365. Just check that it shows up within the Microsoft Office program group.

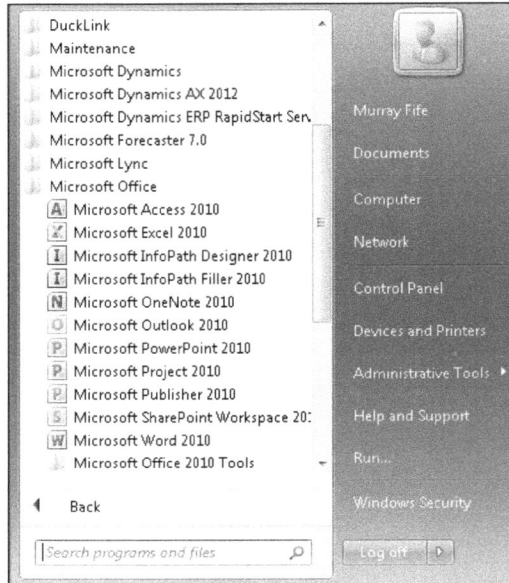

How to do it...

To use a web service within an InfoPath form, follow these steps:

1. Within the InfoPath designer, create a new form and select the **Web Service** template.

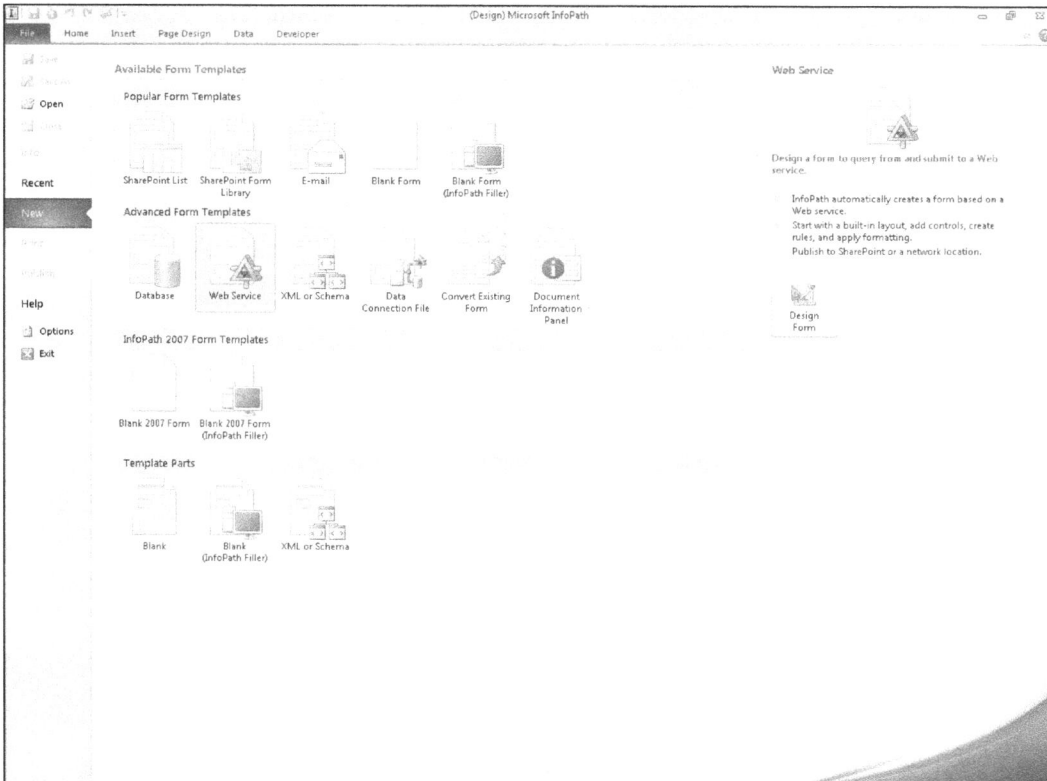

2. This will automatically open up the **Data Connection Wizard**. Select the **Submit** data option, since our example will be sending information to the web service to update Dynamics AX, and then click on **Next**.

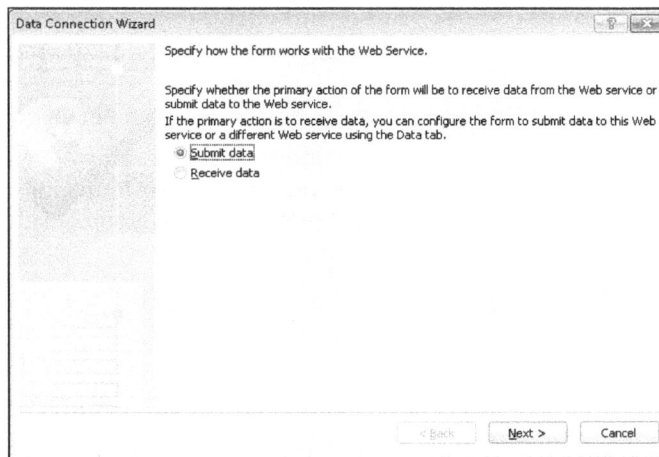

3. When asked for the web service, type in the URL for the **WSDL (Web Services Description Language)** of your web service wrapper and click on **Next**.

> If you don't know how to find the WSDL, just open up the web service that you are calling from InfoPath, and at the top of the page will be a link for **Service Description**. If you click on that, it will take you to the WSDL page.
>
> The URL for this page is the one that you will want to paste into the **Web Service:** field on the **Data Connection Wizard**.

4. If your web service has multiple operations published against it, you will see all of them listed in the next step in the wizard. Select the web service operation that you want your InfoPath form to use when submitting data and click on **Next**.

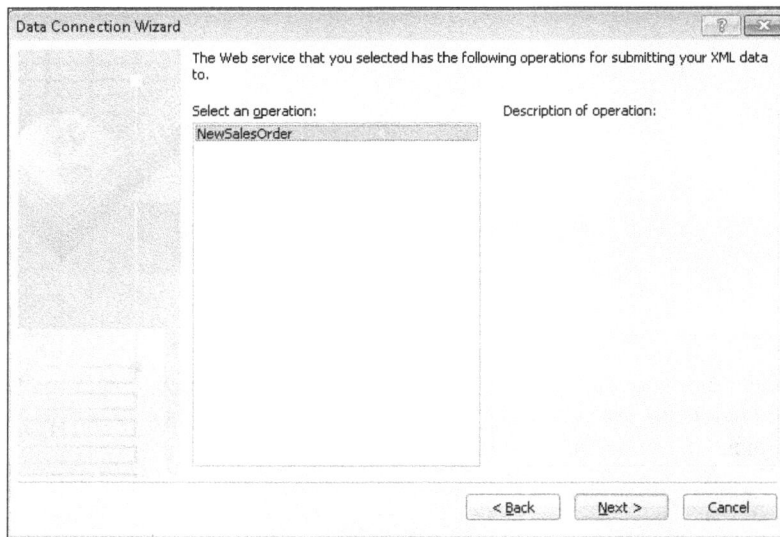

5. Finally, give your data connection a name and click on the **Finish** button.

6. Once the data connection is created, the web service parameters will show up as fields within the **Fields** browser. You can add them to the form individually by dragging and dropping them over, or you can just grab the whole group of fields and drag them onto the form.

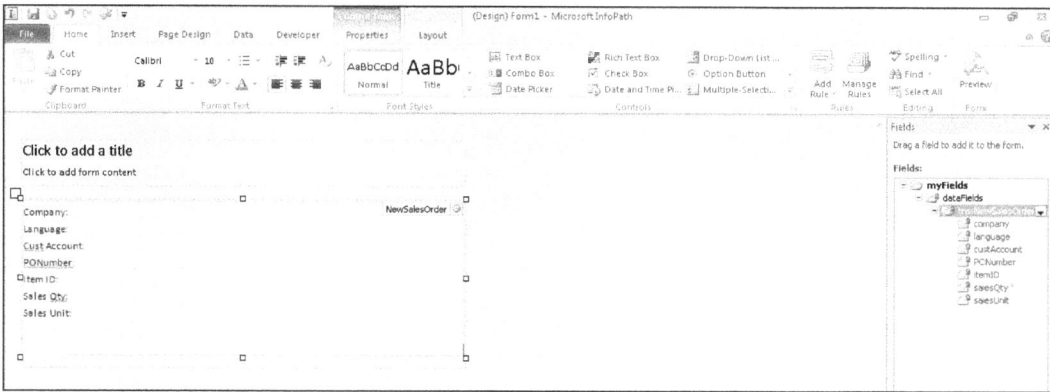

7. To default values in particular fields so that the user doesn't have to type in the values every time, select the **Properties** menu item after right-clicking on the field in the **Fields** browser. This will open up the **Field or Group Properties** window and you can specify the default value in the **Value:** field.

> In our example, we will default the **Company:** and **Language:** fields.

How it works...

To see the form in action, click on the **Preview** button on the **Home** ribbon bar.

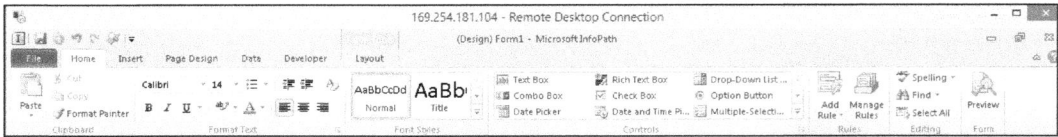

This will open up the form in edit mode and you can fill in the remaining fields. To send the data to Dynamics AX, click on the **Submit** button in the **Home** ribbon bar.

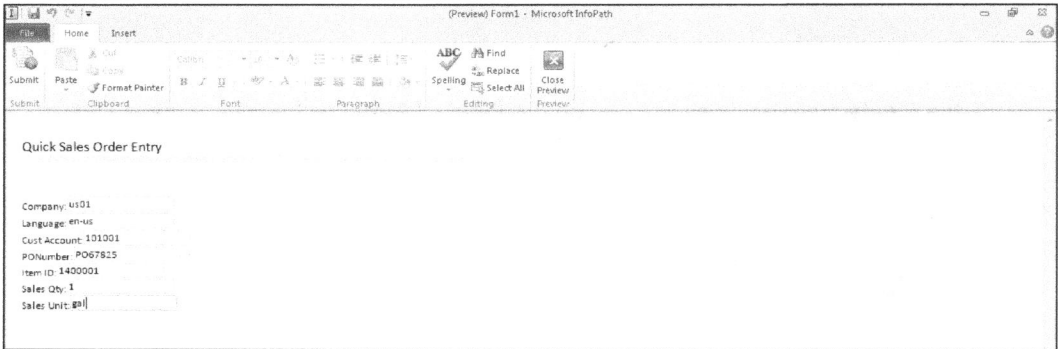

Quick Sales Order Entry

Company: us01
Language: en-us
Cust Account: 101001
PONumber: PO67825
Item ID: 1400001
Sales Qty: 1
Sales Unit: gal

Now, you should be able to see a new order within Dynamics AX that was created by your new InfoPath form.

Creating custom OData queries to retrieve Dynamics AX data

Dynamics AX has a more generic web service call feature called **OData Query** that allows you to query tables and return them through a URL. This is useful because they can be used as read-only data sources for other programs such as InfoPath.

In this recipe, we will show how you can register your own custom query within Dynamics AX, and then access it through the OData Query web service.

How to do it...

To create an OData query, follow these steps:

1. To access a query through the OData Query feature, we open the **Document data sources** form from the **Organization Administration** area page within the `Document Management` folder of the **Setup** group.

2. To create a new query, click on the **New** button in the menu bar.

3. The **Document data sources** reference the queries that are built within AOT. Usually, you don't have to build a whole new query because you can use one of the existing ones as a basis. Select a module that you would like the data source to be associated with, and then select **Custom Query** for the data source type. If you just want to query the table with no filter, you could select the **Query Reference** option, but we want to filter the data before it's sent to us.

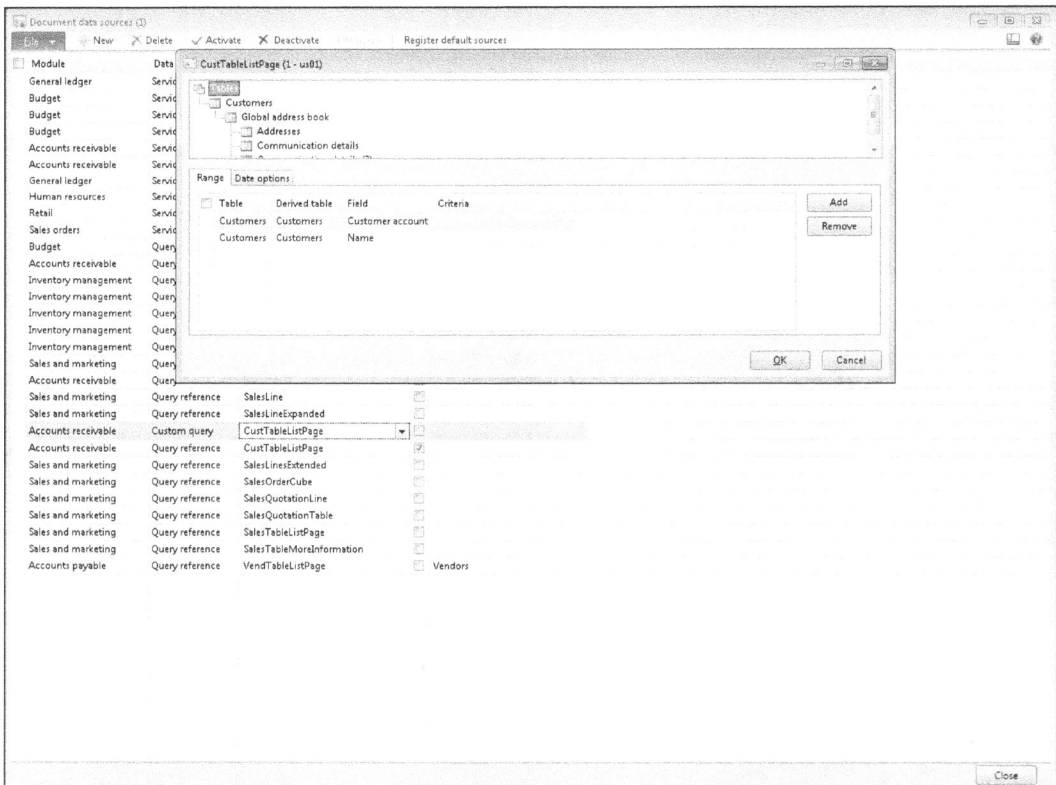

4. In the **Data source name** field, select the query that you want to publish as an OData Query. In this recipe we want a list of customers; so the **CustTableListPage** works for us.

5. On selecting the data source name, AX will open up a query panel, where we can add whatever filters we want, and then we can click on **OK** to save.

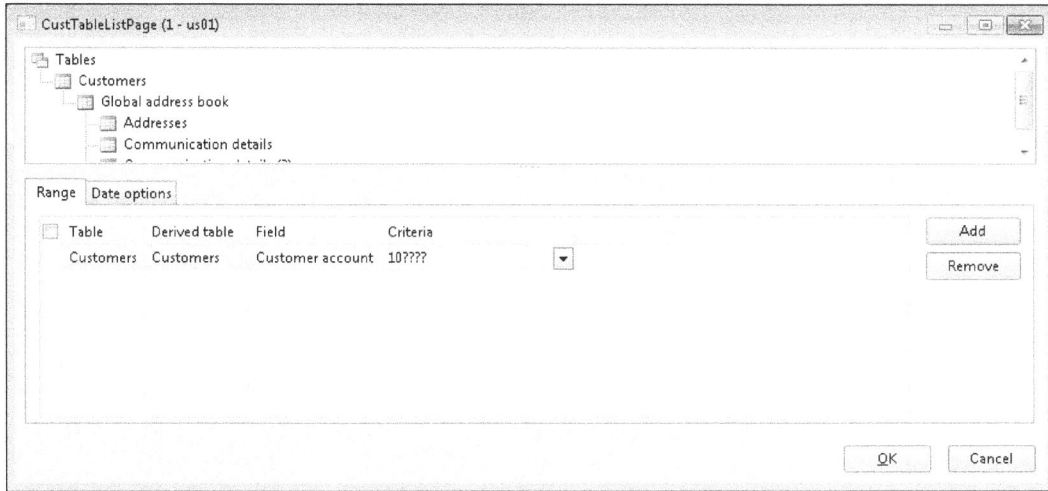

6. You may want to change the data source name to help you recognize what it is associated with, and then maybe add a description.

7. Finally, to enable the document data source to be used in the queries, select the **Activated** checkbox.

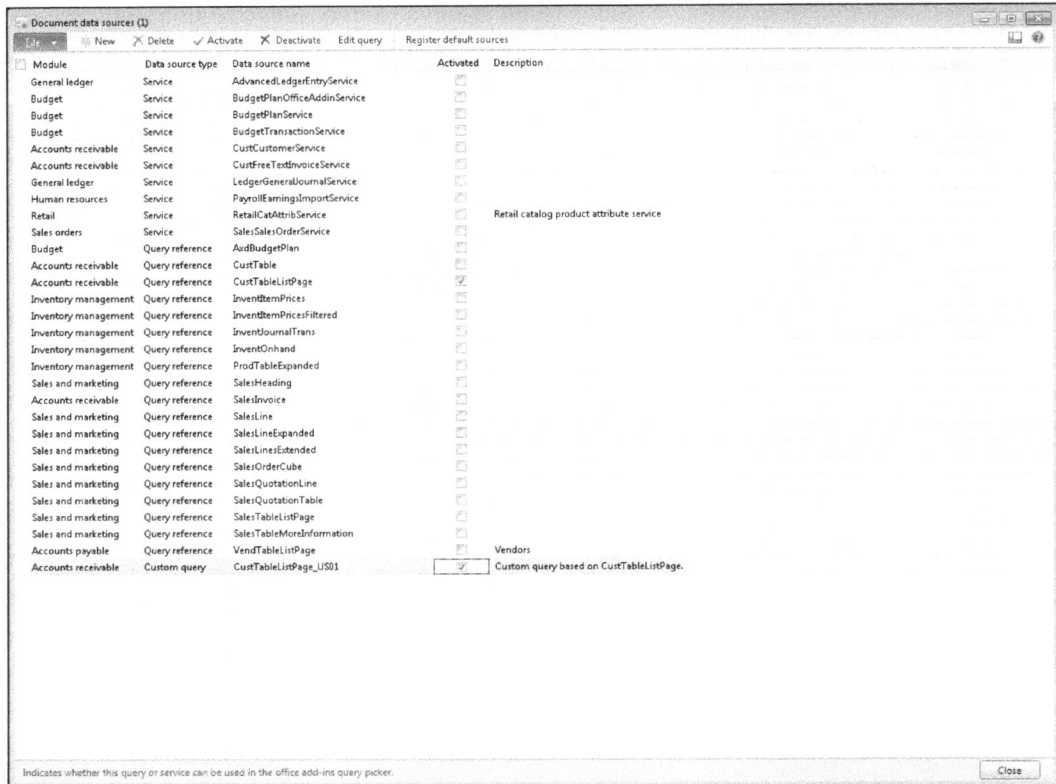

For the following example, we also need to create a second document data source that queries the **EcoResProductListPage**, to return back all of the products in the database.

How it works...

Now that the query is published as a document data source, you can access it through a URL with this format: `http://localhost:8101/DynamicsAx/Services/ODataQueryService/CustTableListPage_US01`.

It will return back all of the data.

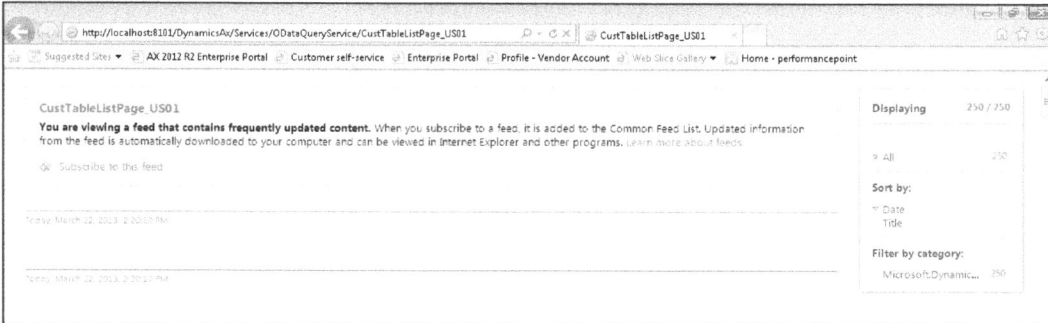

Building InfoPath lookups using OData queries

A feature of InfoPath that makes forms even more useful is the ability to allow fields to be populated with dynamic data coming from static lists, databases, and also web data sources, so that users do not have to remember field values such as part codes and customer numbers. Since you are able to query Dynamics AX data through web queries, we can use these queries to create dynamic lookups in our forms.

In this recipe, we will show how you can turn text fields into drop-down lists that use OData queries as a data source.

How to do it...

To use an OData query as a data source for a field, follow these steps:

1. We need to first define the data source. To do this, select the **From XML File** option in the **From Other Sources** menu in the **Get External Data** group of the **Data** ribbon bar in the form designer.

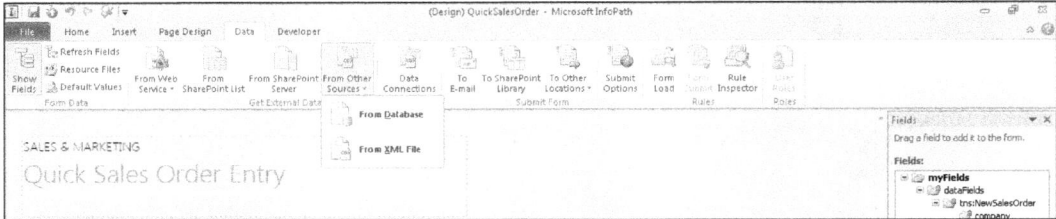

2. When the **Data Connection Wizard** pops up, paste the URL for the OData query that you want to use as a data source and click on **Next**.

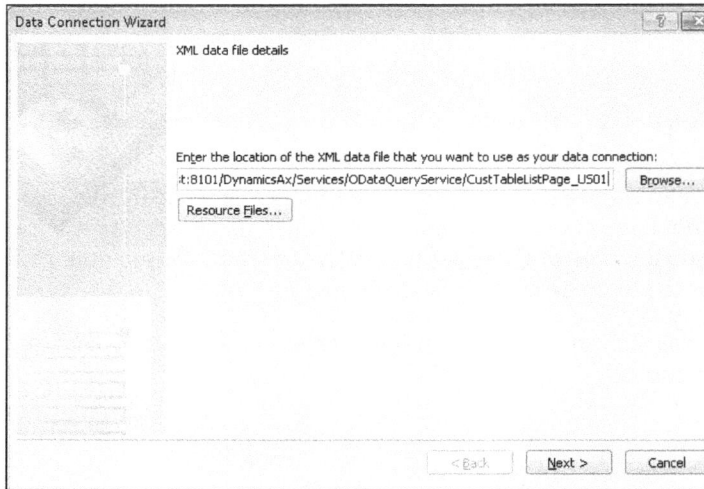

3. To store the data source with the form, select the **Include...** option from the data source location section and click on **Next**.

4. Finally, give your data source a name and click on **Finish**.

5. To use the data source within a field, first you need to change the field's control type to one that will show the data. To do this, right-click on the field and select the **Drop-Down List Box** option from the **Change Control** submenu.

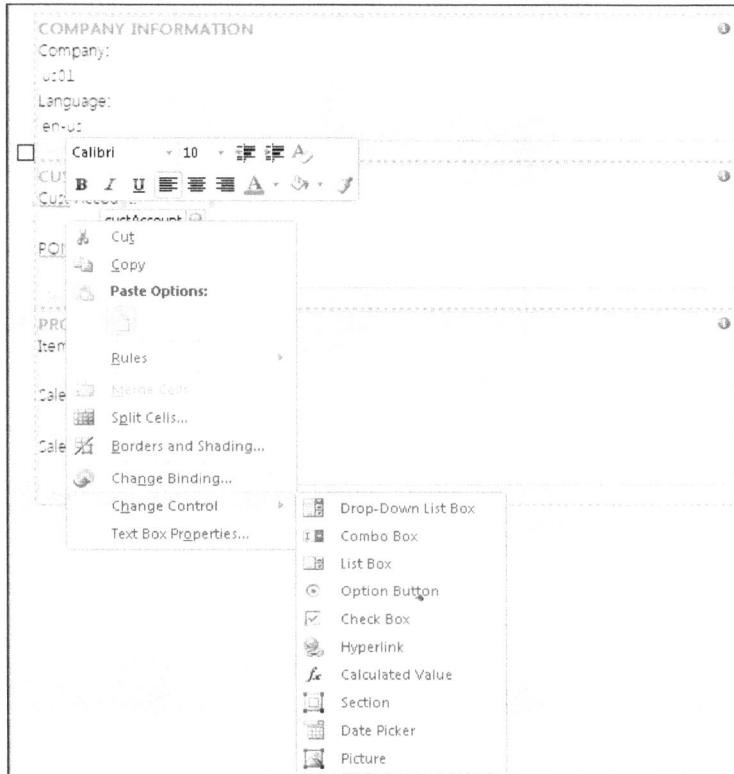

6. Once the control has been changed, right-click on the field again and select the **Drop-Down List Properties** option.

7. Change the **List box** choice from **Enter choice manually** to **Get choice from an external data source** and from the **Data source** dropdown, you will be able to find the XML data source that you just created.

8. To specify what data is shown in the drop-down box, click on the tree navigation icon to the right of the **Entries** field. When the XML tree navigator is displayed, find the **content** node and select it. Selecting the `content` node will make our drop-down box filter out the metadata information in the XML file that is returned from the OData query, so that we can see all the real records.

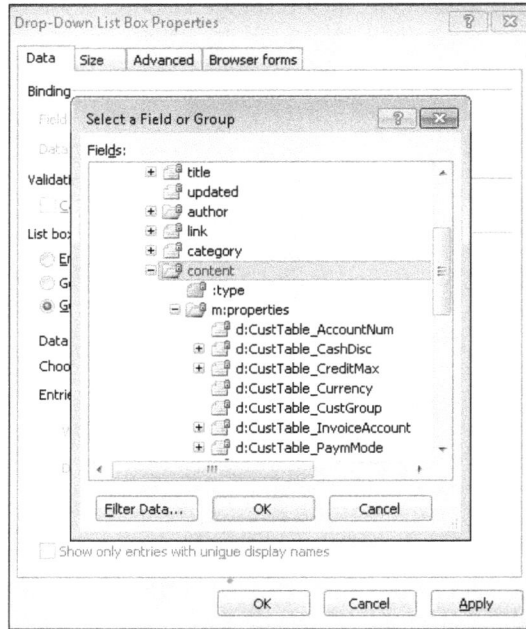

9. Next, click on the tree navigation icon to the right of the **Value:** and **Display name:** fields and select the fields that you want to store in the form, and also to be displayed in the dropdown. This will open up the XML tree navigator again and you can select any of the fields from the query.

10. Finally, you may want to select the **Show only entries with unique display names** checkbox to filter out any duplicates, and then click on **OK**.

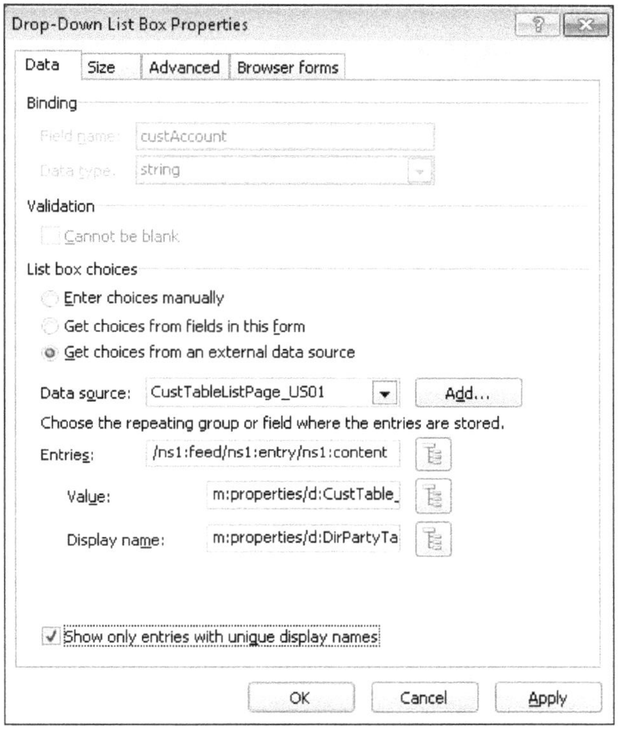

Drop-Down List Box Properties

Data | Size | Advanced | Browser forms

Binding

Field name: custAccount

Data type: string

Validation

☐ Cannot be blank

List box choices

○ Enter choices manually

○ Get choices from fields in this form

◉ Get choices from an external data source

Data source: CustTableListPage_US01 ▾ [Add...]

Choose the repeating group or field where the entries are stored.

Entries: /ns1:feed/ns1:entry/ns1:content [⬚]

Value: m:properties/d:CustTable_ [⬚]

Display name: m:properties/d:DirPartyTa [⬚]

☑ Show only entries with unique display names

[OK] [Cancel] [Apply]

How it works...

Now when you preview the form, all the customer information will be populated for you to pick from.

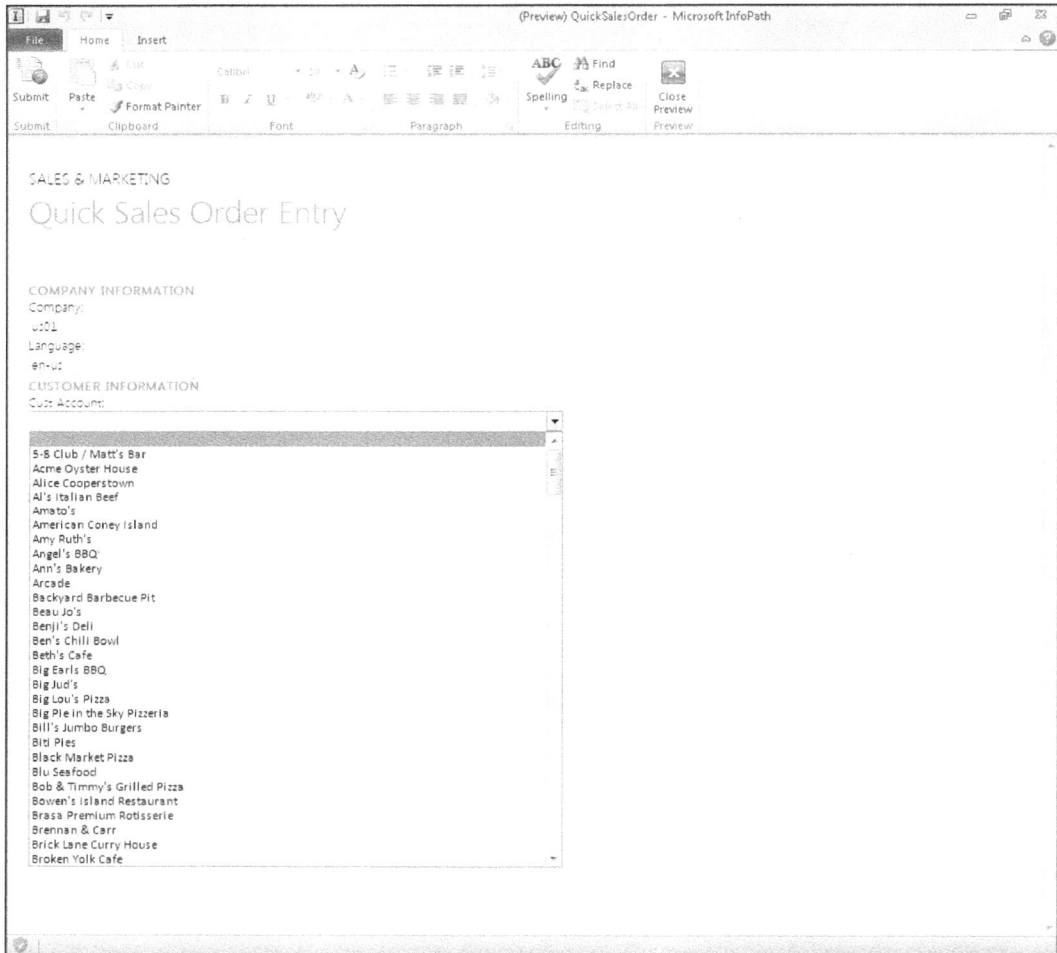

By changing the layout of the InfoPath form to have a little bit of a larger font, adding some formatting columns to the body of the form, changing the drop-down fields to list selections, and adding a submit image, we can create a kiosk form that is populated from Dynamics AX, and also create sales orders based on the selections.

Summary

InfoPath is an incredibly useful tool for creating forms and gathering information. When you use it in conjunction with Dynamics AX and just a little bit of coding, it becomes even more useful because you are able to create forms that feed back into the database.

In addition to what we showed you in this chapter, you can also:

▶ Publish your forms to a SharePoint Forms repository allowing users to access the latest form templates from a centralized location. If you change the template on SharePoint, the users' local copies will also be upgraded ensuring that they always have the latest version.

▶ Host the InfoPath forms on a SharePoint site, allowing users to fill in the forms without even having InfoPath installed. This allows you to create forms that customers, vendors, or employees could fill out that could update Dynamics AX.

► Capture signatures through pen-based input devices such as tablets and Surface devices. The signatures can be stored as JPEG files and even posted to the Dynamics AX attachments if you are clever enough.

► Publish the InfoPath forms to SharePoint rather than Dynamics AX, while still indexing the document against the key Dynamics AX fields. These document libraries could be linked to records just like the traditional file document libraries that were shown in the earlier chapters.

Other ideas on where you may want to capture information through InfoPath forms could include:

► Sales people using them to capture store survey information. Pictures from Surface devices could be added to the InfoPath form data as image attachments.

► Logging of quality issues as Cases within Dynamics AX by mobile users without having to log in to be tethered to a normal PC.

► Capturing lead and prospect information through a simple table-based form.

► Simple inquires such as customer details through web-based forms.

Who would have guessed that such an overlooked product could be so useful!

11
Role Center Personalization and Customization

In this chapter, we will show some of the ways that you can extend out Role Centers by creating new templates, and also how to use some of the in-built web parts to add more information for the users. You will also learn the following:

- ▸ Creating a new Role Center template
- ▸ Creating a new Dynamics AX user profile
- ▸ Adding cues to Role Center profiles
- ▸ Adding cues through the Advanced Filter editor
- ▸ Adding RSS feeds to Role Centers
- ▸ Removing the ribbon bar from Role Centers
- ▸ Removing the navigation bar from Role Centers
- ▸ Embedding Role Centers into Outlook

Introduction

Role Centers give users a single dashboard where they can see all the information that is relevant to them, and it is usually the first thing that they see when they open up Dynamics AX. The flexibility of Role Centers also makes them a very powerful business tool, since the users are able to tweak what they see themselves, and also administrators are able to tweak default Role Center views to deliver the correct information to the users.

In this chapter, we will look at some of the ways that you can extend the Role Centers to better match your business, show how you can tweak the information displayed on Role Centers, and also show some alternative ways that the Role Centers can be used outside the normal Dynamics AX client.

Creating a new Role Center template

Dynamics AX comes prepackaged with over 40 standard Role Centers for a lot of the normal user types that you would expect to see within an organization—CFO, Salesperson, AP Clerk, and so forth. But if you have unique roles within your organization that don't fit the standard roles, Dynamics AX allows you to create your own Role Center template.

In this recipe we will show you how to do just that.

Getting ready

In order to create a Role Center template, you will need to have designer rights to SharePoint. If you don't have these rights, talk to your SharePoint administrator and they should be able to help you.

How to do it...

To create a new Role Center template, follow these steps:

1. Open up the Enterprise portal and from the **Site Actions** menu, click on the **View All Site Content** menu item.

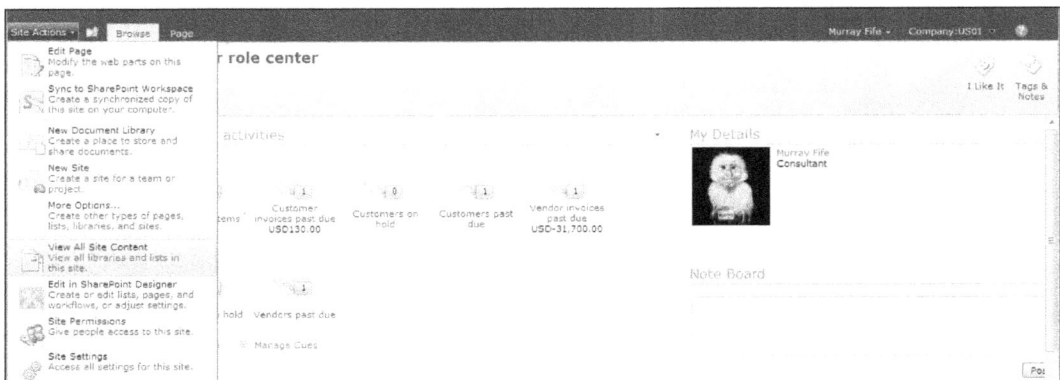

2. This will show you all the site content. All Role Center templates are stored in the **Enterprise Portal** document library. Click on that to open up the library. If you browse through the files there, you will be able to find all the Role Centers. They are easy to spot and all begin with **RoleCenter**.

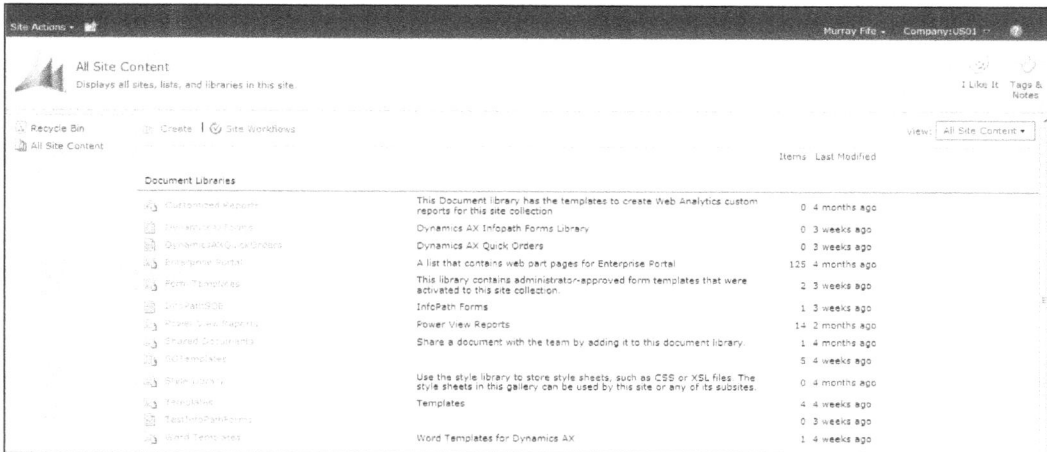

3. From the **Documents** tab on the ribbon bar, click on the **New Document** menu item to create a new template.

4. Give your Role Center template a name. You can change the layout of the template, but it is best just to use the default one.

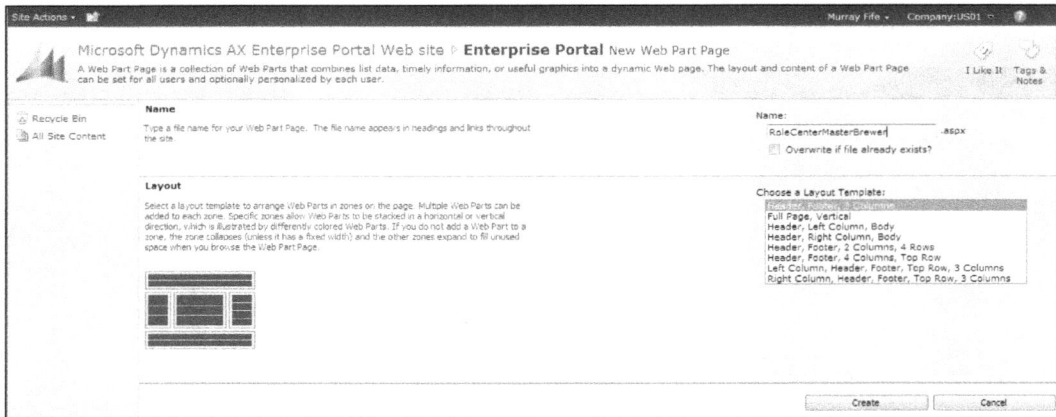

5. After the new Role Center template is created, you will be taken to the edit mode for the page.

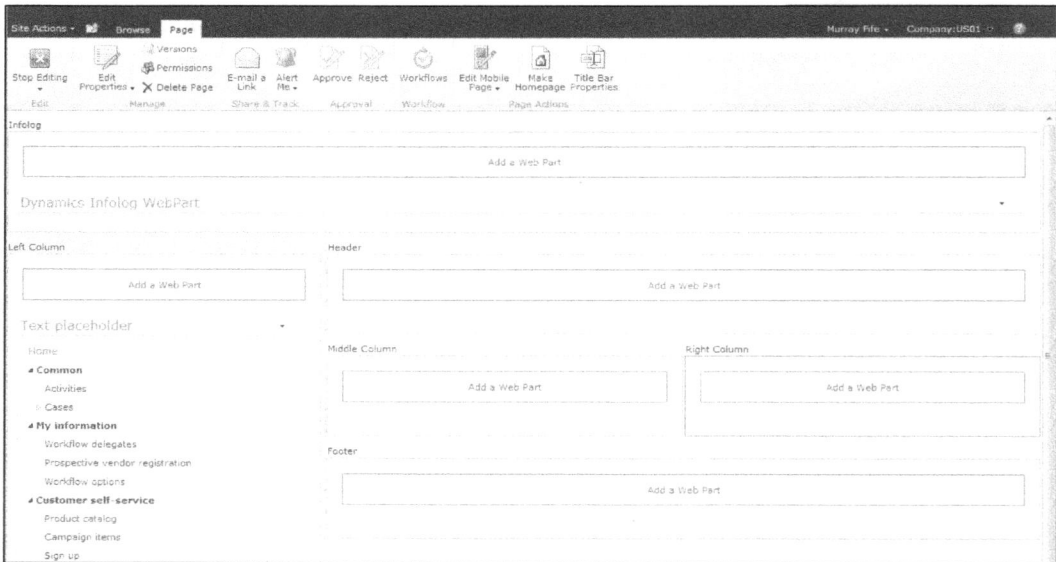

6. If you click on the **Add a Web Part** link on any of the columns, you will be taken to the web part catalog, where you can select any of the standard web parts delivered with SharePoint and also Dynamics AX. Select the **Cues** web part from within the **Microsoft Dynamics AX** category and click on the **Add** button.

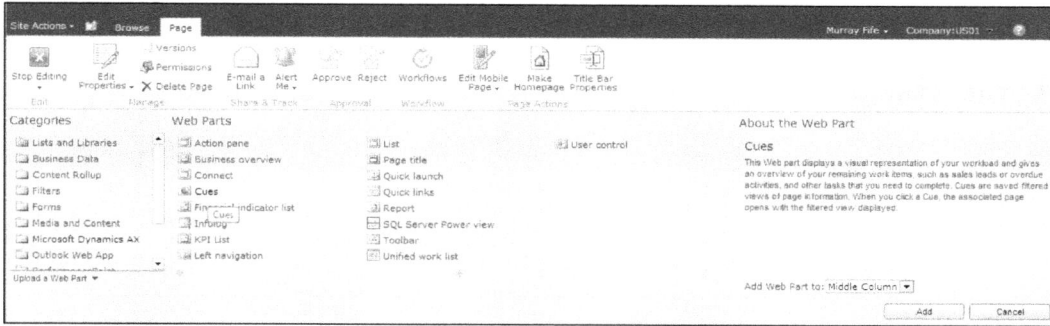

7. You can continue adding web parts until you are satisfied with the template. Then, click on the **Stop Editing** button on the ribbon bar.

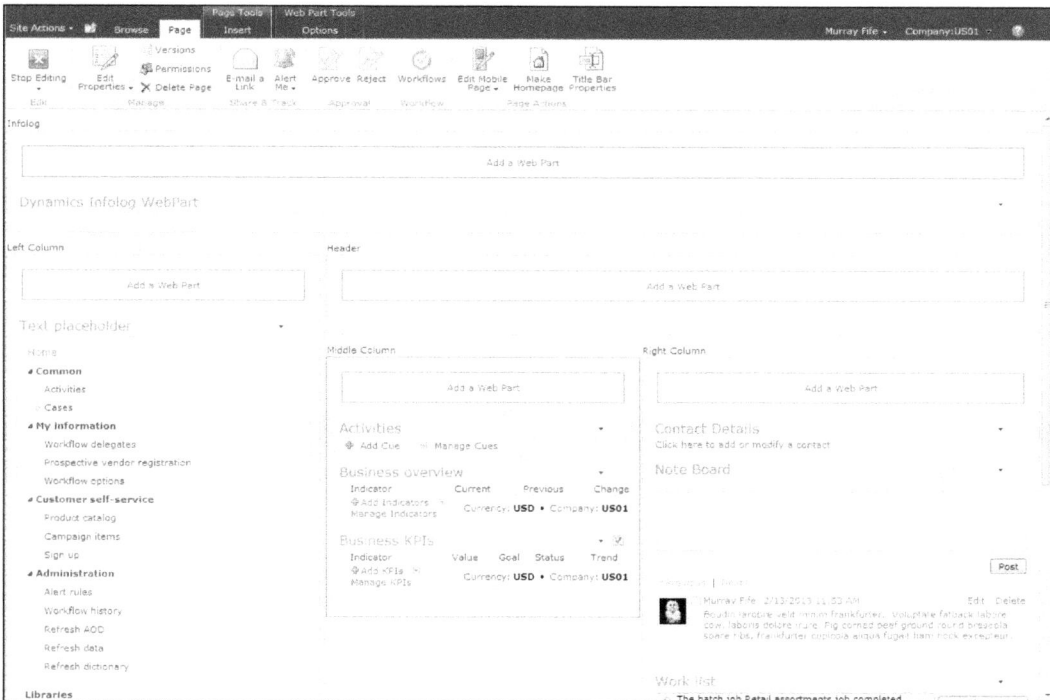

How it works...

This process will create a new template site for you that users are able to access.

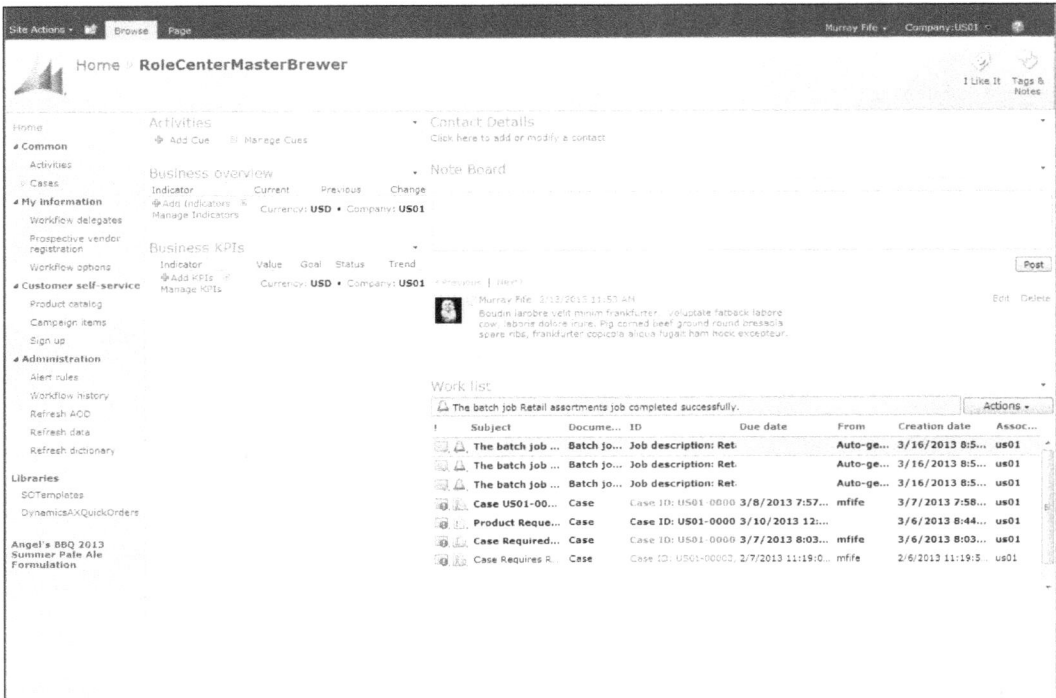

Creating a new Dynamics AX user profile

The Role Center template that is used as the default for a user is associated with the user's profile. For a user to take advantage of the new Role Center that you build, you need to create a new user profile.

In this recipe, we will show you the steps that you need to perform to create a new user profile that is linked to a new Role Center template.

How to do it...

To create a new user profile, follow these steps:

1. First, you need to create a menu item for the Role Center within AOT. To do this, create a new development project for the menu item.
2. Within the project, add a new **URL** object from the **Web** group.

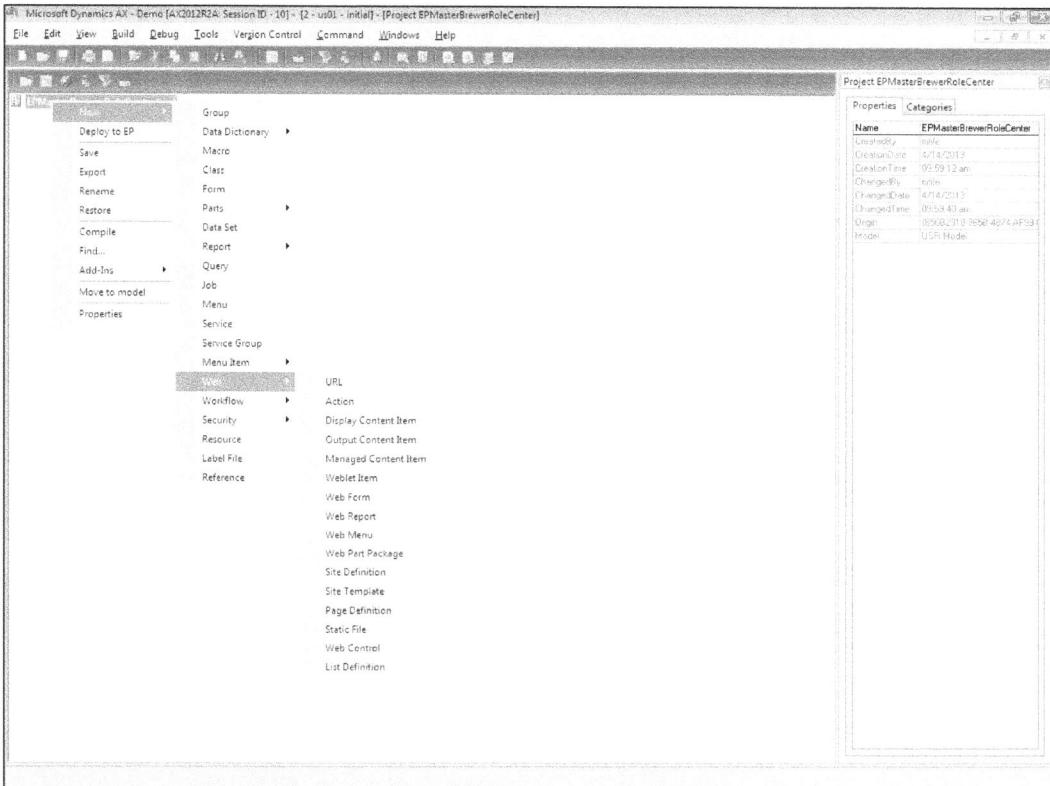

3. Give the object a name, label, and help text.

4. Within the **URL** field, type in the relative path for the Role Center that you created. It will probably be similar to the following: `/Enterprise Portal/ RoleCenterName.aspx`.

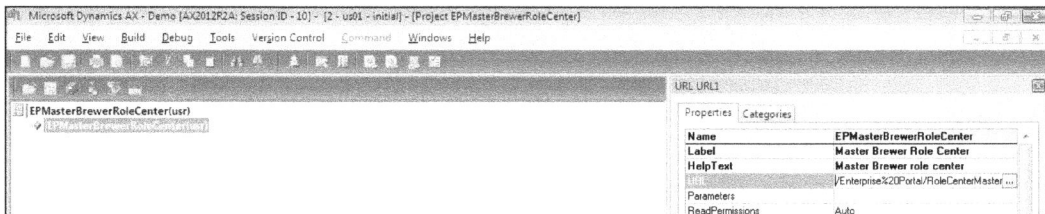

5. Also, make sure that you set the **HomePage** field to **Yes**.

6. Now we need to create a new user profile. From the **System administration** area page, click on the **User profile** menu item in the **Common** group in the `Users` folder. This will open up a list of all the user profiles in the system.

7. Click on the **New** button to create a new record.

8. You can give your new profile an ID and description. Then from the drop-down box in the **Role center** field, you should be able to find the new Role Center menu that you just created.

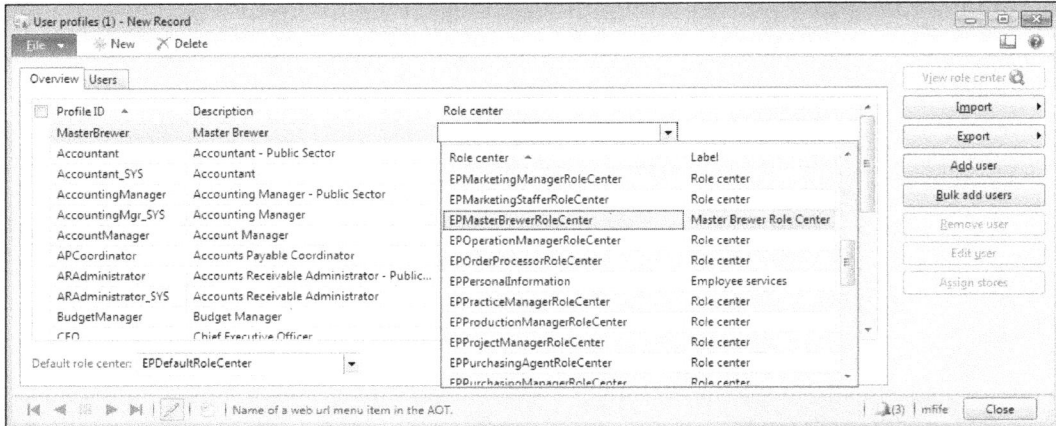

9. If you click on the Users tab, you will be able to see the users are assigned to the selected role. In this case it will be blank. Click on the **Add user** button.

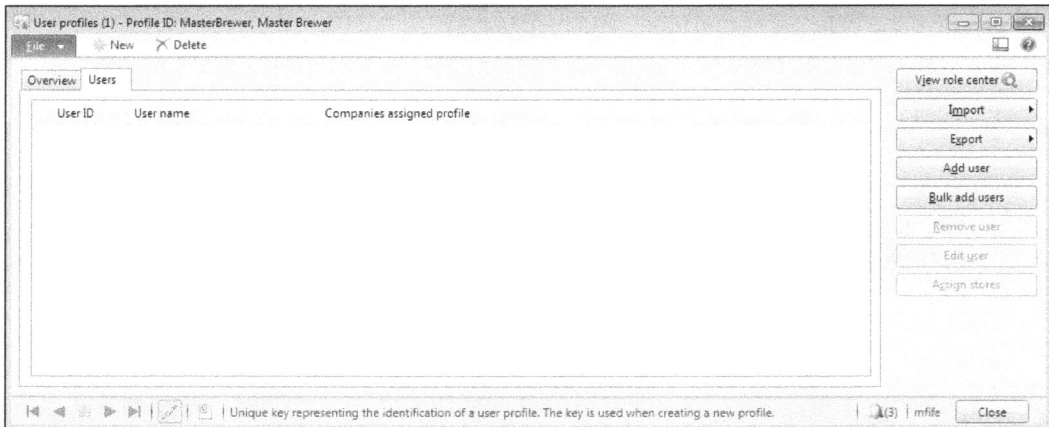

10. Now, you can select the users who you want to assign to the role.

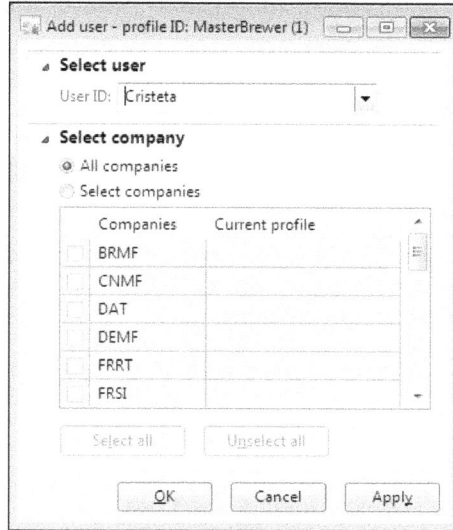

11. Then, click on the **Close** button to finish.

How it works...

The next time your user logs in, their Role Center will be the new template that you created.

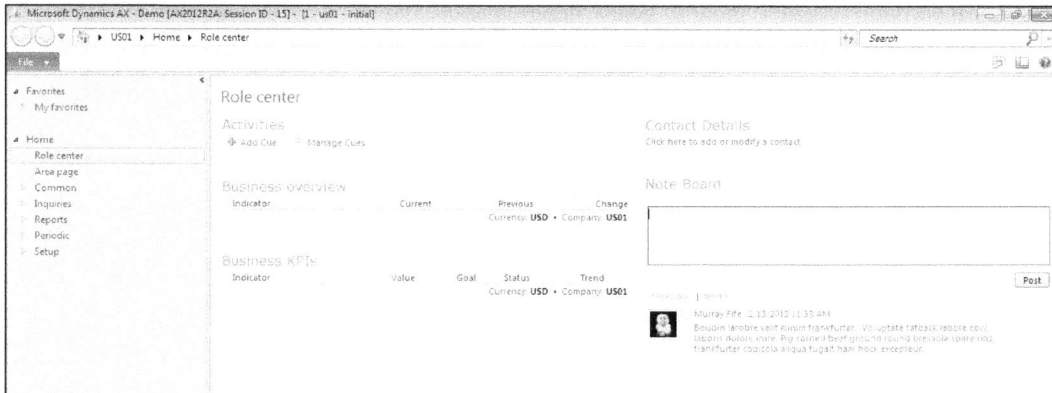

Adding cues to Role Center profiles

Cues are a great way to create your own personal reminders on your Role Centers. Cues allow you to turn the physical stacks of paper, which you probably have sitting on your desk right now that remind you of the amount of work that you have to do, into virtual stacks of records within your Role Center. Any list page that you work in within Dynamics AX may be turned into a cue, but you get to select the records you are interested in working on, so you are in control of what goes into that list.

As you create cues, you can also choose to assign them to everybody within the organization as an informational metric, you can assign them to everyone who has a certain profile, or you can just assign them to your own personal Role Center.

In this recipe, we will show you how to create cues and assign them to user profiles.

Getting ready

Cues are displayed on the Role Centers through the **Cues** web part. If you don't currently have that web part, you may want to add it by entering personalization mode and adding the **Cues** web part.

How to do it...

To add a cue to a user profile, follow these steps:

1. Open up the list page that you would like to publish to your Role Center as a cue.

2. If you don't want to include every record in your cue, filter out the records to just the ones that you are interested in.

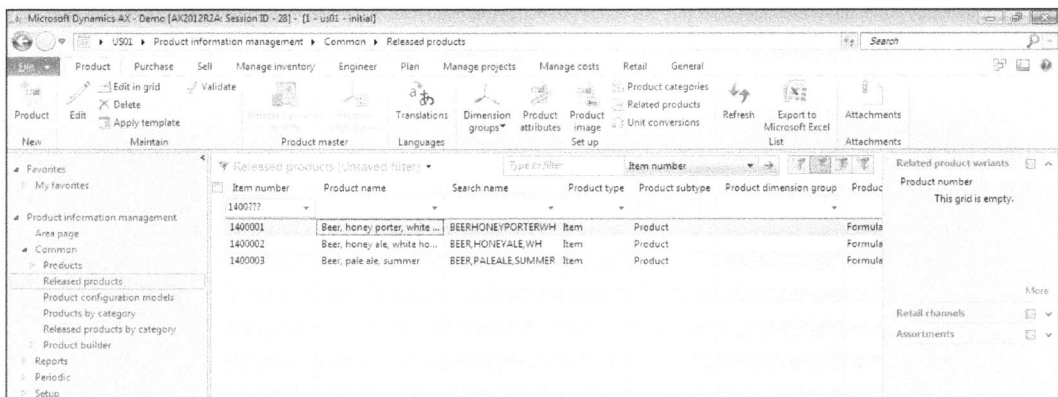

3. Select the **Filter** dropdown from the header of the list, and select the **Save As Cue...** menu item.

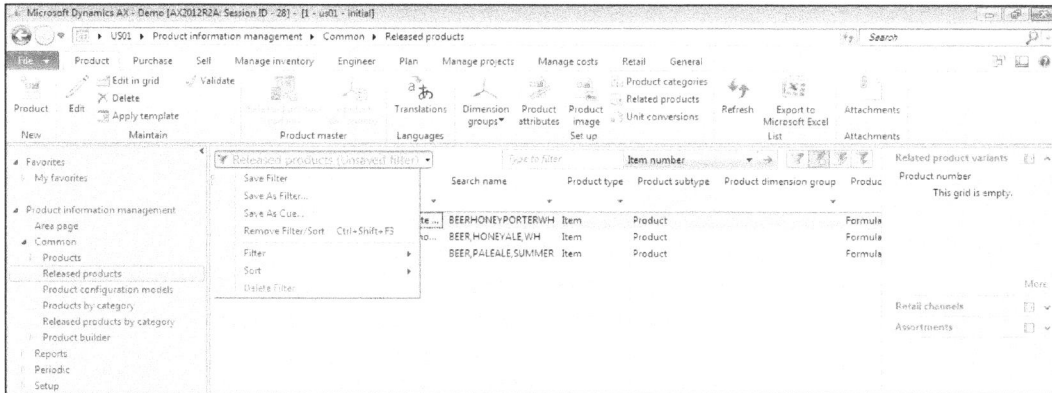

4. Give your cue a name and select the **Specified profiles** option from the **Visibility** group to add a cue to a particular profile. Within the list of profiles, select all of the profile IDs that you want the cue to be added to and then click on the **OK** button.

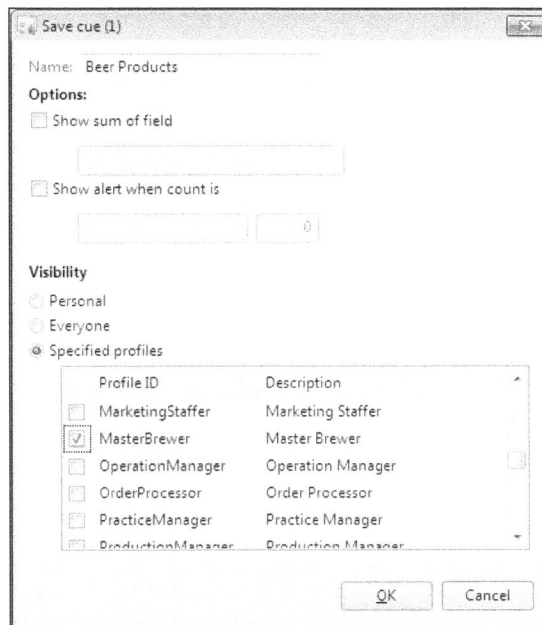

How it works...

When the user opens up their Role Center, they will now automatically have a cue there. Clicking on the cue will take them straight to the list page that it is associated with, with the list filtered just to show the particular records.

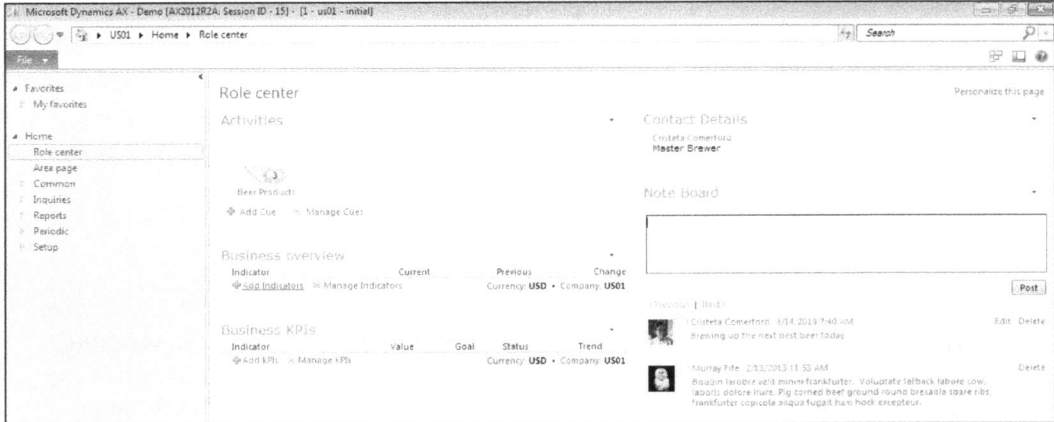

Adding cues through the Advanced Filter editor

Unfortunately, not all forms have the new Filter drop-down menu that was introduced with Dynamics AX 2012; although that doesn't mean that you cannot create cues from their data, because the **Advanced Filter editor** also has the ability to publish filtered data as cues.

In this recipe, we will show how to create a cue from the Advanced Filter editor.

How to do it...

To add a cue through the Advanced Filter editor, follow these steps:

1. First, start off with the list that you want to filter and turn it into a cue. Apply the filter that you want on the data, so that you just see the records that you want to be included.

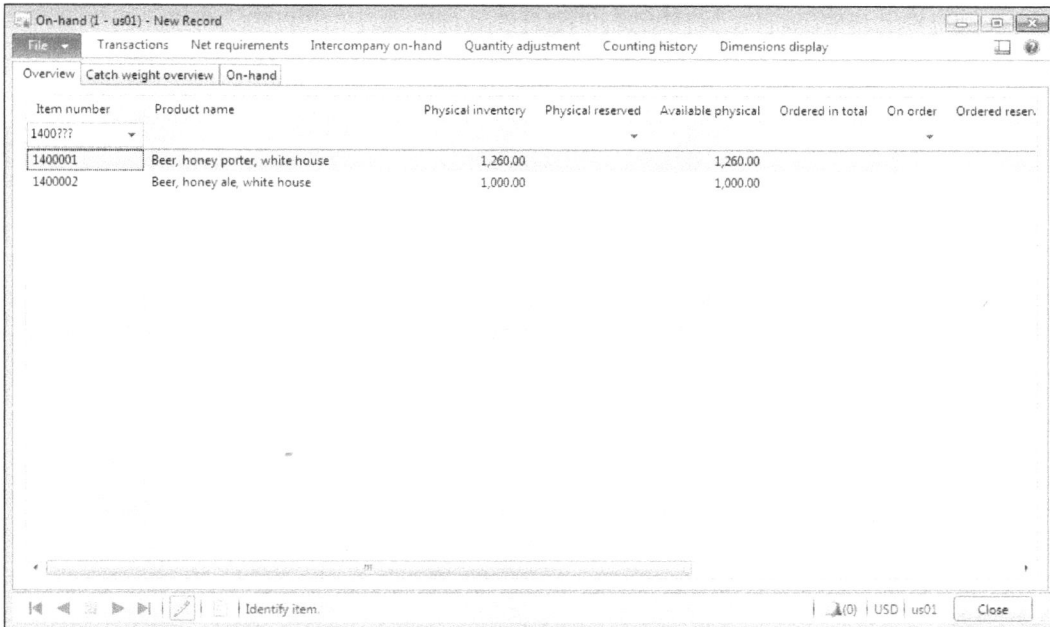

2. Then, from the **File** menu select the **Edit** menu item, and from within the **Filter** submenu select the **Advanced Filter/Sort** menu item.

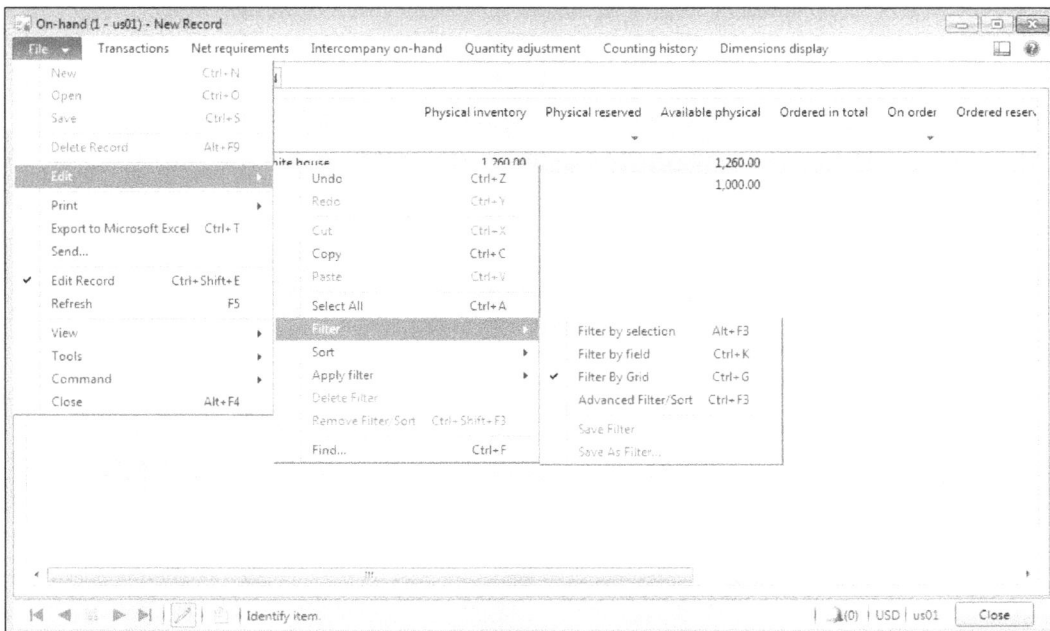

3. This will open up the **Advanced Filter** dialog. Click on the **Modify** button and select the option called **Save as cue...**.

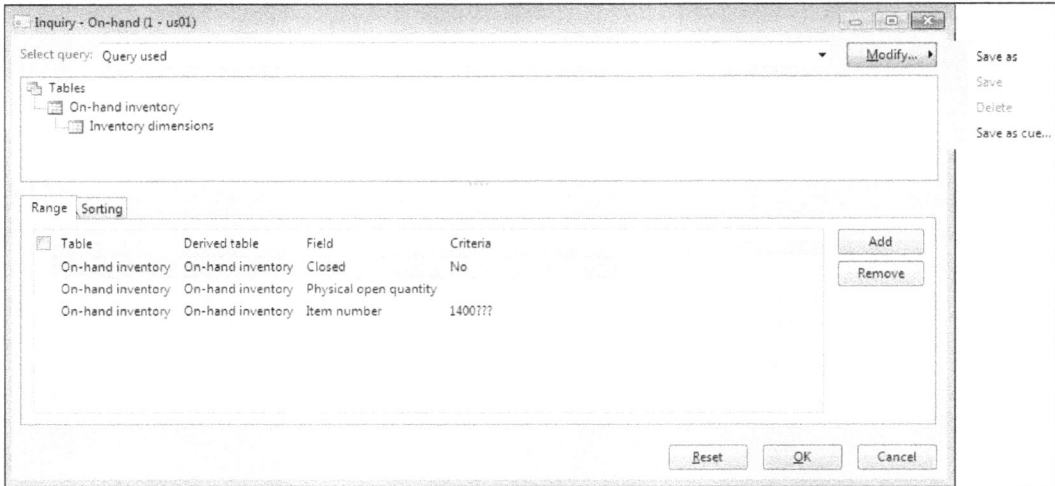

4. Now, you can give your cue a name and choose where you want to send it.

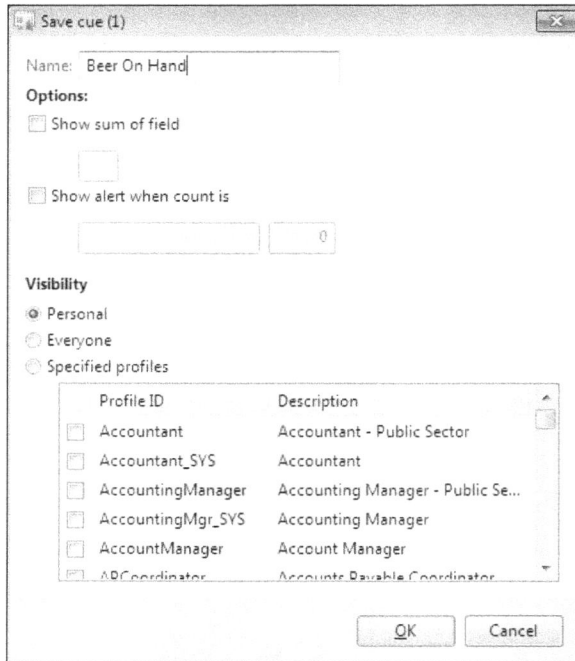

How it works...

The next time you refresh your Role Center, you will see the new cue and it will take you to the filtered data within the form, even if it doesn't have the new AX 2012 style drop-down **Filter** menu.

Adding RSS feeds to Role Centers

Most people just use Role Centers to consolidate Dynamics AX information into one simple dashboard. However, since the Role Centers are built upon SharePoint, you can take advantage of all the other SharePoint web parts that are available to incorporate non-Dynamics AX information that is still important to the business. One such web part is the **RSS Feed Reader** that allows you to display information from other websites that publish their information as feeds. Sources for RSS feeds could include blogs, search engines, and also social media tools.

In this recipe, we will show how you can add an RSS feed from Bing into your Role Center, so that you don't have to manually search to find what is currently new on the Web.

Getting ready

Bing has a search feature that will output the most current searches that match as an RSS feed. The format is:

```
http://www.bing.com/search?q=Query&go=&qb=y&format=rss
```

Before you start adding the RSS feed to the Role Center, it's always a good idea to run the query within a web browser just to check that the format is correct. The result should look something like this:

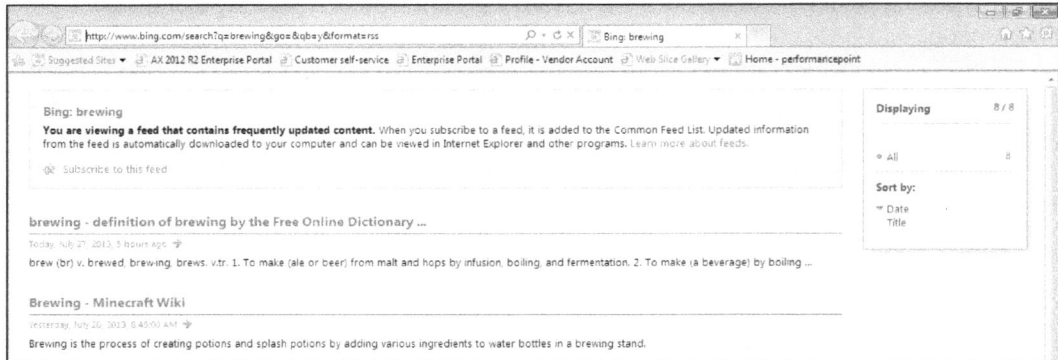

How to do it...

To add an RSS feed to a Role Center, follow these steps:

1. The first step in the process is to add a web part to your Role Center that will return back the RSS information in a human-readable format. To do this, go to your Role Center page, and click on the **Personalize this page** option on the top right hand corner of the Role Center.

2. Now, click on the **Add a Web Part** link in the column that you want to show your feed information in.

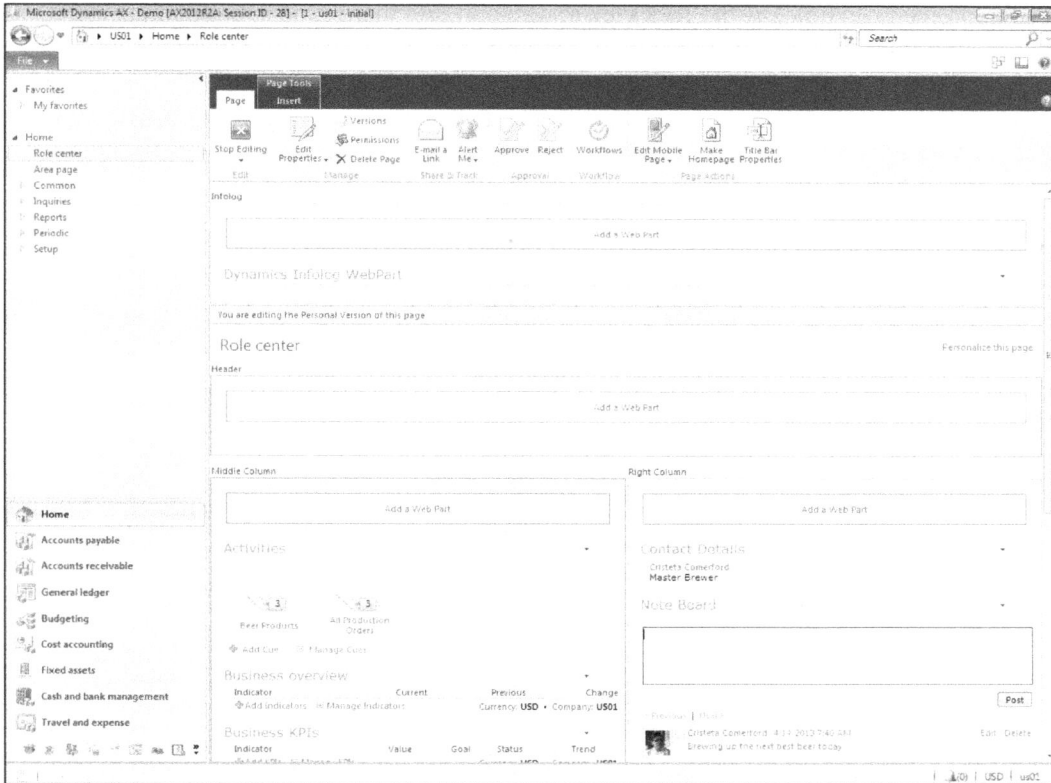

3. Within the **Web Parts** browser select the **RSS Viewer** web part from the **Content Rollup** category, and then click on the **Add** button to insert it into your Role Center.

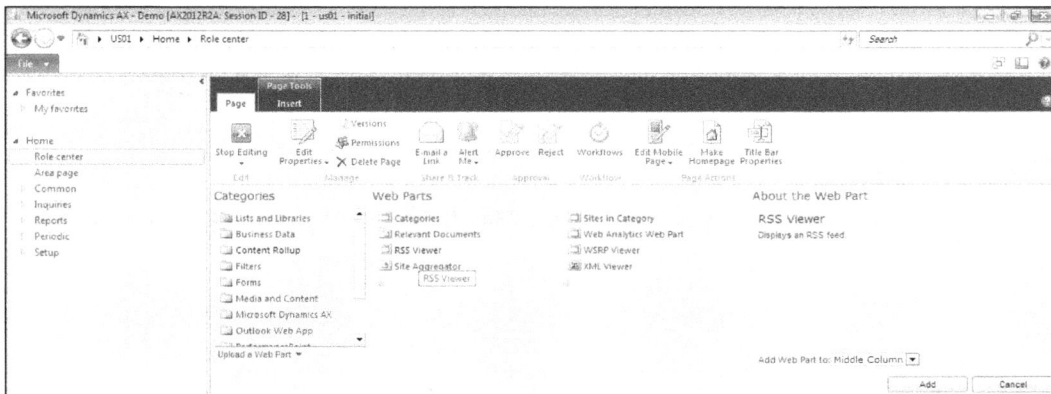

4. You should now see the **RSS Viewer** web part, but there is no information being returned because the feed has not been configured. Click on the **Open the feed pane** link within the body of the web part to open up the options panel.

5. When the **Properties** panel shows up, paste the URL for the Bing RSS search into the **RSS Feed URL** field in the **RSS Properties** group.

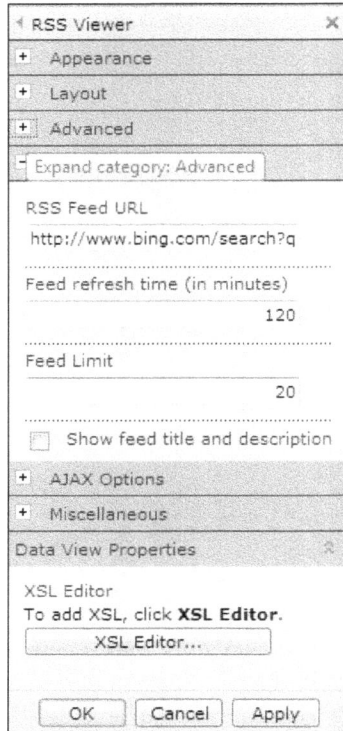

```
◄ RSS Viewer                              ✕

 [+]  Appearance

 [+]  Layout

 [+]  Advanced

 [–]  Expand category: Advanced

 RSS Feed URL
   http://www.bing.com/search?q
 ...............................................

 Feed refresh time (in minutes)
                             120
 ...............................................

 Feed Limit
                              20
 ...............................................

 [ ]  Show feed title and description

 [+]  AJAX Options

 [+]  Miscellaneous

 Data View Properties                      ☆

 XSL Editor
 To add XSL, click XSL Editor.
      [    XSL Editor...    ]


      [  OK  ] [ Cancel ] [ Apply ]
```

6. Also, open up the **Appearance** properties group and give your feed a more appropriate name.

7. Then, click on the **OK** button on the **RSS Viewer** properties panel to save your changes.

8. To return to the view mode, click on the **Stop Editing** button in the **Edit** group of the **Page** ribbon bar.

How it works...

When the user opens up their Role Center, they will now have a link to the latest items from the RSS feed, which in this case are the latest happenings from Bing that they may be interested in.

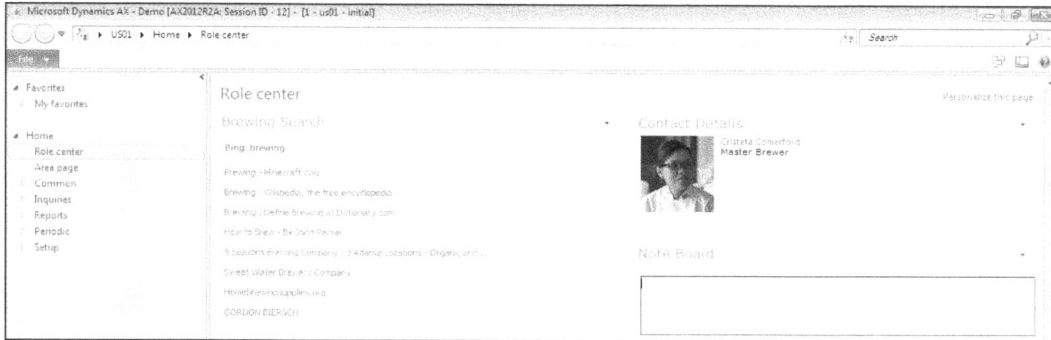

Removing the ribbon bar from Role Centers

A benefit of Role Centers is that they are a lightweight version of Dynamics AX that the users can operate from a browser, without having to install the Rich Client. You may not want to let the users know that they are able to edit the page, or access any of the SharePoint ribbon bar that appears when you run the form in the default web mode. You can easily hide this information with a simple qualifier on the Role Center URL.

In this recipe, we will show how you can open up Role Centers without the SharePoint ribbon bar.

How to do it...

To remove the ribbon bar from Role Centers, follow this step:

1. While navigating to the Enterprise portal, add a `RUNONCLIENT=1` parameter to the end of the URL shortcut; for example: `http://dynamicsax.contoso.com/sites/DynamicsAx/Enterprise%20Portal/?RUNONCLIENT=1`.

How it works...

If you update the default links that the users access to open the Role Centers, the next time they use them, they will see that the ribbon bar is removed.

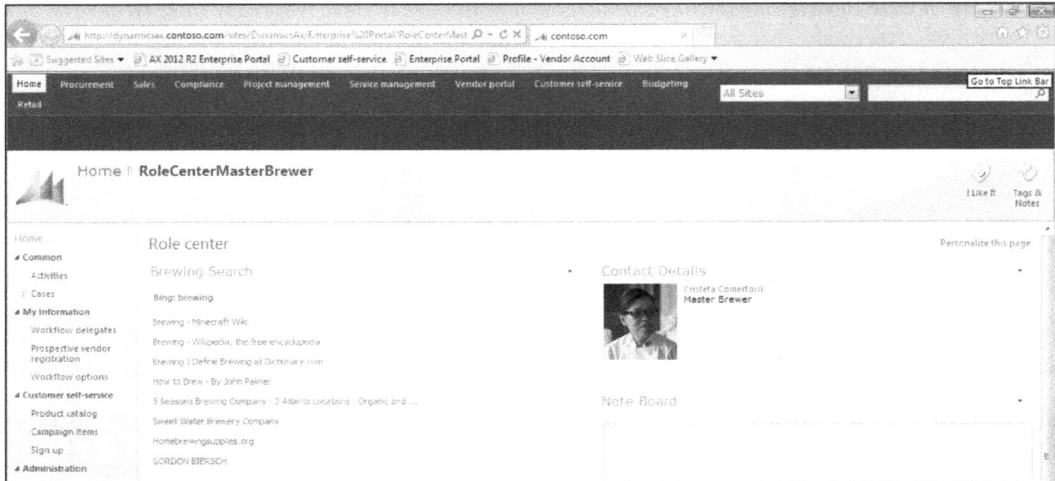

Removing the navigation bar from Role Centers

SharePoint has a URL parameter that will simplify the pages so that you don't see the left navigation panel. This is useful because you may want to open up the Role Center on a tablet or Surface device, and all you want to see is the Role Center dashboard area since you are more constrained for space.

In this recipe, we will show how you can open up Role Centers without the SharePoint navigation panel on the left.

How to do it...

To remove the navigation bar from Role Centers, follow this step:

1. While navigating to the Enterprise portal, add a `IsDlg=1 parameter` to the end of the URL; for example: `http://dynamicsax.contoso.com/sites/DynamicsAx/Enterprise%20Portal/?RUNONCLIENT=1&IsDlg=1`.

How it works...

When the Role Center is opened up with the `IsDlg=1` qualifier, the navigation bar is removed.

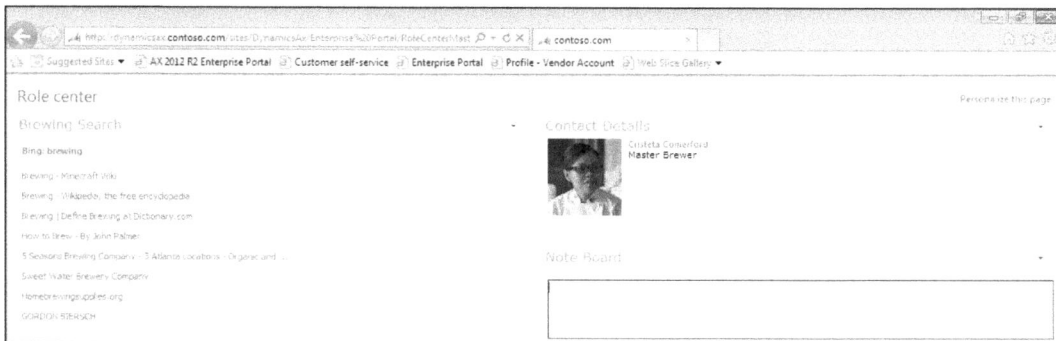

Embedding Role Centers into Outlook

Another benefit of the dialog mode for the Role Centers is that you can embed them in other applications as pure dashboards. Outlook may be one of the most used applications within a business, so why not embed the Role Centers in there making it unavoidable that they cannot miss events within Dynamics AX.

In this recipe, we will show how you can add Role Centers as homepages within Outlook.

How to do it...

To embed the Role Center as a homepage within Outlook, follow these steps:

1. Within the `Outlook` folder tree, right-click on the parent node, and select the **New Folder** menu item.

2. Give the new folder the name `Enterprise Portal`.

3. Right-click on the new folder and select the **Properties** menu item.

4. Within the folder properties, switch to the **Home Page** tab, check the option **Show home page by default for this folder**, and paste the URL for the Enterprise portal into the **Address:** field. Then, click on **OK** to save the changes.

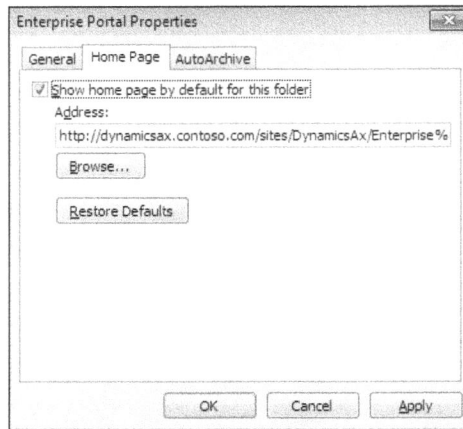

5. Now go to **Options** within the Outlook **File** menu.

6. Select the **Advanced** group within the options and in the **Outlook start and exit** group, click on the **Browse...** button for the **Start Outlook in this folder:** field.

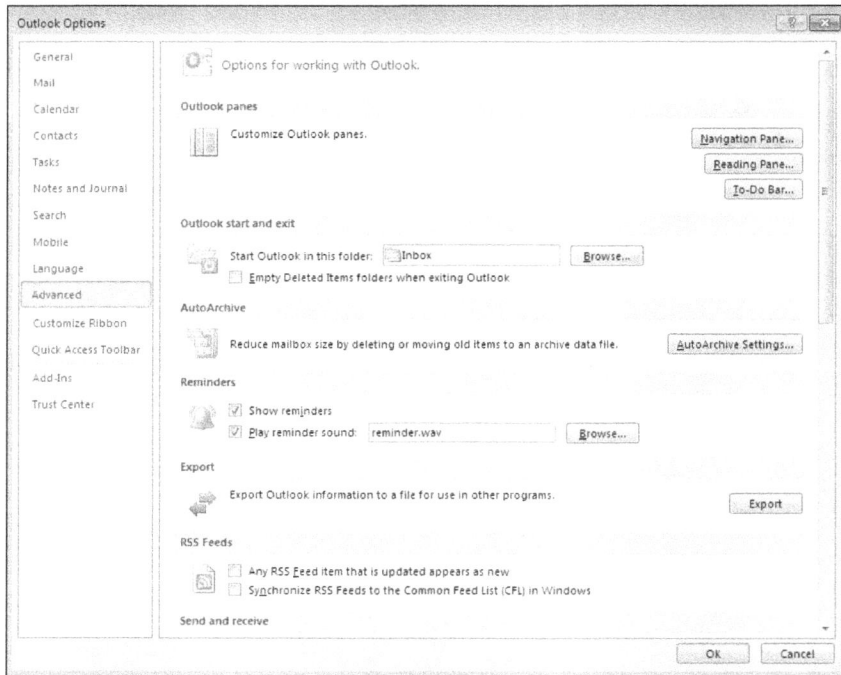

7. Select the `Enterprise Portal` folder that you just created and close the options forms.

How it works...

Now whenever the user opens up Outlook, they will see their Dynamics AX Role Center.

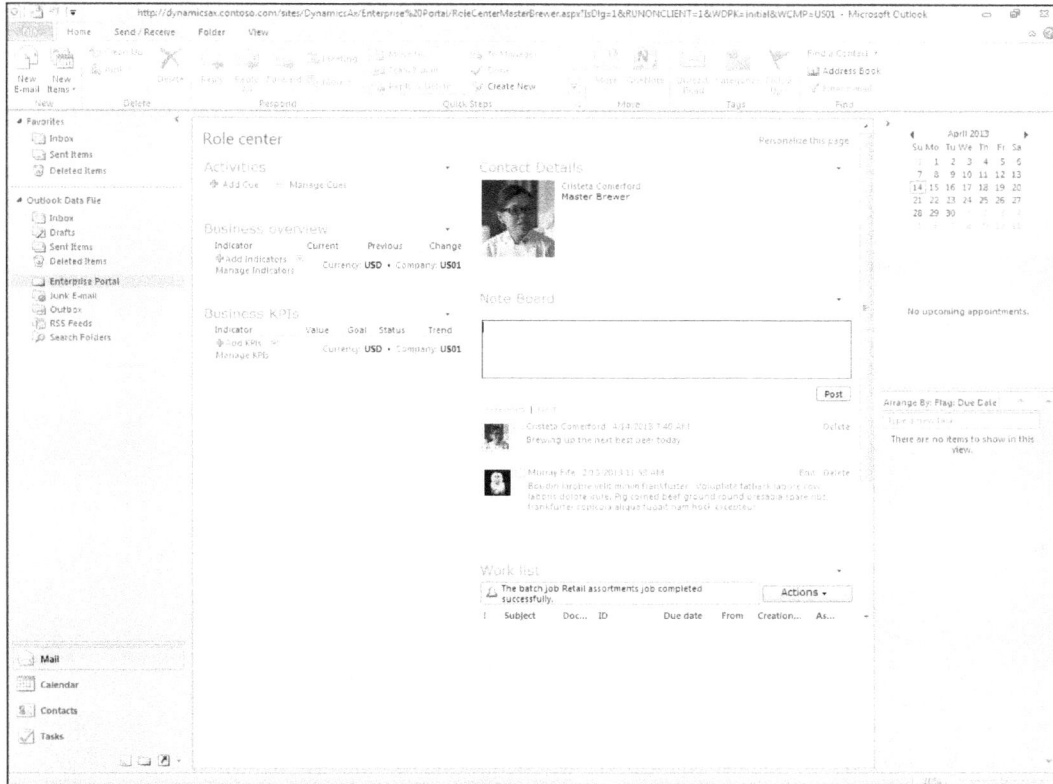

Summary

Role Centers that are delivered with Dynamics AX are a great starting point that you can then extend out to match your business. This could be by creating entirely new Role Centers, adding more content to use them as a central place to view everything that is important to you, or by taking Role Centers out of Dynamics AX and using them either as standalone portals or embedded portals in other applications.

Since Role Centers are based on SharePoint technologies, there is so much more that you can do to customize the information that is delivered through them. Other examples that you may want to try include:

- Adding document libraries
- Adding links to external websites
- Adding internal navigation links to Dynamics AX applications

Also, if you want to do some development in Visual Studio, you can take advantage of Role Center project templates that get installed with Dynamics AX. They will allow you to create your own Enterprise portal web parts to display custom data views within Role Centers.

Index

Thank you for buying
Extending Microsoft Dynamics AX 2012 Cookbook

About Packt Publishing

Packt, pronounced 'packed', published its first book "*Mastering phpMyAdmin for Effective MySQL Management*" in April 2004 and subsequently continued to specialize in publishing highly focused books on specific technologies and solutions.

Our books and publications share the experiences of your fellow IT professionals in adapting and customizing today's systems, applications, and frameworks. Our solution-based books give you the knowledge and power to customize the software and technologies you're using to get the job done. Packt books are more specific and less general than the IT books you have seen in the past. Our unique business model allows us to bring you more focused information, giving you more of what you need to know, and less of what you don't.

Packt is a modern, yet unique publishing company, which focuses on producing quality, cutting-edge books for communities of developers, administrators, and newbies alike. For more information, please visit our website: www.PacktPub.com.

About Packt Enterprise

In 2010, Packt launched two new brands, Packt Enterprise and Packt Open Source, in order to continue its focus on specialization. This book is part of the Packt Enterprise brand, home to books published on enterprise software – software created by major vendors, including (but not limited to) IBM, Microsoft and Oracle, often for use in other corporations. Its titles will offer information relevant to a range of users of this software, including administrators, developers, architects, and end users.

Writing for Packt

We welcome all inquiries from people who are interested in authoring. Book proposals should be sent to author@packtpub.com. If your book idea is still at an early stage and you would like to discuss it first before writing a formal book proposal, contact us; one of our commissioning editors will get in touch with you.

We're not just looking for published authors; if you have strong technical skills but no writing experience, our experienced editors can help you develop a writing career, or simply get some additional reward for your expertise.

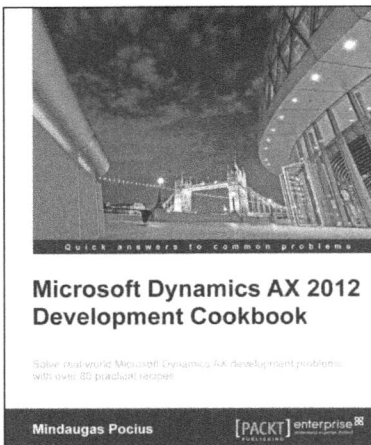

Microsoft Dynamics AX 2012 Development Cookbook

ISBN: 978-1-84968-464-4   Paperback: 372 pages

Solve real-world Microsoft Dynamics AX development problems with over 80 practical recipes

1. Develop powerful, successful Dynamics AX projects with efficient X++ code

2. Proven recipes that can be reused in numerous successful Dynamics AX projects

3. Covers the general functionality of Dynamics AX

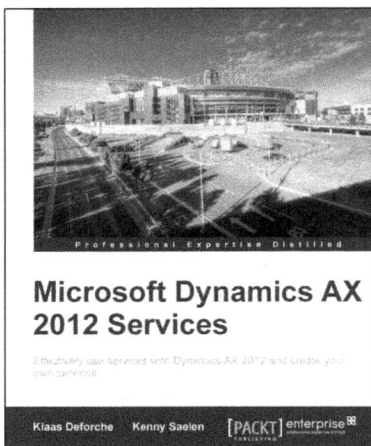

Microsoft Dynamics AX 2012 Services

ISBN: 978-1-84968-754-6   Paperback: 196 pages

Effectively use services with Dynamics AX 2012 and create your own services

1. Learn about the Dynamics AX 2012 service architecture

2. Create your own services using wizards or X++ code

3. Consume existing web services and those you've created yourself

Please check **www.PacktPub.com** for information on our titles

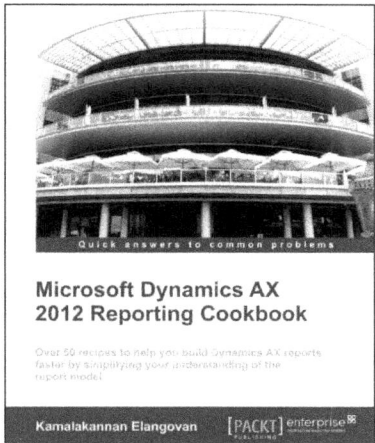

Microsoft Dynamics AX 2012 Reporting Cookbook

ISBN: 9978-1-84968-772-0   Paperback: 300 pages

Over 50 recipes to help you build Dynamics AX reports faster by simplifying your understanding of the report model

1. Practical recipes for creating and managing reports

2. Illustrated step-by-step examples that can be adopted in real time

3. Complete explanations of the report model and program model for reports

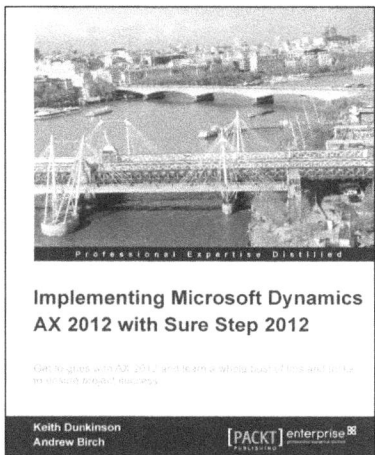

Microsoft Dynamics AX 2012 Reporting Cookbook

Over 50 recipes to help you build Dynamics AX reports faster by simplifying your understanding of the report model.

Kamalakannan Elangovan   [PACKT] enterprise ⊠

Implementing Microsoft Dynamics AX 2012 with Sure Step 2012

ISBN: 978-1-84968-704-1   Paperback: 234 pages

Get to grips with AX 2012 and learn a whole host of tips and tricks to ensure project success

1. Get the confidence to implement AX 2012 projects effectively using the Sure Step 2012 Methodology

2. Packed with practical real-world examples as well as helpful diagrams and images that make learning easier for you

3. Dive deep into AX 2012 to learn key technical concepts to implement and manage a project

Implementing Microsoft Dynamics AX 2012 with Sure Step 2012

Get to grips with AX 2012 and learn a whole host of tips and tricks to ensure project success

Keith Dunkinson
Andrew Birch   [PACKT] enterprise ⊠

Please check **www.PacktPub.com** for information on our titles